NBER SERIES ON LONG-TERM FACTORS
IN ECONOMIC DEVELOPMENT

EDITORS

ROBERT W. FOGEL AND CLAYNE L. POPE

ALSO IN THE SERIES

CLAUDIA GOLDIN

UNDERSTANDING THE GENDER GAP: AN ECONOMIC HISTORY OF AMERICAN WOMEN
(OXFORD UNIVERSITY PRESS, 1990)

RODERICK FLOUD, KENNETH WACHTER, AND ANNABEL GREGORY
HEIGHT, HEALTH, AND HISTORY:
NUTRITIONAL STATUS IN THE UNITED KINGDOM, 1750–1980
(CAMBRIDGE UNIVERSITY PRESS, 1990)

ROBERT A. MARGO

RACE AND SCHOOLING IN THE SOUTH, 1880–1950: AN ECONOMIC HISTORY
(UNIVERSITY OF CHICAGO PRESS, 1990)

IN PREPARATION (TENTATIVE TITLES)

ROBERT W. FOGEL

THE ESCAPE FROM HUNGER AND EARLY DEATH: EUROPE AND AMERICA, 1750–2050

KENNETH L. SOKOLOFF

IN PURSUIT OF PRIVATE COMFORT: EARLY AMERICAN INDUSTRIALIZATION, 1790–1860

FATAL YEARS

RELATION OF THE DIRECTORS TO THE
WORK AND PUBLICATIONS OF THE
NATIONAL BUREAU OF ECONOMIC RESEARCH

1. The object of the National Bureau of Economic Research is to ascertain and to present to the public important economic facts and their interpretation in a scientific and impartial manner. The Board of Directors is charged with the responsibility of ensuring that the work of the National Bureau is carried on in strict conformity with this object.

2. The President of the National Bureau shall submit to the Board of Directors, or to its Executive Committee, for their formal adoption all specific proposals for research to be instituted.

3. No research report shall be published by the National Bureau until the President has sent each member of the Board a notice that a manuscript is recommended for publication and that in the President's opinion it is suitable for publication in accordance with the principles of the National Bureau. Such notification will include an abstract or summary of the manuscript's content and a response form for use by those Directors who desire a copy of the manuscript for review. Each manuscript shall contain a summary drawing attention to the nature and treatment of the problem studied, the character of the data and their utilization in the report, and the main conclusions reached.

4. For each manuscript so submitted, a special committee of the Directors (including Directors Emeriti) shall be appointed by majority agreement of the President and Vice Presidents (or by the Executive Committee in case of inability to decide on the part of the President and Vice Presidents), consisting of three Directors selected as nearly as may be one from each general division of the Board. The names of the special manuscript committee shall be stated to each Director when notice of the proposed publication is submitted to him. It shall be the duty of each member of the special manuscript committee to read the manuscript. If each member of the manuscript committee signifies his approval within thirty days of the transmittal of the manuscript, the report may be published. If at the end of that period any member of the manuscript committee withholds his approval, the President shall then notify each member of the Board, requesting approval or disapproval of publication, and thirty days additional shall be granted for this purpose. The manuscript shall then not be published unless at least a majority of the entire Board who shall have voted on the proposal within the time fixed for the receipt of votes shall have approved.

5. No manuscript may be published, though approved by each member of the special manuscript committee, until forty-five days have elapsed from the transmittal of the report in manuscript form. The interval is allowed for the receipt of any memorandum of dissent or reservation, together with a brief statement of his reasons, that any member may wish to express; and such memorandum of dissent or reservation shall be published with the manuscript if he so desires. Publication does not, however, imply that each

member of the Board has read the manuscript, or that either members of the Board in general or the special committee have passed on its validity in every detail.

6. Publications of the National Bureau issued for informational purposes concerning the work of the Bureau and its staff, or issued to inform the public of activities of Bureau staff, and volumes issued as a result of various conferences involving the National Bureau shall contain a specific disclaimer noting that such publication has not passed through the normal review procedures required in this resolution. The Executive Committee of the Board is charged with review of all such publications from time to time to ensure that they do not take on the character of formal research reports of the National Bureau, requiring formal Board approval.

7. Unless otherwise determined by the Board or exempted by the terms of paragraph 6, a copy of this resolution shall be printed in each National Bureau publication.

(Resolution adopted October 25, 1926, as revised through September 30, 1974)

CONTENTS

LIST OF ILLUSTRATIONS

Figures

Tables

Illustrations

PREFACE

PREHISTORIC man appears to have lived an average of 20–25 years. Today, the average length of life in the United States is 75 years. This tripling of life expectancy is perhaps the single most beneficial feature of the changes that social scientists term "modernization." It was not a smooth journey: warfare and famine have evidently afflicted the human race since its inception, and plagues and epidemics joined the episodic horrors when man settled into dense communities. These periodic crises were, moreover, just a supplement to the crushing burden of "normal" mortality.

In the industrialized world, about half of the progress in life expectancy since prehistoric times has occurred during the twentieth century. Many western European countries had good vital registration systems at the turn of the century, and these suggested that life expectancy at birth was approximately 50 years. In the United States, life expectancy in the 1900 Death Registration Area, which contained the 26 percent of the population with reliable data on mortality, was also in this range. Nevertheless, there were suspicions that the Death Registration Area was not a good representative of national mortality conditions.

Vital registration systems produced data for large geographic aggregates, not for individuals or families or social classes. Our information about the mortality of specific groups before the twentieth century is drawn mainly from unusually privileged groups such as the European aristocracy, from family genealogies of unusually long-lived families, or from local records. We lack a detailed portrait of the mortality conditions faced by common folk and of the principal differences among groups. As a result, we have an underdeveloped appreciation of the momentous progress that has been made in the twentieth century, and too vague an understanding of the sources of that progress.

A data set that recently became available for the United States provides an unparalleled opportunity to depict mortality conditions in the late nineteenth century. The U.S. Population Census of 1900 asked married women how many children they had ever borne ("Mother of how many children?") and how many of those children were still living ("Number of these children living"). This pair of questions has become the principal basis of mortality estimation in contemporary developing countries, thanks largely to the pioneering methodological work of William Brass. But early Census officials evidently had little knowledge of how these questions could be used, since no tabulations of them were ever made.

A public use sample constructed from microfilmed records of the 1900 U.S. Census of Population lets us apply the devices of modern demography to records from the past. This sample was produced at the University of Washington under the direction of Samuel Preston, Steven Graham, and Richard Johnson. A total of 100,438 individuals are included in this sample (Graham 1980). Women in the sample reported the birth of 81,916 children, of whom 61,778 had survived to the time of the census.

The time and place are opportune. As noted, the data pertain to an epoch about halfway between modern and prehistoric mortality circumstances. Important scientific developments in the late nineteenth century were just beginning to transform mortality conditions, but their penetration was far from complete by 1900. Old ideas about disease causation were formidable obstacles to the advance of health, and social institutions had only begun to realize their potential for improving survival chances.

The United States is an excellent stage for viewing this unfolding drama. Its population contained a relatively equal mixture of urban and rural residents and was spread over a wide array of disease environments. And it featured a high proportion of people who had been born in other countries and who carried with them childrearing behaviors and other customs that influenced their mortality levels. The United States also lagged far behind most European countries in the quality of its vital registration data, so that the 1900 census sample fills many gaps in American demographic history. In fact, the sample converts the United States from the industrialized country with the poorest mortality data at the turn of the century to the country with perhaps the richest and most detailed data on infants and children.

This book serves two related functions. One is to present better information than was previously available about levels, trends, and differences in child mortality for the United States at the turn of the century. This function involves careful description of the data and methods of analysis, some of which were developed specifically for processing these data. In one sense, we are presenting a monograph that could have been a publication from the census of 1900, had Census officials only possessed modern means of processing and interpreting the data that they collected. This component of our work, concentrated in Chapters 2 and 3, is likely to have greatest appeal to demographers and others who are eager to, as the Chinese say, learn truth from facts.

But presenting these data inevitably raises questions about why they look as they do: for example, why was child mortality so high, and why were social-class differences so muted and residential differences so pronounced? In working back and forth between our data and accounts of living conditions of the time, we have constructed an interpretation of some of the main results. This dual focus on data and interpretation is reflected in the organization of the volume.

Chapter 1 presents a description of the major arenas in which the struggle to reduce child mortality was being enacted. The great killers of children in the 1890s were infectious diseases, although they were not always recognized as such. The United States, like European countries, was in the midst of a revolution in bacteriology. The germ theory of disease, which had received striking empirical validation in the 1880s, was beginning to replace earlier theories of disease causation that stressed the importance of miasmata, atmospheric contaminants mainly to be found in public places and detectable principally by their odor.

The germ theory allowed the possibility of much more effective public and private interventions to reduce the incidence of infectious diseases; it was not only more "modern," it was also fundamentally correct. Enlightened public officials and up-to-date physicians saw clearly the implications of the theory for public and personal health-care practices. But the old ideas gave way slowly and continued to be reflected in the daily practices of health professionals of the time. The 1890s were a period of tumult and contention among competing ideas of disease, and advocates of the germ theory often despaired at the backwardness of some of their colleagues.

Parents appear to have been, in general, highly motivated to enhance their children's survival chances (unlike, it is alleged, some European parents of the nineteenth century), but they had few means at their disposal for doing so. One of the surest means available at the time was extended breastfeeding, although the practice faced increasing competition from the use of cow's milk. Chapter 1 reviews what little is known about the breastfeeding practices of different groups at the time. It also notes that the attempt to purify milk brought into the home, which was such an important component of the public-health effort during the twentieth century, had barely begun in the 1890s.

Chapter 1 also reviews evidence from other studies regarding the influence of social factors on child mortality in the late nineteenth century. Much of this evidence comes from other countries, or from later periods in the United States, since there were very few data on these matters in the United States at the time. We do, however, establish that food was abundant and relatively cheap in the late nineteenth century, so that the high levels of child mortality were unlikely to have had a dietary source.

Chapter 2 presents our basic estimates of levels and trends in child mortality for blacks and whites in the years preceding 1900. The census sample provides the first opportunity to gauge the representativeness of mortality data from the Death Registration Area (DRA). By comparing our estimates of child mortality for the U.S. as a whole to those for the states that constituted the DRA (estimates also constructed for the census sample), we are able to show that the DRA had substantially higher mortality than the nation as a whole for whites and, especially, for blacks. Ironically, the DRA gave much more satisfactory estimates when both races were combined because its very low proportion of blacks, 1.9 percent, offset much of the bias that existed for each race separately.

We validate the basic quality of data in the census sample by showing that, for the DRA, the sample produces levels of child mortality very similar to those coming from vital registration in the Area. The registration data are certainly the most important independent test of the quality of census data. Furthermore, we show that states in the DRA had higher levels of reported mortality, levels that were closer to our own estimates, than did states whose mortality estimates were drawn solely from a census question on household deaths in the year before the census. The latter information is so incomplete as to be virtually unusable.

Our census sample suggests that child mortality had been declining in the two decades before 1900 for whites and for the total population. No such improvement is evident for blacks, but any assessment of mortality trends for the black population is plagued by data problems. Marital disruption was frequent for blacks, making marital duration a less reliable indicator of the timing of children's deaths. Furthermore, there are more questions for blacks than for whites about the suitability of the models of age-specific death rates that we use to establish trends.

Chapter 3 presents information about child mortality differences among social and residential groupings that can be constructed from questions asked on the 1900 census. The census sample provides the first opportunity to examine these differences, and the results are sometimes surprising. In particular, we show that the South had mortality levels that were slightly better than those of the Northeast; that second-generation women (i.e., those born in the U.S whose mothers were born abroad) had child mortality levels that were typically well below average; and that there was relatively little differentiation in child mortality levels according to the father's occupation. Other results were more predictable: residents of large cities had much higher child mortality levels than rural residents; children of foreign-born women had higher mortality than those born to natives; and wives of men who were unemployed in the year preceding the census had much higher child mortality than wives of fully employed men.

Chapter 3 shows that immigrants to the U.S. typically achieved lower child mortality than those who remained in the countries from which they emigrated. It also shows that the pattern of interstate differences in child mortality in the 1890s was correlated with interstate differences in the heights and weights of World War I recruits, most of whom were young children in the 1890s. Regional factors that served to raise child mortality also appear to have reduced rates of physical growth.

In presenting results about the relation between mortality and various social and residential conditions in Chapter 3, we discuss a number of reasons why these conditions may have influenced mortality, including reasons that were offered by those writing at the time. The task of sorting out which of these conditions was most influential, and which appear to be unrelated to mortality once other variables are controlled, however, belongs to Chapter 4. There is no single best way to answer these questions, and Chapter 4 uses a variety of criteria.

Whatever approach is used, race stands out as a dominant influence on mortality at the time. Blacks had higher child mortality for reasons that are not primarily explicable in terms of other measured characteristics, such as their low levels of literacy and poor occupational standing. Size of community also remains influential throughout the analysis; residents of larger cities clearly paid a price in terms of child health. Other variables that continue to have a strong influence on child mortality levels when the remaining variables are controlled are father's unemployment, the presence of boarders in the household, the average income level in one's state of residence, and one's region of residence. Once all other variables are controlled, residence in New England or the Mountain region was associated with unusually high mortality, while the South Atlantic is found to have been a region of low mortality.

The results are almost as noteworthy for what is not closely related to mortality as for what is. The husband's occupation, the wife's literacy, and the wife's ethnicity all lose most of their association with child mortality when other variables are introduced. We do show that some of the occupational differences are significant in urban areas, but the process of occupational labelling is evidently sufficiently imprecise in rural areas, and in the nation as a whole, that occupational differences in child mortality are small and generally insignificant. A similar result pertains when we use very detailed occupational titles to assign a mean occupational income and mean occupational months unemployed to men in the sample. Neither of these variables is significant, nor do their coefficients even take the proper sign, in multivariate analysis.

When multivariate relations are examined separately for rural and urban areas, we show that the comparative advantage of the South Atlantic relative to New England is more pronounced in rural areas. We speculate that New England's rural disadvantage may be attributable to its high rural population densities. The income level of a state is also much more influential in rural mortality than in urban, suggesting that it is principally reflecting rural living conditions. The husband's literacy is shown to have a sizable influence on child mortality in urban areas, whereas his ability to speak English is far more important in rural areas.

Chapter 5 shows that England and Wales in 1911 had much sharper occupational differences in mortality than did the United States in 1900. Part of the explanation is that occupation-specific incomes were substantially more unequal in England. But even apart from income differentials, occupational class appears to have conveyed far more information about conditions of life in England than in the United States. England's early industrialization evidently had created a far more differentiated class structure than was true of the United States (except for the notable distinctions associated with race). We suggest that larger occupational differences in mortality in England may be partly explained by a higher degree of residential segregation by occupation.

Chapter 5 also compares American child mortality differences at the turn of the century to those typically observed in present-day developing countries. We show that the relative and absolute mortality advantage of literate mothers and of members of the professional classes is far greater today. We argue that, in view of the relatively primitive state of knowledge about ways to prevent infectious disease in 1900, there were many fewer steps available to these groups in the United States that would enable them to enlarge the advantage conveyed by their purely economic circumstances. The pattern of higher urban mortality in the U.S., now decisively reversed in developing countries, is further evidence of the extent to which the U.S in 1900 remained in the grip of natural forces.

Chapter 6 summarizes a main theme that runs throughout the volume: child mortality was high in the United States in the late nineteenth century not because parents neglected their children or because resources were severely limited. Mortality was high simply because people lacked the know-how to reduce it. Social efforts to improve child mortality were at an early stage, and individual parents and their physicians had few means at their disposal to prevent infectious diseases. The inability of privileged groups in the U.S. to achieve sharply superior mortality levels is, we believe, further evidence for this proposition.

Portions of Chapter 2 appeared in the *Journal of the American Statistical Association* 79, no. 386 (1984):272–81. Portions of Chapter 5 appeared in the *Journal of Economic History* 45(4) (1985):885–912, and in *Proceedings, International Population Conference of the International Union for the Scientific Study of Population. Florence, Italy, 1985*, 4 (1985):373–88. We are grateful for permission to reproduce them here.

In preparing this volume, we incurred debts to many people. Stephen Graham and Avery Guest from the University of Washington kindly made some of the data available to us in a form that was almost ideal for analysis. Michael Strong of the University of Pennsylvania skillfully provided our principal link with computers in the production of tables and estimation of parameters. We benefitted enormously from comments on the manuscript by Timothy Guinnane, Susan Watkins, Claudia Goldin, Robert Fogel, Clayne Pope, Eileen Crimmins, George Alter, Richard Easterlin, Gretchen Condran, Charles Rosenberg, Douglas Ewbank, Maris Vinovskis, and Jack Repcheck. Millicent Minnick typed the seemingly endless iterations of text and tables with grace and skill. Finally, we are indebted to the National Institute of Child Health and Human Development for grants that supported the production and analysis of these invaluable data.

FATAL YEARS

ONE

THE SOCIAL AND MEDICAL CONTEXT OF CHILD

MORTALITY IN THE LATE NINETEENTH CENTURY

B Y THE LATE nineteenth century, epidemics of cholera, ty-
phus, yellow fever, and plague were claiming many fewer
lives in the modernizing states of Europe and North America.
Governments had successfully asserted their rights to quarantine infected populations when these episodic horrors appeared, and improved standards of military hygiene had also blunted the diseases'
spread (Kunitz 1983, 1986). Increasingly, the diseases of consequence
were of an endemic infectious nature, the products of pathogens that
were ever-present in communities and that took their greatest toll
among infants and young children. These diseases were sufficiently
dangerous to produce mortality levels that were, by present standards, appallingly high. Nearly two out of every ten children died
before reaching their fifth birthday. American child mortality was
substantially higher in 1900 than it is today in either Asia or Latin
America.

Although the Death Registration Area (DRA) that was formed in
1900 covered only an unrepresentative 26 percent of the population,
it is the only source of information about the medical causes of children's deaths. The published 1900 United States Census furnished
information assembled by registrars and enumerators on deaths by
age, sex, and cause for the DRA during the year preceding the census
of June 1, 1900 (U.S. Bureau of the Census 1902b). Despite imperfect
diagnoses and incomplete recording of deaths, the data are instructive regarding the orders of magnitude of various diseases.

Table 1.1 shows that, within the DRA, deaths below age 15 were
highly concentrated at the youngest ages. Approximately 88 percent
of these deaths occurred at ages 0–4, and 59 percent were infant
deaths. Among the leading causes of death were gastrointestinal diseases, which caused 20 percent of all deaths for children aged 0–14
and 25 percent of deaths for infants. These diseases included such
conditions as cholera infantum, enteritis, and diarrhea. Another
leading group of causes was respiratory diseases, which included
pneumonia and bronchitis. Proportionally, these struck children

TABLE 1.1

Leading Causes of Death among Infants and Children: U.S., Death Registration Area, 1899–1900.

	Below age 1		Ages 1–4		Ages 0–4		Ages 5–14		Total ages 0–14	
	N	%[a]	N	%[a]	N	%[a]	N	%[a]	N	%[a]
All causes	60,524	100.00	29,216	100.00	89,740	100.00	12,485	100.00	102,225	100.00
Cause unknown	903	1.49	131	0.45	1,034	1.15	81	0.65	1,115	1.09
Selected gastro-intestinal diseases	15,112	24.97	4,108	14.06	19,220	21.42	804	6.44	20,024	19.59
Colitis	282	0.47	106	0.36	388	0.43	12	0.10	400	0.39
Diarrhea	1,097	1.81	247	0.85	1,344	1.50	105	0.84	1,449	1.42
Dysentery	269	0.44	298	1.02	567	0.63	72	0.58	639	0.63
Enteritis	5,431	8.97	1,453	4.97	6,884	7.67	167	1.34	7,051	6.90
Gastritis	408	0.67	146	0.50	554	0.62	48	0.38	602	0.59
Peritonitis	137	0.23	143	0.49	280	0.31	326	2.61	606	0.59
Cholera morbus	196	0.32	155	0.53	351	0.39	74	0.59	425	0.42
Cholera infantum	7,292	12.05	1,560	5.34	8,852	9.86	0	0.00	8,852	8.66
Selected respiratory diseases	11,618	19.20	9,328	31.93	20,946	23.34	1,966	15.75	22,912	22.41
Influenza	317	0.52	165	0.56	482	0.54	96	0.77	578	0.57
Croup	211	0.35	994	3.40	1,205	1.34	277	2.22	1,482	1.45
Pneumonia	6,664	11.01	6,220	21.29	12,884	14.36	1,235	9.89	14,119	13.81
Bronchitis	3,322	5.49	1,469	5.03	4,791	5.34	145	1.16	4,936	4.83
Other respiratory diseases	1,104	1.82	480	1.64	1,584	1.77	213	1.71	1,797	1.76
Convulsions	3,200	5.29	780	2.67	3,980	4.44	86	0.69	4,066	3.98
Malformations, etc.	16,162	26.70	1,605	5.49	17,767	19.80	309	2.47	18,076	17.68
Premature birth	5,829	9.63	0	0.00	5,829	6.50	0	0.00	5,829	5.70
Malformation	1,117	1.85	20	0.07	1,137	1.27	6	0.05	1,143	1.12
Debility/atrophy	5,750	9.50	589	2.02	6,339	7.06	41	0.33	6,380	6.24

Hydrocephalus	813	1.34	905	3.10	1,718	1.91	246	1.97	1,964	1.92
Inanition	2,653	4.38	91	0.31	2,744	3.06	16	0.13	2,760	2.70
Selected childhood diseases	2,480	4.10	6,583	22.53	9,063	10.10	2,705	21.67	11,768	11.51
Measles	659	1.09	1,448	4.96	2,107	2.35	276	2.21	2,383	2.33
Scarlet fever	113	0.19	1,054	3.61	1,167	1.30	575	4.61	1,742	1.70
Diphtheria	359	0.59	3,090	10.58	3,449	3.84	1,775	14.22	5,224	5.11
Whooping cough	1,345	2.22	987	3.38	2,332	2.60	75	0.60	2,407	2.35
Smallpox	4	0.01	4	0.01	8	0.01	4	0.03	12	0.01
Tuberculosis	608	1.00	641	2.19	1,249	1.39	756	6.06	2,005	1.96
Other diseases										
Meningitis	2,262	3.74	2,011	6.88	4,273	4.76	711	5.69	4,984	4.88
Jaundice	251	0.41	16	0.05	267	0.30	12	0.10	279	0.27
Kidney disease	222	0.37	297	1.02	519	0.58	13	0.10	532	0.52
Erysipelas	289	0.48	37	0.13	326	0.36	8	0.06	334	0.33
Cerebro-spinal fever	390	0.64	449	1.54	839	0.93	257	2.06	1,096	1.07
Venereal disease	278	0.46	25	0.09	303	0.34	0	0.00	303	0.30
Brain diseases	404	0.67	222	0.76	626	0.70	123	0.99	749	0.73
Heart diseases	889	1.47	206	0.71	1,095	1.22	775	6.21	1,870	1.83
Tetanus	169	0.28	16	0.05	185	0.21	93	0.74	278	0.27
Bowel obstruction	213	0.35	67	0.23	280	0.31	80	0.64	360	0.35
Dentition	216	0.36	137	0.47	353	0.39	0	0.00	353	0.35
Accident/injuries	960	1.59	996	3.41	1,956	2.18	1,271	10.18	3,227	3.16
Death rates (per 10,000 population)	1496.3	—	179.8	—	458.0	—	36.0	—	184.9	—

Source: U.S. Bureau of the Census 1902b: Table 8.
Note: Death rates are for the period 1900–1902 and are calculated from data in Glover 1921.
[a] Percentage of all causes of death.

aged 1–4 most heavily, accounting for 32 percent of all deaths in this age group. Respiratory diseases also accounted for 19 percent of deaths among infants and 16 percent of deaths among children aged 5–14. Other identifiable infectious diseases, including measles, scarlet fever, diphtheria, whooping cough, and smallpox, were also important, constituting 11.5 percent of all deaths among children below age 15. Despite the availability of diphtheria antitoxin since the mid-1890s, this disease accounted for 11 percent of the deaths in the age group 1–4 and 14 percent in the group aged 5–14. Scarlet fever, measles, and whooping cough remained life-threatening to children in this era. Smallpox, on the other hand, had been largely eliminated as an important cause of death, almost certainly because of vaccination.

Other important causes of death were meningitis (5 percent of child deaths) and accidents/injuries (3 percent of child deaths). Tuberculosis, although significant as a cause of adult deaths (representing 15 percent of all deaths to persons aged 15 and over), contributed only 2 percent of all deaths below age 15. There is evidence, however, that tuberculosis was severely underestimated as a cause of, or contributor to, child and even infant mortality, because its symptoms in children were less apparent than they were among adults. Autopsies in several cities around the turn of the century showed that 10 percent or more of infants who died were infected with tuberculosis (von Pirquet 1909). Woodbury (1925:35) reports that offspring of tuberculous mothers in Baltimore in 1915 had 2.65 times the infant mortality rate of offspring of nontuberculous mothers.

Among the deaths attributed to malformations and other congenital conditions, some were undoubtedly truly congenital defects, largely affecting infants in the first days and weeks of life. Other terms within this category such as inanition (or inability to absorb nutrition, mostly affecting infants) and debility/atrophy were quite imprecise. This category ("Malformations, etc.") accounted for 27 percent of infant deaths, but only 5.5 percent of deaths to those aged 1–4 and 2.5 percent of deaths at ages 5–14. Finally, "Convulsions" represented about 4 percent of all deaths and about 5 percent of infant deaths. Death through convulsions was usually only the final and fatal effect of infection or some other condition, often (though it was not widely acknowledged at the time) including dehydration resulting from gastrointestinal disturbances.

Theories of Disease Causation

Table 1.1 depicts an overwhelming assault on young children by infectious diseases in 1900. Deaths were, of course, only the tip of the iceberg, a signal of the enormous burden of morbidity that lay below. According to the prominent economist Irving Fisher, "Every observer of human misery among the poor reports that disease plays the leading role" (Fisher 1909:124). A 1908 survey of schoolchildren in New York found that 66 percent needed medical or surgical attention or better nourishment (cited in Fisher 1909:74).

Yet the late nineteenth century was also a time of dramatic discoveries in bacteriology. The nature of infectious disease came into much sharper focus as disease-causing agents, invisible to the naked eye but increasingly visible under the microscope, were identified as the source of many common afflictions. The germ theory received its first important empirical support in the early 1860s, when Louis Pasteur showed that the growth of microorganisms in a broth could be prevented by avoiding atmospheric contamination. This demonstration was quickly put to practical use in antiseptic procedures in hospitals, promoted especially by Joseph Lister (Rosenberg 1987: ch. 5). Lister's visit to the U.S. during the centennial year of 1876 was instrumental to the country's gradual acceptance of antiseptic procedures. Case fatality rates from surgery declined precipitously in the last decades of the nineteenth century, and surgical patients began to outnumber medical patients in some hospitals (Vogel 1980).

Although antiseptic practices came to be accepted in U.S. hospitals, the ideas on which they were based were not always greeted so warmly. Phyllis Richmond (1954) describes the indifferent and even hostile reception to the germ theory by American medical society. Medical journals carried little information about the European developments, and medical research was poorly organized and underfunded. Textbooks were slow to recognize the role of disease-causing microorganisms; an official health manual for the military in 1884 made virtually no mention of germs, and when they were mentioned the reference was usually erroneous. A survey of leading American physicians in 1877 by H. I. Bowditch, himself the developer and promoter of the "law of soil moisture" as an explanation of the geographic distribution of disease, asked, "Has any law of development of disease been discovered by attention to which, in coming centuries, we may hope to greatly lessen or destroy the disease?" Thirty-nine physicians replied "no," 6 "yes," and 3 did not reply (Bowditch 1877:117).

According to Charles Rosenberg (1987), the notion that diseases were caused by minute particles seemed meaninglessly random, a contradiction of collective wisdom distilled from centuries of medical experience. Briefly stated, that experience emphasized the importance of atmospheric miasma (or miasmata), produced by environmental filth, as agents of disease. Sources of filth included sewers, cesspools, swamps, slaughterhouses, and decaying vegetation (Richmond 1954). Exposure to miasmata disrupted the body's balance, and physicians often attempted to restore its balance through purgatives, diuretics, and emetics.

The miasmatic theories focussed attention on what were often real nuisances and sometimes led to effective health interventions (Duffy 1971). Ridding the environment of foul odors often removed disease-causing agents as well. The 1850 Report of the Sanitary Commission of Massachusetts persuasively and accurately laid the cause of many public-health problems at the doorstep of contaminated water and improper ventilation (Rosenkrantz 1972). Careful empirical studies occasionally led to the establishment of more precise relationships between environmental agents and disease consequences, as in Semmelweis's 1848 demonstration of the role of unclean instruments in mortality from childbed fever. Likewise, careful epidemiologic investigations of yellow fever in the 1860s produced sensible decisions about preventive measures even without clear knowledge of the nature of the disease (Coleman 1987).

But confusion about the causes of infectious disease often led to misdirection and wasted effort, as best revealed by the preoccupation with sewer gas in the 1870s and 1880s. In his 1880 address to the Medical Society of the State of Pennsylvania, Benjamin Lee blamed sewer gas for most major diseases (Richmond 1954:447). Great emphasis was placed on the building of "stench traps." Evidently the concern was embraced by much of the populace. In his 1877 book, entitled *Public Hygiene in America*, Bowditch says, "There seems to be arising among citizens a kind of panic relative to the drains of their own house, and they have a great horror of the least odor of sewer gas" (Bowditch 1877:38). For George Waring, one of the most influential sanitary engineers in the last decades of the nineteenth century, sewer gas came to be what miasma had been to people of earlier eras. His anticontagionist platform was finally discredited only in 1898–1902, when the source of yellow fever was identified as mosquitoes rather than filth (Cassedy 1962b).

The old ideas grew increasingly untenable after 1882 and 1883 when Koch identified the tuberculosis bacillus and the cholera organism. By 1890, the microorganisms causing typhoid, pneumonia, and diphtheria had also been identified. The germ theory produced a number of bogus cures for disease in the next decades, but it also scored a grand success with the development of diphtheria antitoxin, which could arrest the development of a case if caught at the very early stages. The discovery and rapid deployment of the antitoxin after 1894 had an enormous popular impact, and the physician's image as a healer improved greatly (Vogel 1980; Rosenberg 1987: ch. 6). Rothstein (1972) argues that the success of diphtheria antitoxin brought about the triumph of bacteriology in medicine. In 1895, impressed by the new successes of bacteriology, Charles Buchanan could write, "Today the germ theory of disease is the very foundation upon which the magnificent superstructure of modern medicine rests—ay, we might almost say that it is at once the foundation and the structure" (cited in Brieger 1966:145).

But it would be incorrect to assume that the role of germs in disease was readily and universally acknowledged, let alone that a wide array of preventive and therapeutic procedures based on the germ theory were implemented. The last two decades of the nineteenth century were a period of tumult and contention among contrasting ideas of disease causation (Duffy 1967). Some theories attempted to combine contagious and miasmatic mechanisms (Meckel 1990: ch. 1). According to Hermann Biggs, who organized the first municipal department of pathology and bacteriology in New York City in 1892 and was later New York State Commissioner of Health, doctors were very slow to comprehend the meaning of Koch's discovery, and even in 1902 a large proportion of physicians failed to grasp the discovery's significance (cited in Rothstein 1972: 268). Tuberculosis and pneumonia, each responsible for massive loss of life, were typically considered "constitutional diseases" and were largely unnoticed by the general public, whose eyes were fixed on the much less consequential but more dramatic episodic killers such as Asiatic cholera and yellow fever. Likewise, the loss of so many infants from vague-sounding causes was generally accepted as the inexorable working of fate (Duffy 1967). Although the contagious nature of the epidemic diseases was obvious and led to quarantine measures that were often effective, the endemic diseases appeared to be a more constant component of the human condition. Sick patients expected their physicians to prescribe doses of cathartics or analgesics to restore the body's balance, and the physicians usually obliged (Rosenberg 1987: ch. 6).

Germs were strangely missing from many contemporary explanations of disease. Explanations of differences in death rates among racial and ethnic groups were typically couched in terms of the different "constitutions" of the various groups rather than the different intensities of disease to which they may have been subject. This was an era of extreme racism, fed by a misunderstanding of the new science of genetics. The Presidential Address to the first meeting of the American Pediatric Society in 1889 set the tone for much health-oriented discourse:

> [America's] self-assumed destiny is to raise humanitarian and social de-
> velopment to a higher plane by amalgamating, humanizing, and civiliz-
> ing the scum of all the inferior races and nationalities which are congre-
> gating under the folds of our flag. (Jacobi 1889:898)

This sense of mission was not shared by all in the medical establishment. In 1897 George Shrady, editor of the *Medical Record*, told read-
ers that the public-health movement was wasting vast sums of
money on "worthless and undeserving persons" (cited in Starr
1982:182).

Constitutional explanations were most frequently invoked when
considering mortality differences between blacks and whites. Fred-
erick Hoffman, an actuary for the Prudential Insurance Company
and a very prominent vital statistician in the early twentieth century
(Cassedy 1965), published a monograph in 1896 for the American
Economic Association entitled *Race Traits and Tendencies of the American Negro*. It ascribed the high mortality of blacks to constitutional
inferiority and to immorality. Blacks had higher tuberculosis death
rates because of their "smaller or tropical lung" (Hoffman 1896:76).
They were constitutionally more susceptible to typhoid and malaria
(now clearly seen as a disease against which blacks had a genetic advantage through the sickle-cell trait) (ibid.: 102). Parents broken
down by disease consequent on vice, immorality, and debauchery
imparted enfeebled constitutions to their offspring (ibid.: 67). No-
where in the account are germs to be found, and only a grudging
gesture is made towards the notion that the extreme poverty of
blacks might figure into their high mortality:

> The facts here brought together for southern cities as well as for the is-
> lands of the West Indies so fully support each other as to warrant the
> conclusion that the excessive infant mortality among the colored popu-
> lation is largely a result of individual neglect, as well as in part due to
> inherited organic weakness, and only to a limited extent to the condi-
> tions of life. (Ibid.:69)

Hoffman's views were by no means exceptional for the period (cf.
Kiple and King 1981). Southern physicians—those closest to the actual situation of blacks—were the group most inclined to blame the
environment for high black mortality, whereas most other commentators viewed it as a product of an inevitable genetic weeding-out
(ibid.:89). DuBois's classic study, *The Philadelphia Negro*, ridicules the
genetic position and cites the wretched housing and sanitary conditions in which northern urban blacks were forced to live as the main

source of excessive black mortality. He also implicates deficient personal cleanliness (DuBois 1899:161, 163).

Assumptions of racial superiority that informed attitudes toward disease were not limited to black-white comparisons. Immigrant groups from southern and eastern Europe were widely assumed to be of inferior stock and to suffer excessive mortality as a result. These ascriptions were probably facilitated by the persistence of theories of disease that stressed the maintenance of balance among bodily parts and systems. The "holistic" theories of health made it easier to imagine that individuals varied in their vulnerabilities to an array of diseases, and genetics in its popular form of eugenics made it seem plausible that these vulnerabilities would vary along racial or ethnic lines. As a result, it was easy to blame the victim, especially if he or she came from "inferior" stock. In contrast, the germ theory stressed specific symptoms and clinical courses in relation to specific disease entities and focussed on discrete ways of preventing or treating discrete diseases (Maulitz 1979; Rosenberg 1987). By the middle of the twentieth century, it had eroded the basis for ethnic and racial labelling of disease susceptibilities.

The Practice of Medicine

Although the bacteriological discoveries of the late nineteenth century revolutionized medical science, they had a much smaller impact on medical practice (Rothstein 1972). Rosenberg (1987) concludes that digitalis, quinine, and especially opium and its derivatives were the medical profession's most effective drugs at the end of the nineteenth century, as they had been a half-century earlier. Diagnosis was aided by many new tools in 1900: chemical and bacteriologic tests for microorganisms that had been identified as disease-causing, microscopes, x-rays, stethoscopes and otoscopes. Yet the tests were not often applied in private practice, in part because there was little that could be done to alter the course of a disease once it was identified. A popular physician's handbook by Cathell, in its eleventh edition of 1902, warned that there was no bread and butter for the practicing physician in "histology, pathology, microscopical anatomy, refined diagnostics, and bacteriomania" (Rothstein 1972:266). Many physicians would walk out of scientific meetings in contempt when the subject of bacteriology arose (ibid.:265).

Physicians had reason to worry about their bread and butter because their profession did not enjoy the esteem and privileges that it does today. Although there are no definitive sources, income estimates in 1899/1900 for groups of occupations presented in Appendix A show physicians to be in a group that earned more than manual workers, on average, but less than many other professionals such as surveyors, lawyers, and even college professors. At proprietary schools and some of the weaker university departments, physicians were being recruited from working men and the lower classes, to the dismay of professional leaders endeavoring to raise the status of doctors (Starr 1982:117). Although all jurisdictions had adopted a licensing statute of some sort by 1901, "the ports of entry into medicine were still wide open and the unwelcome passed through in great numbers" (ibid.:116). These entry points included openings for "irregulars" such as homeopaths, allopaths, osteopaths, and eclectics, who constituted some 16–24 percent of all practitioners (Leavitt and Numbers 1978:75). The famous Flexner Report of 1910 concluded that the country needed "fewer and better doctors" (Caldwell 1988:170).

Just as doctors had few drugs in their arsenal to cure disease, so too did hospitals have few means at their disposal to alter the clinical course of a disease. In fact, exposure in the hospital to others' infections often produced a turn for the worse. Writing a ten-year retrospective on the Babies Hospital of New York City, superintendent Luther Emmett Holt (1897) anguished over the difficulties facing children who required a prolonged stay because of the likelihood of their developing an acute disease while in the hospital. The population at large was aware of these dangers. Leavitt (1979) recounts an episode in Milwaukee in 1894 when a crowd of 3000 furious people, armed with clubs, assembled to protect a child whom health authorities intended to take to the hospital during a smallpox epidemic. The child's mother had already lost a child in the hospital, and she was frantic not to let the city "kill" another of her children. The mob prevailed, and the ambulance retreated. Members of the middle class quite sensibly preferred to avoid hospitals and to be treated at home whenever possible (Rosenberg 1987), although Vogel (1980) reports a change in middle-class attitudes in Boston beginning around the turn of the century. DuBois (1899:162) reports that, in part because of their brusque treatment, "Many a Negro would almost rather die than trust himself to a hospital."

While doctors and hospitals were poorly equipped to deal with the array of adult afflictions with which they were confronted, they were even more poorly equipped to deal with infants and children. The first professor of pediatrics at Harvard described the state of knowledge about diseases of children in 1891 as consisting of "a poor subterfuge of unreal facts forming structures of misleading results which in the scientific medicine of adults would not for a second be tolerated" (Rotch 1891:819). Abraham Jacobi, the first president of the American Pediatric Society, bemoaned the absence of attention in medical curricula to diseases of children, even though children would typically form the majority of a doctor's patients (Jacobi 1890:818). The high death rates of infants and young children seemed to many lay people and doctors alike to be an inevitable concomitant of this vulnerable stage of development. In 1887, less than a half-dozen general hospitals in the U.S. had wards for infants (Holt 1897). While children's hospitals were established in eight major cities during the 1880s, some of these would not accept patients below age 5 (Jacobi 1909:832).

Yet matters were to change rapidly. The first journal in English dealing with the specific medical problems of children, *Archives of Pediatrics*, was begun in 1884, and the American Pediatrics Society was formed in 1888 (Bremner 1971:811). In the 1890s, diphtheria antitoxin, the first successful therapeutic agent for a disease affecting children, became available. And diphtheria had become an important disease, rising in the course of the nineteenth century to a crude death rate approximately equal to that of cancer today. In Boston City Hospital, the fatality rate for diphtheria admissions declined from 47 percent in 1888 to 10 percent in 1899. Citywide, mortality from diphtheria fell from 18.03 deaths per 10,000 inhabitants in 1894 to 3.15 in 1898 (Vogel 1980:63). The antitoxin did much to enhance the esteem of physicians, and the recognition that a common affliction could be arrested through medical intervention seemed to reduce the fatalism that had surrounded diseases of children. By 1906, W. C. Hollopeter (a professor of pediatrics in Philadelphia) could write with some exaggeration that

> Pediatrics is second to no branch in energy, enthusiasm, and progress, not only in the annual literary output but in the teaching in the clinic and laboratory . . . diphtheria is now viewed with serenity. . . . in fact in most intelligent communities any appreciable number of cases of measles or scarlet fever is viewed with reproach as the result of faulty domiciliary, school, or public hygiene. Twenty years ago, such cases and epidemics were looked upon as unavoidable calamities." (Hollopeter 1906:820)

We have little quantitative information on the specific kinds of preventative or curative measures that were deployed at the turn of the century. By 1900, only two effective drugs were available: smallpox vaccine and diphtheria antitoxin. The high death rate from diphtheria in 1900–1902 is evidence that the deployment of the antitoxin had been far from completely effective. With regard to vaccination, a broad-based 1930 survey of children's health showed that only 21 percent of city preschool children and 7 percent of rural preschool children had been vaccinated against smallpox (White House Conference on Child Health and Protection 1931:1082). The figures were unlikely to have been higher in 1900, although schoolchildren undoubtedly showed higher coverage than preschoolers. The poor coverage of this preventative measure was ironically revealed in 1899–1900, when 3 of 12 medical students at Tulane University died of smallpox (Duffy 1971:395). Nevertheless, smallpox mortality had declined rapidly because those vaccinated protected not only themselves but also many of the unvaccinated.

Obstetrics seemed little more developed than pediatrics, and undoubtedly a sizable fraction of infant deaths were attributable to problems of childbirth that today would be readily prevented. Even by the standards of the time, obstetrics seemed backwards. A 1912 survey of physicians showed that obstetrics was considered the weakest area in medical schools (Kobrin 1966:218). According to Meckel (1990: ch. 6), pregnant women in the late nineenth century rarely visited a physician for preventive reasons, and there was a special reluctance to do abdominal exams on women. Vaginal exams were out of the question. Forceps and anesthesia had improved somewhat the tools at an obstetrician's disposal, but their utilization was based more on trial and error than on systematic science (Leavitt 1986:144). Most obstetricians believed that antiseptic practices were nearly impossible to implement in private practice (Dye 1987:55). Standards of cleanliness in hospitals by 1900 were probably higher than what could be achieved in home deliveries, a state of affairs that was beginning to draw increasing numbers of births into hospitals (Leavitt 1986:161).

Midwives presided at a large percentage of births at the turn of the century and were still delivering about 50 percent of babies born in 1910, heavily concentrated among immigrants and blacks (Kobrin 1966:217). A 1902 deliberation by the secretary of the New York State Board of Medical Examiners about midwives in New York City, who were delivering 47 percent of babies born, referred to the "undivided opinion that great evils are wrought to the community by reason of the incapacity and negligence of the midwives" (Lewi 1902:984). Midwives in Providence, Rhode Island, presided at 42 percent of births in 1910. A commentator complained bitterly about their unsanitary practices, including dressing the cord with snuff and giving babies a mixture of molasses and urine to drink as a physic (Stone 1912:988). More systematic investigations into the knowledge and practices of midwives by the Children's Bureau found them largely unprepared to deal with complications of childbirth and often uninformed about hygienic practices. In a predominantly black area of Mississippi, fewer than 10 percent of midwives used antiseptics as late as 1917 (Dart 1921). Midwives serving Polish women in Wisconsin often failed to wash their hands (Sherbon and Moore 1919:35). Yet obstetricians were often ill-prepared themselves. The advantages of midwives included their availability and cheapness and the possibility that they would help out in the early days of the infant's life.

We have found no data to support (or refute) the claim of inferior outcomes among children delivered by midwives, who disproportionately served immigrant mothers, blacks, and women in remote rural areas. Physicians undoubtedly had a professional interest in disparaging the work of midwives. In the twentieth century, various cities attempted to educate midwives toward better practice, and to make them intermediaries between mothers and public health facilities. Licensing requirements, the institution of which accelerated from 1890 to 1910, also improved the practice of midwifery. When these reforms were accomplished, babies delivered by midwives could have below-average mortality (Chapin 1919:157).

With physicians and hospitals having so few tools at their disposal in 1900, it is not surprising that people resorted to home remedies on a wide scale. Approximately $75 million worth of patent medicines were purchased in 1906 (Adams 1906:882). DuBois (1899:114) bemoaned the vast quantities of patent medicines purchased by blacks in Philadelphia, as well as their frequent resort to the "old class of root doctors and patent medicine quacks." In 1890, seventeen factories were busily producing "Microbe Killer," consisting nearly entirely of water except for traces of red wine and hydrochloric and sulfuric acids (Starr 1982:128). Patent medicines reached their apogee in the very age when reasonable explanations of disease first became available (ibid.). The two were perhaps not unconnected, since recognition that germs played a role in disease, however misunderstood, probably made a cure seem within closer reach.

While medical practice in the doctor's office, hospital, and home was by present standards ill-informed and often unwise, there were enlightened members of the medical profession who saw clearly the implications of the germ theory for medical practice, and who combined the theory with sensible empirical observation, especially about the importance of feeding practices. Two such individuals were authors of pediatric texts at the turn of the century. Dr. Luther Emmett Holt, superintendent of the Babies' Hospital of New York City, was the author of a popular home manual, *The Care and Feeding of Children* (1894), as well as a widely used pediatric text, *The Diseases of Infancy and Childhood* (1897), which went through a number of sub-sequent editions. Dr. Henry Koplik had established the first infant milk dispensary in the United States in New York City in 1889 and was the author of *The Diseases of Infancy and Early Childhood* (1902), which also went through subsequent editions (Bremner 1971:812, 827). Here we review some of the information and advice contained in these texts to gain a sense of the best practice of the period.

Holt noted that gastrointestinal infections were epidemic in most large cities during the warm months and were believed to be bacterial in origin (Holt 1897:317). "In large cities more than one-half of deaths among infants under the age of twelve months are caused by summer diarrhea. . . . Th[e] high rate of mortality of bottle-fed infants, is not alone due to the difference in the nature of the food; no matter how carefully it is handled before it reaches the infant, milk passes through many channels, and in each of these it is exposed to infection. The intense heat of summer also favors the increase of infective agents" (Koplik 1902:316). Koplik probably overestimated the importance of summer diarrhea, as suggested by Table 1.1, although there is substantial evidence to support his conclusion that summer diarrhea was caused largely by contamination of artificial feeding media, especially cow's milk, and was most prevalent after weaning. There was, however, debate concerning the specific microorganisms involved, and some suspicion that normal intestinal bacteria (e.g., E. Coli) might become virulent. Mechanical irritation (caused by "improper food") was also suspected to be a cause.

Treatment, though sometimes crude and impractical, could have been effective. The first recommendation was prophylaxis: to keep the child from being exposed to infective organisms. Both Holt (1897:324–25) and Koplik (1902:321–22) felt strongly that providing pure food and milk was an important step. "No greater work of philanthropy can be done among the poor in summer than to provide means whereby pure, clean milk for young children can be supplied at the price now paid for an inferior article" (Holt 1897:325). Prompt attention to mild cases of diarrhea was encouraged, since many severe and fatal cases were felt to have been treatable at an earlier, milder stage. Sensible hygienic practices around sick people, e.g., washing of hands and changing and thorough washing of clothing and bedclothes, were also encouraged (Koplik 1902:333).

In brief, prophylaxis demands (1) sending as many infants out of the city in summer as possible; (2) the education of the laity up to the importance of regularity in feeding, the dangers of overfeeding, and as to what is a proper diet for infants just weaned; (3) proper legal restrictions regarding the transportation and sale of milk; (4) the exclusion of germs or their destruction in all foods given, but especially in milk, by careful sterilization in summer, and scrupulous cleanliness in bottles, nipples, etc.; (5) prompt attention to all mild derangements; (6) cutting down the amount of food and increasing the amount of water during the days of excessive summer heat. (Holt 1897:325)

Once a child had become ill, rest, fresh air, quiet, and cleanliness were recommended, usually in a location outside the city. For feeding, a sugar solution with barley or rice water, or some other milk substitute such as wine whey, malted food, albumen water, acorn cocoa, or animal broths, were recommended. Cow's milk and all other foods were to be stopped, since they were believed to be irritating to the infant's gastrointestinal system. Elements of holistic balance theories remained, however, as purgatives and irrigation of the intestines, now considered damaging practices, were proposed to cleanse the intestinal tract (Holt 1897:325–32, 335–37; Koplik 1902:321–25).

In terms of actual treatment of sick infants (as opposed to prevention of illness), there seemed to be only partial recognition that dehydration and consequent systemic shock were the greatest dangers. Subcutaneous saline injections (sometimes from something resembling a modern intravenous apparatus) were recommended for the most severe cases, but there were recognized dangers of local infection from that treatment (Koplik 1902:323–24). Baths were seen as efficacious and necessary for the reduction of high fevers (Holt 1897:331, 336–37). Drug therapy, using alcohol, strychnine and atropine (to stimulate the heart), and bismuth and resorcin (to alleviate vomiting) were symptomatic and not very effective. Overall, medical advice was most helpful in prevention and early treatment. Therapy in severe cases was of limited effectiveness, even when medical advice and help was sought by mothers of sick infants. It was not until the 1920s and 1930s that fluid and electrolyte therapy was developed to deal with the dehydration and electrolyte imbalances that were shown in 1915 to be the immediate cause of death for infants and children with severe diarrhea (Meckel 1990: ch. 2).

A second major cause of infant and child deaths in 1900 was respiratory infections (see Table 1.1). Chief among these were pneumonia and bronchitis. "In the early life the lungs are more frequently the seat of organic disease than any other organs of the body. Pneumonia is very common as a primary disease, and ranks first as a complication of the various forms of acute infectious disease of children. It is one of the most important factors in the mortality of infancy and childhood" (Holt 1897:477). Lobar, pleuro-, and bronchopneumonia were recognized as bacterial infections; and the symptoms, diagnosis, and prognosis were reasonably well understood. The fact that pneumonia was also frequently a complication of another condition (e.g., measles, whooping cough, diphtheria) was known, as were possible consequent complications (e.g., meningitis) (Holt 1987:477–537; Koplik 1902:375–409). Pneumonia was observed to be serious, with a high case fatality rate.

But there was little that medical professionals could do about pneumonia and other respiratory diseases in the era prior to the discovery and use of sulfa drugs in the 1930s and antibiotics in the 1940s. "The treatment of lobar pneumonia is pre-eminently expectant. The disease is self-limited, and complications cannot be prevented. . . . The temperature should be treated not with a view to its actual reduction, but in order to mitigate its ill effects" (Koplik 1902:389). The term "self-limited" was used in medical literature at the turn of the century to describe conditions for which no effective intervention was available.

Acute bronchitis is fundamentally an inflammation of the bronchial tubes and was so recognized at the turn of the century (Koplik 1902:302). Again, treatment was symptomatic, or "supporting and expectant" (ibid.:364). The condition was seen as self-limiting. Prevention, by keeping children generally healthy and warm, was appropriately stressed. It was felt that mild attacks (i.e., bronchitis of the large tubes) should not be neglected and allowed to become life-threatening by moving down to the smaller bronchial tubes (Holt 1897:466–67). Croup was frequently another name for bronchitis (ibid.:470), although it was usually seen as a disease of the larynx. In general, respiratory diseases were known to be contagious, more common in colder months, and potentially very serious. Medical advice stressed prevention via good general health, warm clothing and shelter, and symptomatic treatment. But respiratory diseases, once contracted, had to be allowed to run their course.

Some considerable amount was known about the so-called "specific infectious diseases," if only that they were infectious. The latter implied isolation and quarantine as possible preventives. Among the diseases that were relatively well defined were measles, scarlet fever, diphtheria, whooping cough, mumps, rubella, typhoid fever, chicken pox, tuberculosis (in various forms), smallpox, and meningitis. Of these, smallpox had been greatly reduced as a childhood disease, mostly through vaccination (Koplik 1902:162–66). Among the remaining diseases, diphtheria alone had a specific treatment. The discovery of diphtheria antitoxin to counteract the effect of the bacillus was made by Emil von Behring in 1890 and, as noted earlier, began to pass into widespread use after 1894 (Rosen 1958:330). In addition, prophylaxis via isolation, quarantine, and disinfection was quite effective. "In no infectious disease can so much be accomplished in the way of prevention as in diphtheria" (Holt 1897:981). Koplik notes large declines in the diphtheria case-fatality rate after the use of antitoxin therapy (Koplik 1902:223). In extreme cases, the membrane growth in the larynx, which was the proximate cause of death from diphtheria, could be successfully surgically removed or bypassed (ibid.:227–34). Nonetheless, as we have seen, diphtheria in 1900 still accounted for over 5 percent of total deaths among children below age 15 in the Death Registration Area. Here is a clear example of the slow diffusion of a medical innovation within the structure of American medicine at the turn of the century.

Although a good deal was known about the remaining specific infectious diseases, not much could be done about them in terms of prevention or specific therapy. Typically, the best that could be recommended was maintaining children in good health and preventing exposure via quarantine, and practicing good hygienic practices in the home and sickroom. Hospitalization was not necessarily a good alternative. "The result of hospital treatment in many diseases is notoriously bad" (Crandall 1896:532). In some cases the diseases were viral (e.g., smallpox, influenza, chicken pox, measles), and hence the microorganism had not been identified.

For several bacterial diseases as well, such as scarlet fever and whooping cough, the pathogens had not yet been found (Koplik 1902:118–19, 201). The tuberculosis bacillus had been identified by Koch, but "no specific remedy for tuberculosis has as yet stood the test of experience" (Holt 1897:1051). "It will be seen that treatment of tuberculosis of the lung in young infants and children must be simply symptomatic" (Koplik 1902:247). The same could be said for other, nonrespiratory forms of tuberculosis. Isolation of patients, use of tuberculosis tests to determine exposed and infected individuals and animal hosts, provision of pure milk (free from the tuberculosis bacillus), maintenance of good health among potential victims, and disinfection of areas where tuberculosis had been present were all urged as effective preventive measures. (Holt 1897:1050–51). The decline in tuberculosis death rates in the late nineteenth and early twentieth centuries, to the extent that they occurred in the United States, were probably partly due to such prophylactic activities.

Overall, for most diseases, prevention was more important than specific therapy in 1900. Isolation of infectious patients and disinfection of their quarters were becoming much more common in hospitals and even homes (Chapin 1901:527; Rosenberg 1987). Specific treatments were effective in a few cases, namely diphtheria and some gastrointestinal infections. But medical advice was mainly effective in prevention, an activity that, of course, extends into the realm of public health. It was here that the new knowledge of disease mechanisms was beginning to have its greatest payoff.

The Practice of Public Health

In the last two decades of the nineteenth century, increased recognition that most diseases were spread from person to person provided a sounder basis for public preventative measures. And many government units did assume responsibility for such measures. S. W. Abbott (1900) cites an 1879 statement by sanitarian John Billings that "a standing committee on public health would be about the last committee that either congress or a state legislative would think of organizing." But Abbott notes that by 1900 such committees formed a part of the organization of state legislatures in many of the older states and were supplemented by committees responsible for water supply, sewerage, drainage, and other public health concerns. Only five states were without a board of health by 1900 (ibid.:11). In Abbott's mind there was no doubt that the discoveries of Pasteur provided the impetus for many such changes (ibid.:67). Rosenkrantz's (1972) account of public health in Massachusetts, on the other hand, suggests that governments would have assumed greater responsibility for public health even without the germ theory, as urbanization and immigration produced vivid social contrasts that activated humanitarian impulses. Increased governmental responsibility for health was a logical component of the Progressive Era of the 1890s and 1900s, when greater social responsibility for improving conditions of life was assumed in many areas (Wiebe 1967).

John Duffy (1971:401) suggests that the germ theory awakened the upper classes to the realization that bacteria did not respect social or economic conditions and that a person's health was dependent on that of others. This realization gave impetus not only to the institution of public-health programs but also to social reforms and antipoverty programs. Evidence of the public's support for public-health initiatives, whatever its source, was vividly revealed in a Chicago referendum. In 1889 the Illinois legislature created the Chicago Sanitary District with boundaries well beyond those of the city. The purpose of the Chicago Sanitary District was to address the technical problems of sewerage disposal and to avoid political impediments to sanitary reform. Further, the twenty-five-mile Sanitary and Ship Canal was authorized to drain more of the city's wastes away from its water supply in Lake Michigan. The canal was begun in 1892 and completed in 1900. In a combined referendum on the Sanitary District and the canal and the election of Sanitary District trustees in 1889, the people of Chicago endorsed the project by a vote of 70,958 to 242 (Galishoff 1980:48). Public acceptance of such large and expensive projects is some evidence that they were considered effective by contemporaries in reducing sickness and death rates (Cain 1977; Galishoff 1980; Tarr, McCurley, and Yosie 1980; Anderson 1984). The great sanitary engineer Charles Chapin wrote in 1901 that the need for sewers was so well appreciated by the public that health officers scarcely needed to press the case for them (Chapin 1901:297).

Such public support did not extend to all potentially valuable health programs. Several commentators despaired at the public's apparent indifference to sanitizing the milk supply (Chapin 1901:399; Coit 1893:867). The greater support for improvements in sewers than in milk supplies may reflect the continued grip of miasmatic theories on the public's consciousness. Health officers frequently felt the need to galvanize public opinion in favor of health reform. In these matters they often had little support from physicians, who sometimes saw public intervention in health as a usurpation of their authority (Starr 1982: ch. 5). Chapin (1901) repeatedly stressed that health officials were more advanced in their recognition of the value of bacteriology than physicians of the era. Other special interest groups such as dairymen also resisted state intervention on behalf of the public's health (Rosenkrantz 1972).

The implementation of public-health measures was, of course, a political process, and subject to the vagaries of the polling place and political alliances. The federal government played a minor public-health role in the nineteenth century, although some urged an expanded role upon it. The Supreme Court, for example, had declared a federal role in compulsory vaccination to be unconstitutional (Chapin 1901:573). And although state governments had often formed committees to oversee public health, the state's role was mainly didactic (Abbott 1900:12), and it had little power to enforce decisions (Chapin 1901:269). Expenditures by state boards of health rarely reached one cent per capita in 1898 and never exceeded nine cents (Abbott 1900:36).

As in England (Szreter 1988), the principal burden of instituting public health-programs fell on municipal governments. Some $2.1 million was spent by municipal health departments in 32 large cities around 1900, about twenty cents per capita (Abbott 1900:92). But municipal governments were not always enlightened. Hollopeter wrote despairingly in 1906 that, "so long as politics as a distinct profession remains on so low a plane in our cities, so long will crime and graft crush out young life and retard the advance of true hygiene" (Hollopeter 1906:821). Judith Leavitt (1979) presents a provocative account of the politics of public health in Milwaukee. During the smallpox epidemic of 1894, patronage, class, and ethnic divisions in the city were responsible not only for depriving the health department of its most effective means of controlling the epidemic—forcible isolation of infective patients—but also for impeaching the competent, but politically unpopular, health commissioner. Leavitt argues that the incident permanently damaged Milwaukee's ability to advance the public's health. A more successful example of health officials' political acumen is the relationship established between Herman Biggs, health commissioner of New York City, and the Tammany Hall political machine (Duffy 1974).

The activities of public officials in health improvement took many forms. Charles Chapin's marvelous 969-page work, *Municipal Sanitation in the United States* (1901), is a compendium of the activities of state and municipal officials and of legislation bearing on public health, as well as a guidebook to proper practice at the time. The last two decades of the nineteenth century witnessed advances on a wide front, although there is probably no area of public health where a majority of the progress between 1850 and 1950 occurred by 1900. Public water supplies were available to 42 percent of the nation's population in 1896 (up from 17 percent in 1870), although many of those to whom public water was available remained unconnected. Sewers were available to only 29 percent of the population (Abbott 1900:37, 40).

Bacteriologic testing of New York City's water began in 1891, but tests showed no improvement over the decade. Despite the referendum of 1889, the last two decades of the nineteenth century were a dark period for water quality in Chicago, with typhoid death rates reaching their all-time high of 1.74 per 1000 in 1892. In New Orleans, there was no public water supply until 1906, and there were no sewer hook-ups until 1907. Cisterns collecting rainwater were the main source of water, and they often ran dry or became contaminated with dirt on the roofs of dwellings that served as collectors (Lentzner 1987).

Even when public water supplies were available, the water was often unfiltered or improperly filtered. At the turn of the century, there was still a debate over whether slow sand filtration or mechanical filtration was more effective against bacterial contamination.

Chlorination was not begun until 1902 and sedimentation not until 1904. Although aeration of drinking water was recommended, it was later determined to be ineffective against many of the most dangerous waterborne human pathogens. In 1870 there was virtually no filtered water in the United States. By 1880, about 30,000 persons in cities with populations over 2,500 were using filtered water. This number grew to 310,000 by 1890 and to 1,860,000 by 1900. But the major improvements came thereafter. By 1910 approximately 10,800,000 persons were served by filtered water, and the number had risen to over 20 million by 1920 (Whipple 1921:166–68). For Chapin, there was no question about what the aim of water improvement programs should be: "The most serious contamination of water is disease germs. Of these the typhoid bacillus is by far the most important. It is possible that certain diarrheal affections may be carried in drinking water, but the evidence is not clear" (Chapin 1901:263). But he also suggests that it is important to rid the water of color, suspended matter, taste, and odor (ibid.:274).

Probably of greater importance than water quality for infant and early child mortality is the quality and cleanliness of the milk supply. Milk could and did spread typhoid, scarlet fever, diphtheria, strep throat, and tuberculosis (North 1921). Progress in improving milk supplies was quite slow in the nineteenth century, perhaps in part because of the sheer technical difficulties of monitoring the supply in its many stages from the birth of a calf to its final consumption by babies and children. Chapin (1901:366) argues that milk was far more urgently in need of protection than any other food, but that little progress had been made in that direction. In addition to the difficulties of monitoring the supply, Chapin cites a widespread apathy on the part of consumers concerning the quality of milk. They were said to be far more attentive to price than to quality (ibid.:399), a refrain echoed in many other accounts of the period. Pasteurization was also widely believed to harm the taste of milk (North 1921:274).

In 1911, only 15 percent of the milk supply in New York City—one of the most progressive cities in public health—was pasteurized, even though the process had been known since the 1860s (Lentzner 1987:229). Before 1908, when pasteurization was made compulsory in Chicago, only a fifth of the milk sold had been pasteurized (ibid.:246). Pasteurization was made compulsory in New York in 1912. Other strategies were available for improving the quality of milk: the inspection of dairies, first instituted in Minnesota in 1895 (Chapin 1901:401), and licensing of milk sellers, begun in New York City in 1895 (Lentzner 1987:216). This latter effort did not appear to have much impact on mortality, as Lentzner shows. Greater purity of milk was sometimes attained by heating it in the home, a practice introduced from Germany in the late 1880s (Ewbank and Preston 1989). No mention of bacteria in regard to milk supplies was made by the New York City Board of Health until 1896, and it was not until 1909 that the Board enlarged its concept of adulterated milk to include bacteria (Shaftel 1978:283). Samples of milk supplies intended for consumption from around the country in 1905–10 showed that 8.3 percent contained tubercle bacilli (North 1921).

State and municipal health authorities took other steps in the last two decades of the nineteenth century. As noted above, all states had physician licensing regulations by 1901. Licensing of midwives also began late in the nineteenth century, and the percentage of infants delivered by midwives in Washington, D.C. declined from 50 percent in 1896, when licensing was instituted, to less than 10 percent in 1915 (Chapin 1919:159). School health programs were begun in some municipalities. Boston began organized medical examinations in schools in 1894, and New York City introduced compulsory vaccination for schoolchildren in 1897 (Bremner 1971:813). Rochester, New York, established the first municipally operated milk station in 1897 (ibid.:812). New York City fostered the removal of tuberculous patients from their households in the 1890s, leading (according to Herman Biggs) to a sharp decline in tuberculosis mortality for children under age 15 (Morse 1906:891). The first municipal bacteriologic laboratory was established in Providence in 1888, and free distribution of diphtheria antitoxin by cities was common by 1901 (Chapin 1901:598).

Health education was also a component of public-health efforts. Chapin (1901:520) stresses the key role that sanitary officials were playing in disseminating the results of biological research even among the medical profession. As early as the 1870s, the Bureau of Health in Philadelphia issued a pamphlet on the care and feeding of children, stressing the advantages of breastfeeding; 40,000 copies were distributed (Condran, Williams, and Cheney 1984). The focus on education campaigns, however, was to become much sharper in the first decade of the twentieth century. The proceedings of a 1909 Conference on the Prevention of Infant Mortality (1909) is principally devoted to the question of how to convince mothers to use better health practices in the home, especially with regard to infant feeding. C.E.A. Winslow noted at the conference that less progress had been made in reducing infant mortality than mortality at other ages, and argued that the reason is that the campaign must be preeminently one of popular education. "It is much harder to bring education to the mothers of a community than it is to lead pure water into its houses" (Winslow 1909:224). The educational efforts were to become prominent in the twentieth century, particularly after the formation of the Children's Bureau in 1912. A 1914 pamphlet on infant care issued by the Children's Bureau became the largest seller of any publication ever issued by the Government Printing Office (Bremner 1971:36).

Governmental efforts to improve the public's health in the nineteenth century undoubtedly reduced infant and child mortality, along with that of other age groups. But the connections have been hard to demonstrate. Writers of the time were quick to attribute mortality improvements to their favorite health programs, but systematic analysis of impact was rarely undertaken. Inadequacies of mortality data were partly to blame. Sanitary engineers were on solid empirical ground when they attributed declines in typhoid death rates to improvements in the water supply, and some professed to find a "multiplier effect" on other causes of death as well (e.g., Sedgwick and MacNutt 1910). Preston and van de Walle (1978) identify an apparent link between nineteenth-century water supply and sewage improvements in the three largest cities of France and cohort-specific mortality gains. But Lentzner (1987) is unable to draw such a close connection in three major American cities. As Condran, Williams, and Cheney (1984) stress in their fine study of Philadelphia, many changes were often occurring simultaneously, social and economic as well as those specifically in the health sector, and disentangling the diverse influences is often difficult. By concentrating on several specific linkages between diseases and public-health activities, some of which were regionally differentiated within Philadelphia, the authors are able to show the effects of public-health programs on mortality from typhoid, smallpox, and infant and child diarrhea.

Public-health activities were not confined to the largest cities. Swedlund (1985) documents the late nineteenth-century work of public-health authorities in Franklin County, Massachusetts, an area consisting mainly of small urban agglomerations. Chapin (1901) claims that rural hygienic efforts were most effective in states with a township system, where traditions of local government were better developed. Whether a state department of health was "energetic" was a key factor in the effectiveness of township health authorities. He adds that "while a scheme of sanitary administration is normally provided for the larger portion of our population, it must be admitted that it is not as a rule very efficient in really rural communities. Little attention is paid to sanitation in the country, and it is almost entirely in compact villages, towns, and cities that effective administration is found" (Chapin 1901:13).

Privies were typically used in rural areas to concentrate human waste, although they were altogether absent among blacks in rural East Virginia, where shallow surface wells—merely holes dug in swampy land—compounded the hazards (Frissell and Bevier 1899). Later studies in rural areas by the Children's Bureau found a wide variety of practices regarding drinking water. Wells were the typical source, but often they were too shallow or inadequately protected from contamination by surface water. Rivers, rainwater, and melted snow were also sources of water in rural areas (Paradise 1919; Bradley and Williamson 1918; Dart 1921; Sherbon and Moore 1919; Moore 1917). Despite the often primitive conditions, the rural health environment may not, of course, have been inferior. Whereas municipal authorities were beginning to protect urban residents from one another by legislation and public works, rural residents were already substantially protected from one another by distance.

The late nineteenth century was unquestionably a period of accelerated activity in urban public health, and some of this activity became more precisely targeted and effective as a result of the emergent germ theory. But one receives a somewhat distorted view of these activities by relying on enlightened classics such as Chapin's (1901) work. Acceptance of the germ theory and of state responsibility for health was quite slow, and the period was full of contention about the best ways to advance health. According to the medical historian James Cassedy (1962b:305):

> [In the 1890s] a handful of far-seeing health officers like Charles V. Chapin of Providence and Herman M. Biggs of New York were already looking into the potent implications of the newly proved germ theory for their day-to-day sanitary work. Yet, these pioneers did not find quick success or ready acceptance in the United States for their contagionist conclusions. On the contrary, for most of the last quarter of the 19th century it was the concept of anti-contagionism which continued to hold the dominant position in the thinking of American doctors and sanitarians.

In a fifty-year retrospective on the American Public Health Association, the editor writes ruefully that "miasma theory is just today giving up its hold upon the health authorities of cities and states" (Ravenel 1921:77).

The Practice of Parenting

Infants and young children in the late nineteenth century spent the vast majority of their time under parental supervision inside the home. The resources that parents brought to child care were critical for the child's chances of survival. The extreme dependence of the child on the mother is best illustrated by what happened when she died in childbirth or shortly thereafter. While we have no evidence about this from the nineteenth century, a study of registered births (about 13,000) in Baltimore during 1915 found that the infant mortality rate among babies whose mothers died within two months of childbirth ($N = 32$) was 625 per 1000 (Rochester 1923:151). Of the 366 children admitted without their mothers to New York City's Infant Hospital in 1896, 97 percent had died by April 15, 1897 (Henderson 1901:105). The death of a mother was only the extreme instance of parental incapacity, of course, and contemporary accounts described widespread health problems of American women that affected their maternal performance (see Leavitt 1986; ch. 3 for a review).

Mortality was also very high if the mother was forced to work outside the home in the first year of a baby's life. In Baltimore, the infant mortality rate was 59 percent above average among women employed outside the home (Rochester 1923:313). In contrast, it was 5 percent below average for women employed inside the home during their baby's infancy, suggesting that it was not work per se but the mother's separation from the infant that was critical for its survival.

Almost certainly the chief dependency of the infant was on the mother's milk. At the turn of the century, the difference in mortality between breastfed babies and others was enormous. The Children's Bureau study of infant mortality in eight cities between 1911 and 1915, in which the Baltimore study represented about half of the observations, found that death rates among those not breastfed were 3–4 times higher than among the breastfed (Woodbury 1925). While the Children's Bureau study provided the first good statistical documentation of this relation (and is still frequently cited for its precision in measuring it), casual observation had been more than sufficient to establish much earlier the health importance of breastfeeding. Advice about the importance of breastfeeding was common among physicians in the 1840s (Dye and Smith 1986), and health authorities frequently advertised the advantages of breastfeeding in the late nineteenth century. Increasingly, the advantages of breastfeeding and the enormous hazards of impure milk were based upon sound epidemiologic studies (e.g., Park and Holt 1903). A study of the history of infant feeding in the U.S. concludes that physicians at the turn of the century generally advocated that a mother breastfeed her child (Apple 1980:407).

Undoubtedly, an important advantage of breastfeeding was the protection it gave against diarrheal diseases, which struck with particular vengeance in summer (Lentzner 1987). Valuable evidence from Berlin in 1901 showed that the seasonality of infant mortality was essentially absent among breastfed children: the ratio of July/August deaths to February/March deaths was 2.90 for infants fed on cow's milk and 1.06 for infants who were breastfed (Schwartz 1909:168).

Breast milk had its competitors, however. Cow's milk was sometimes fed to infants despite its lack of cleanliness, and many other substitutes or supplements were introduced at an early age. Apple (1980) describes attempts beginning in the 1890s to use scientific methods to "humanize" cow's milk. The Walker-Gordon Milk Laboratory was established in 1891 in Boston to prepare modified cow's milk formulas according to physicians' prescriptions and to deliver the bottles directly to consumers. By 1903, Walker-Gordon labs could be found in ten other American cities.

There is scant statistical evidence regarding the extent of breastfeeding in the late nineteenth century. The first survey of which we are aware found 65 percent of mothers in New York City in 1908 to be breastfeeding their children at age 9 months, about when the benefits of breastfeeding fade (Schwartz 1909:169). The later Children's Bureau study provided much more detail, though it also pertained exclusively to cities, and mainly eastern cities at that. Table 1.2 is reproduced from Woodbury's (1925) summary of the Children's Bureau's study. It shows that, of an infants' first nine months of life, 57 percent were spent exclusively on breastmilk, 25 percent exclusively on artificial feeding, and 18 percent in a mixed mode. Foreign-born women breastfed somewhat more frequently, with Italians, Poles, and Jews at the top of the list and Portuguese and French-Canadians at the bottom. Polish women in rural areas also appeared to breastfeed longer than German or native American women (Sherbon and Moore 1919:53). Before the Children's Bureau's urban studies, the superior mortality experience of Jews or children in largely Jewish areas had been noted, despite their often poor and crowded circumstances. Several contemporaries attributed it to the fact that Jews had been urbanized for many generations and were better adapted to urban life (Hamilton 1909:78; Devine 1909:103). The extended period of breastfeeding of Jewish mothers is likely an important mechanism through which this "adaptation" worked. Ritual washing before eating and maintenance of sanitary habit in purchasing and preparing food may also have contributed to the better mortality among Jewish children (for extended discussions, see Condran and Kramerow 1990; Schmeltz 1971).

Rural women were probably breastfeeding children for longer periods than urban women. Here again we must rely on Children's Bu-

TABLE 1.2

Type of Feeding, by Color and Nationality of Mother: Children's Bureau Study, 1911–15

Color and nationality of mother	Total months lived from birth to end of ninth month	Percentage of months of exclusive breast-feeding	Percentage of months of partial breast-feeding	Percentage of months of artificial feeding
White	180,397.5	57.6	17.1	25.2
Native	102,285.5	56.2	15.4	28.3
Foreign-born	78,112.0	59.4	19.3	21.1
Italian	11,943.0	68.6	18.3	13.1
Jewish	10,688.0	61.5	27.1	11.3
French-Canadian	8,666.0	42.7	13.3	44.0
German	6,514.0	56.5	22.0	21.5
Polish	10,391.5	65.9	22.7	11.1
Portuguese	5,410.5	48.8	19.3	31.9
Other	24,471.0	60.3	16.5	23.2
Not reported	18.0	27.8	33.3	38.9
Black	11,815.0	54.8	25.5	19.7
Total	192,212.5	57.4	17.6	24.9

Source: Woodbury 1925.

Note: Infants from birth to end of ninth month, in eight cities, from a Children's Bureau study, 1911–15.

reau studies conducted nearly two decades after the date of our sample. Bureau inquiries into infant feeding practices in six rural areas around 1916 showed in every case that rural mothers were breast-feeding for longer periods. Whereas Woodbury (1925:88) found that 35 percent of infants aged 9 months were entirely weaned in the eight cities, the equivalent percentages ranged from 0 percent in a mountainous region of North Carolina (Bradley and Williamson 1918:75) to 23 percent in one Wisconsin county (Sherbon and Moore 1919:53). Rural areas in Kansas (Moore 1917), Montana (Paradise 1919), and Mississippi (Dart 1921) were intermediate. Rural black mothers appeared to differ little from rural white mothers in their breastfeeding practices. While long breastfeeding was probably an aid to the survival of rural children, rural mothers were often charged with introducing solid foods at too early an age and being indiscriminant about the types of foods given infants. Such practices were more common in Mississippi and North Carolina than in Kansas or Montana. Supplementation appeared to begin earlier for babies of black or German mothers.

Children's survival depended on fathers as well as mothers, as indicated in part by the very high mortality of children born out of wedlock. Rochester's study of Baltimore found that the infant mortality rate for illegitimate children was 300.7 per 1000, compared with 103.5 per 1000 for legitimate births (Rochester 1923:170). She believed the former figure to be an underestimate because of the greater difficulty of tracking illegitimate births.

Much of the excess mortality of out-of-wedlock births results from the stresses that illegitimate origin placed on the infant-mother relation. Mothers of illegitimate births were far more likely to work during the child's first year of life, and the child was also more likely to be placed in an institution. In the extreme case, Baltimore children born of unmarried mothers in institutions ($N = 56$) had an infant mortality rate of 625 per 1000 (Rochester 1923:173). Much of the impact of separation of mother and infant, of course, worked through breastfeeding practices. Legitimate children were more likely to be breastfed at every age. At 6 months of age, for example, 53.2 percent of legitimate births in Baltimore were fed exclusively breast milk, compared to 25.4 percent of out-of-wedlock births (ibid.:391).

Health behaviors towards children were part of a larger fabric of emotional and behavioral relations. In the colonial period, the father was the principal parent, and books containing child-rearing advice were directed towards him (Demos 1986:10). Illness and death were apparently accepted in a passive attitude of Christian resignation (Dye and Smith 1986:343). But attitudes began to change in the second half of the eighteenth century. A valuable review and synthesis of the diaries left by middle-class women finds that by the year 1800, mothers had developed a more intense emotional relation with their children than had been true fifty years earlier (Dye and Smith 1986). Nevertheless, nineteenth century mothers appeared to regard serious illness as inevitable. But increased anxiety about child survival throughout the century was evident, perhaps reflecting a growing belief that good mothering could somehow aid a baby's survival. By the first decade of the twentieth century there was general awareness that many infant deaths were preventable, and a growing belief that society at large must assume responsibility for a child's survival and well-being (ibid.). By 1900, women working through women's clubs, municipal reform groups, and social welfare organizations had begun to give public voice to their concerns about child death and to turn it from a private tragedy into a social and political issue (ibid:331). A rallying cry for the assumption of social responsibility was John Dewey's statement in The School and Society (1899): "What the best and wisest parent wants for his own child, that must the community want for all of its children." Katz (1986:113) argues that, by the 1890s, children had captured the energy and attention of social reformers to a greater extent than during any other period of American history. While agitation for the assumption of social responsibility for infant mortality had clearly begun by 1900, the principle was not fully accepted until the first decades of the twentieth century (Dye and Smith 1986:331).

Some contemporary commentators disputed the view that mothers at the turn of the century saw infant death as preventable and were motivated to take steps to avoid it. Writing about her experiences with Irish mothers in New York's Hell's Kitchen in 1902, Josephine Baker comments that they "seemed too lackadaisical to carry their babies to nearby clinics and too lazy or too indifferent to carry out the instructions that you might give them. I do not mean that they were callous when their babies died. Then they cried like mothers, for a change. They were just horribly fatalistic about it when it was going on. Babies always died in summer and there was no point in trying to do anything about it" (Baker 1939:17). Bremner's (1974) volume reprinting articles from the late nineteenth and early twentieth centuries about the state's role in caring for orphaned or abandoned children includes many charges of neglect and abuse on the part of adoptive as well as natural parents.

In the eyes of many public officials, parents could not always be relied upon either to send their children to school or to avoid exploiting them in the labor market, and regulatory legislation was required. "In any complete system of child saving, compulsory education must occupy a large place. Parents must not be left at liberty to educate their offspring, the future citizens, whose ignorance and evil habits are a menace to order and political institutions" (Henderson 1901:102). By 1900, 32 states had compulsory school attendance laws, with most having penalties for noncompliance. Yet compulsion was unnecessary for the large majority of parents, who were already voluntarily sending their children to school. As a result, the laws had little effect on actual attendance (Katz 1986:130–31).

Child labor outside the home was rising in the late nineteenth century on the heels of new industrial opportunities. The practice was not entirely a product of economic motives but also reflected a belief that children were best kept out of trouble if kept busy. In 1870, one in eight children aged 10–15 was employed. By 1900, the number was one in six. Of boys aged 10–15, 26 percent were employed more than half time, as were 10 percent of girls (Bremner 1971:605). The practice was most common in the South, and by 1900 one-third of workers in southern mills were children (ibid.:601). Goldin and Parsons's (1987) analysis of the Carroll Wright sample, consisting of 6800 industrial families in 1889–90, suggested that location in an area with a high demand for child labor (e.g., textile producing) sharply reduced the future wealth of children. The children received less schooling and were not compensated in other ways for the sacrifice. In such areas, father's earnings were reduced and current consumption increased. Accounts of abuse of child workers were common and galvanized public sentiment. By 1899, 28 states had passed some legislation regarding child labor. Although 60 percent of the children working in 1900 were in agriculture, the legislation normally applied only to manufacturing and generally set the minimum working age at 12 (Bremner 1971:601–5).

Parental motivation was also suspect when it came to day care. Henderson (1901:99) warned that day nurseries may become agreeable to mothers who are thereby liberated to work, and that fathers, "disposed to shirk duty, may willingly let their wives go out to labor for support while the home is neglected." Only infants of widows, or of women whose husbands are disabled, should be admitted. "For both sanitary and moral reasons, the infants of unmarried mothers cannot ordinarily be accepted" (ibid.:100). The widespread abandonment of children in nineteenth century Paris was cited as an example of what may happen if the state (through foundling hospitals) made it too easy for parents to shirk their duties.

When the state did acquire jurisdiction, either partial or complete, over a child, there was little doubt what its main mission was. According to Letchworth (1897:94), "It is not necessary at this time to emphasize the importance of saving homeless and wayward children. It is now conceded on all sides that, if we would make social progress and strengthen the foundations of good government, into the minds of this unfortunate class must be instilled principles of morality, thrift, industry, and self-reliance." Bremner's (1974) collection of articles about the state's role in child care makes it clear that character development was the central concern, in order that the child not lead a wayward life of crime or idleness as an adult and thereby remain a drain on public resources. In the extreme, male wards of the state who posed serious threats to the public order could be castrated (e.g., Barr 1905; Fisher 1909)—not an uncommon operation. This emphasis on developing a sense of morality and civic responsibility probably reflects the principal public concern with an individual parent's performance as well.

There are undoubtedly both neglectful and careful parents in any era, and it is impossible to characterize the balance at the end of the nineteenth century, or to say how it may have differed from the balance today. Johansson (1987) summarizes arguments for and against

1. Child labor was rising in the late nineteenth century. Shown here is a fully equipped eight-year-old miner from Clarksburg, West Virginia.

2. Urban children were also involved in income-producing activities, as shown in this Jacob Riis photograph of a family group making artificial flowers, ca. 1890.

the proposition that many European parents in the sixteenth to nineteenth centuries did not strive vigorously to keep all of their children alive. She suggests that neglect was used as a form of birth control, especially in Catholic areas where other forms of birth control were strictly proscribed. But there is no evidence on behalf of this claim from the 1870s or later, and none from the United States, where, she suggests, land abundance reduced pressures to avoid dividing the patrimony among offspring.

The view that parental concern for and activity on behalf of child survival increased during the nineteenth century in the United States, as enunciated by Dye and Smith (1986), seems reasonably well supported. The Children's Bureau's studies in the 1910s showed a tremendous parental interest in means to enhance child survival and were remarkably free of any suggestions of parental neglect. A Bureau of Labor study of indigent families in Washington, D.C. noted that virtually all of their children had life-insurance policies, principally to cover the all-too-frequent burial expenses. In view of the incentives that such policies might be thought to create, it commented that "in this class, parental love would win the victory in any hour of temptation" (U.S. Bureau of Labor 1906:614). That children were sometimes viewed instrumentally, as a source of family income, does not imply any lack of concern for their physical well-being and may even have increased the care they received. Ginsberg (1983), for example, suggests that boys were treated better than girls in nineteenth century Massachusetts (as revealed in their lower mortality) because they had higher earning capacities.

The dominant refrain of writers about health and parenthood in the late nineteenth and early twentieth centuries was not one of neglect but of ignorance. Parents were usually assumed to be motivated to enhance their children's survival chances but to lack essential information or tools to improve them. In the words of Park and Holt (1903:906), "Mothers are often anxious and willing, but ignorant and stupid." These claims grew to a crescendo in the first decade of the twentieth century when, in Irving Fisher's phrase, "the world [was] gradually awakening to the fact of its own improvability" (Fisher 1909:14). In the year that Fisher published his *Report on National Vitality* for the Committee of One Hundred on National Health, the Conference on the Prevention of Infant Mortality was dominated by concern about how to get information to mothers that would enable them to provide better care for their babies. One author affirmed that "the problem of infant mortality is not one of sanitation alone or housing, or indeed of poverty as such, but is mainly a question of motherhood" (Wile 1909:144).

As recognition of the nature of infectious diseases grew, and as evidence was assembled on the role of breastfeeding, of bad milk and water, of diphtheria antitoxin, and of other influences on child health, the frustration of social reformers grew when practices fell short of the ideal. Polish mothers (Hedger 1909:40), Irish mothers (Baker 1939:17, writing about conditions in 1902), rural mothers (Fox 1919:187), and even college-educated mothers (Hollopeter 1906:821) were all charged with ignorance about hygiene and/or proper feeding practices. Obviously, professional self-interest also played a part in these claims, which often laid the basis for professional intervention. By the time the Conference on the Prevention of Infant Mortality was held in 1909, popular education was held to be the key to a successful attack on infant mortality, although some saw the process as taking generations (Phelps 1909:42). Nevertheless, the first decade of the twentieth century was full of optimism about what could be accomplished. In Irving Fisher's words, "The crowning achievement of science in the present century should be, and probably will be, the discovery of practical methods of making life healthier, longer, and happier than before" (Fisher 1909:64).

To fulfill this promise required first of all the diffusion of information about methods that had clearly proven effective in enhancing child survival. The chorus of charges of ignorance that were leveled at mothers must be understood in the light of the new conception of disease processes in the late nineteenth century. These new conceptions displaced some of the emphasis on properties of the general environment—such factors as slaughter houses and sewer gas—and refocused it on properties of human interaction, including the intimate associations found within the home.

Social and Economic Influences on Mortality

It would be misleading to treat America's mortality levels and trends in the late nineteenth century as though they were entirely products of public-health and medical practices. These factors were undoubtedly important in the acceleration of the mortality decline during the late nineteenth century, but many other factors were also at work. Immigrants were arriving at an unprecedented pace; the population was relocating to urban areas; economic growth was fitful and, although it suffered a major setback in the 1890s, was in the longer run providing individuals with the wherewithal to enjoy healthier lives. Clues about the importance of these factors have been provided by many previous studies of other nations or of subnational groups in the United States.

Urbanization

Using a consistent definition of urban population (places larger than 2,500 people), the proportion of the U.S. population living in urban areas grew from 18 percent in 1860 to 40 percent in 1900 (U.S. Bureau of the Census 1975, Series A57–72). This spatial reorganization had two major consequences for mortality. First, the concentration of many people into small areas accelerated the spread of communicable diseases. This effect operates both through greater direct personal contact resulting from crowding, and through increased contamination of water and food. Second, urbanization facilitated the deployment of programs designed to improve health conditions. Like other social services, health services must be "delivered," and their delivery cost was markedly reduced when population concentration reduced the "friction of space." Further, urban populations could form more effective political pressure groups for securing valued objectives. As noted above, public-health activities were weakest in sparsely populated rural areas.

There is abundant evidence that urbanization initially had an unfavorable effect on longevity both in the United States and in western Europe. It is believed that larger urban areas in western Europe in medieval and early modern times had very high mortality and were sometimes not self-reproducing (Wrigley 1969:95–98; deVries 1984: ch. 9). More extensive information for the nineteenth century shows that urban mortality was typically well above rural (United Nations 1973:132–34). For example, the *department* of Seine, containing Paris, had an average female life expectancy of 31.3 years for the period 1816–45, while the average for France as a whole was 39.2. For 1881–90, expectation of life at birth in Sweden was 43.4 years in urban areas and 51.6 in rural areas, and for 1871–80 the infant mortality rate was 193 per 1000 births in urban areas but 119 in rural. Similarly, in Norway from 1896 to 1900, the infant mortality rate 125.7 per 1000 in urban and 83.0 in rural areas. In England and Wales in 1841, male expectation of life at birth was 40.2 years for the country as a whole but only 35.0 in London, 25.0 in Liverpool, and 24.0 in Manchester. In contrast, the expectation of life at birth was 44 years for the largely rural, agrarian county of Surrey. As late as 1881–90, Manchester still had an expectation of life at birth for males of only 29 years, while selected "healthy districts" had an expectation of 51 years and the country as a whole was at a level of 44 years. In Scotland for the period 1871–80, the male expectation of life at birth was 41.0 for the whole country but 30.9 for the city of Glasgow. (Preston and van de Walle 1978; Glass 1964; Weber 1899:347). An investigation by Williamson (1982a) of living standards in Britain during the industrial revolution suggested that city size, density, and an employment mix favoring mining and manufacturing all significantly raised infant mortality in 1905.

Similar results were reported in 1899 by Adna Ferrin Weber for the United States, Prussia, and France. He also noted the positive relation between city size and mortality levels (Weber 1899:343–67), as did Higgs and Booth (1979) for the United States. Woods et al. (1988) find that 50 percent of the variance in infant mortality rates in the 590 registration districts of England and Wales in the 1880s and 1890s could be explained by population density alone. On urban mortality, Weber wrote: "It is almost everywhere true that people die more rapidly in cities than in rural districts" (1899:343). The causes were not always clear, but: "There is no inherent or eternal reason why men should die faster in large communities than in small hamlets. . . .

Leaving aside accidental causes, it may be affirmed that the excessive urban mortality is due to lack of pure air, water and sunlight, together with uncleanly habits of life induced thereby. Part cause, part effect, poverty, overcrowding, high rates of mortality, are usually found together in city tenements" (ibid.:348).

According to data from the U.S. Death Registration Area in 1900–1902, the expectation of life at birth was 48.2 years overall for white males, 44.0 years in urban areas, and 54.0 years in rural areas. The national average white female expectation of life at birth was 51.1 years, with 47.9 years in cities and 55.4 years in the countryside (Glover 1921). For seven upstate New York counties for the period roughly 1850–65, urban child mortality rates were substantially above rural rates. The probability of dying before reaching age 5 was .229 in urban places and .192 in rural areas. (Haines 1977: Table 3).[1] Vinovskis (1981: ch. 2 and Table 2.5) found a rough direct relationship between town size and mortality among Massachusetts towns in 1859–61, although he also found that rural/urban mortality differentials were smaller in the first half of the nineteenth century than they had been in the seventeenth and eighteenth centuries. Condran and Crimmins (1980) calculated the ratio of rural to urban death rates for seven states with reasonable registration data in 1890 and 1900.[2] The ratio of average (weighted for population size) urban to rural total death rates was 1.27 in 1890 and 1.18 in 1900. The urban/rural ratio for infant death rates was higher, at 1.63 for 1890 and 1.49 for 1900; the ratios were 2.07 for 1890 and 1.97 for 1900 for early childhood death rates (ages 1–4 years). So the differentials appeared to be shrinking in these states over the last decade of the century and were much greater for infants and young children than for adults. In nineteenth century France, rural and urban mortality levels tended to converge (partly in a cohort fashion) as public health and especially sanitation improvements were introduced (Preston and van de Walle 1978). They were also converging in England and Wales (Woods and Hinde 1987).

The advantage of rural areas was not attributable to superior health programs, as noted above, nor was it likely to have been a result of superior knowledge about disease prevention and treatment. A number of contemporary accounts single out rural residents and farmers as particularly unhygienic. A survey of bathing in Michigan in 1877 found little resort to the practice among farm families, in contrast to customary weekly baths in the upper classes (Leavitt and Numbers 1971:313). Abbott (1900:71) says of farmers that "there are few occupations in which hygiene is more neglected." The ignorance and indifference of farmers and their wives to child health was still being decried as late as 1919 (Fox 1919:187). The superior mortality of rural residents is most plausibly attributed to their simply being more widely separated from one another's germs.

Of course, rural areas differed profoundly from one another, as later inquiries by the Children's Bureau made abundantly clear. One study of a prosperous rural county in Kansas in 1916 described large farms connected to one another and to towns by excellent roads; highly literate women keenly interested in literature on child survival; wells drilled more than 100 feet into the ground; 95 percent of infants delivered by physicians; and an infant mortality rate of 40 per 1000 (Moore 1917). A study of a mountain region in North Carolina in the period 1911–16 found residents cut off from contact with one another by terrible roads in winter; human waste draining directly into water sources; most births attended by ill-trained midwives; abundant use of patent medicines and home remedies; 64 percent of residents infected with hookworm; and an infant mortality rate of 80 per 1000 (Bradley and Williamson 1918). Even more primitive conditions existed in a county in Montana, but that study's author notes that the infant mortality rate of 71 per 1000 was below that of any of the eight cities studied by the Children's Bureau (Paradise 1919:70).

Industrial and Occupational Structure

Although the hazards of urban living in the nineteenth century seem clearly documented, the effect of industrialization per se on mortality, especially infant and child mortality, is much less clear-cut. In the nineteenth century, rising incomes and technological change led to a proliferation of occupational roles. Some of the new occupations carried with them increased health risks relative to those present on the farm, while others entailed reduced risks. Miners, laborers using heavy machinery, and workers exposed to toxic substances in the workplace are those for whom industrial changes were probably the least advantageous. Most white-collar occupations, on the other hand, entail reduced risks of job-related accidental death, although their sedentary character elevates the risk of cardiovascular disease. The Registrar General of England and Wales, in a survey of occupational mortality differentials for the period 1860–82, found that mortality among farmers was clearly below the national average, but also that mortality among some presumably hazardous occupations such as coal miners and workers in iron and steel manufacturing was also somewhat below the national average. The same was apparently also true for Belgium and Germany (Haines 1979b:29–36). Part of the explanation for low death rates for men in heavy industry may be that they changed jobs after injury or illness. Based upon poorer data for the United States in the period 1890–1910, Uselding (1976) concludes that mortality was generally (though not consistently) elevated for workers in mining, manufacturing, and mechanical industries, as well as in transport and communications. Yet in a study of the coal mining and heavy industrial areas of northwest Europe in the late nineteenth century, Wrigley found that mining and industrial districts in France and Germany seldom had mortality rates that differed much from those of the surrounding rural areas. First and foremost, high mortality was characteristic of large cities, some of which happened also to be partly industrial, e.g., Paris, Berlin, and Marseilles (Wrigley 1961: ch. 4).

Less work has been done on the impact of industrial and occupation structure on infant and child mortality, and the limited results are contradictory. In England and Wales, random samples of 125 registration districts in 1851, 1861, and 1871 revealed that correlations between the infant mortality rate and the proportion of males in mining and metallurgy were insignificant. In contrast, the correlations of those mortality rates with the proportion of the population in urban areas were positive and significant (Haines 1979b:35). Williamson (1982a), however, found that industrial employment had a sizable and significant positive effect on infant mortality, independent of city size, for 72 selected urban areas in England and Wales in 1905.[3]

Just as the functional roles of men diversified in the course of development, so did those of women. In the later stages of industrialization and income growth, less of a woman's time was typically spent in household activities and more in market production outside the home. This change may have had a beneficial influence on child mortality through higher household income but an adverse effect through reductions in time spent on child-rearing. Recently, evidence has begun to emerge suggesting that women's work outside the home is associated with higher risk of child death in developing countries (Caldwell 1981; United Nations 1985).

We have already noted that infants born to working mothers suffered elevated mortality in the Children's Bureau study of 1911–15. Woodbury (1925) attempts to break down this effect into constituent parts. He finds that infant mortality was 2.5 times higher for children of working women. Allowance for breastfeeding differences reduced the ratio to 2.0, for the nationality distribution to 1.7, and for husband's income to 1.6. He attributes the remaining 60 percent excess in infant mortality to a "lack of care." Even before the careful Children's Bureau study, mother's work had been thought to be an important factor in child death. The very high infant death rate of 305 per 1000 in Fall River, Massachusetts, where many women worked in textile mills, was often cited as evidence of the hazards of women working (e.g., Hedger 1909:36). Swedlund (1985) notes that Fall River mothers weaned their children very early. The 1909 Conference on the Prevention of Infant Mortality devoted a good deal of time to the topic of women's work, despite the admission by one participant that the main reason a woman worked was that "she has not money enough to feed and clothe her children" (Hedger 1909:36). The large amount of attention devoted to the subject is also surprising because so few women worked for pay outside the home after giving birth. In the Children's Bureau study, only 4.5 percent of the months lived by infants were spent with the mother working (Woodbury 1925). In terms of "attributable risk" (the total number of excess deaths resulting from mother's work), the hazard was small. And as we show in Chapter 3, the risk appears substantially lower in the nation as a whole in 1900 than in the urban areas later studied by the Children's Bureau. The concentration on women's work as an influence on child health by contemporaries probably says more about social expectations regarding parenthood and the family than it does about major factors in mortality.

Ethnicity and Nativity

The United States in the late nineteenth century was rapidly urbanizing and industrializing, and a large number of immigrants was crossing its borders, principally into its cities, seeking employment and other opportunities. Many of them moved into cramped quarters with poor heating, sanitation, and ventilation. Although crude death rates for the foreign born were often unexpectedly low, reflecting middle-heavy age structures and possibly migrant selectivity, more refined measures do reveal a special toll (Ward 1971:109–17). For example, the 1900–1902 Death Registration Area life tables gave an expectation of life at age 10 of 51.6 years for native white males and 49.1 years for foreign-born white males. Comparable figures for females were 53.3 years and 50.5 years respectively (Glover 1921).

Higgs (1979) used annual registration statistics for 18 large American cities in the period 1871–1900 to relate short-term fluctuations in overall crude death rates to the business cycle via the procyclical demographic variable of immigration. Surges in immigration to the United States in the nineteenth century were more closely related to booms in the American economy than to depressed conditions in Europe (Easterlin 1961), although this view is not universally accepted. An increased influx of immigrants seems to have operated to raise death rates in American cities in the late nineteenth century. Such a relationship also appears for an earlier period, 1840–80, in Boston (Meckel 1985). One possible explanation is that the transport of individuals from one disease environment to another could result in increased exposure to new pathogens for both migrants and natives. Another is that the foreign born were more likely to have lower incomes and poorer housing and nutrition; to live in less desirable, less healthy, and more crowded urban areas; and to have language barriers that impeded the diffusion of useful health information.

Different customs of child-raising are probably reflected in ethnic differences in child mortality. Woodbury (1925) cites the practice of Portugese mothers in feeding their babies crackers immediately after birth, and of Italian mothers in swaddling their babies, as particularly injurious practices. Aykroyd (1971:485) cites the dangerous turn-of-the-century practice of German mothers of replacing milk with cereal gruels in the diet of a child with diarrhea. Breastfeeding customs also differed, as we have seen, and were likely responsible in good measure for the exceptionally low mortality of babies born to Jewish mothers and the exceptionally high mortality of those born to French-Canadians. Apart from breastfeeding, however, there seems to be little that can be said quantitatively about the different modes of child-rearing as they might influence ethnic variation in child mortality.

America had another important aspect of ethnic diversity: its black population. Originally involuntary immigrants to the American colonies, most (79.5 percent) were still living in the relatively healthier rural areas in 1900. In the Death Registration Area, however, 82 percent of the black population was urban. Although the Death Registration Area contained only 4.4 percent of the total American black population, its records have formed the basis of present views of black mortality at the turn of the century. The 1900–1902 Death Registration Area life tables give an expectation of life at birth of 32.5 years for black males, in contrast to 48.2 years for white males and 44.0 years for urban white males. The corresponding numbers for females were 35.0 years for blacks, 51.1 years for whites, and 47.9 years for urban whites (Glover 1921). As we show in the next chapter, however, the DRA data almost certainly overstate black/white mortality differences.

Most blacks lived in rural areas of the South in the families of unskilled laborers or sharecroppers. Blacks had received little or no land after the Civil War, and few had been able to acquire it in the next three decades, in part because of discrimination in credit markets. The initial postwar enthusiasm for educating their children had waned among black parents because there was found to be little economic payoff to schooling in a society that denied blacks jobs of skill and responsibility (Ransom and Sutch 1977: chs. 2, 9). Daily conditions of life among southern blacks are vividly described in two inquiries by the U.S. Department of Agriculture in the late 1890s. In eastern Virginia, blacks lived in one- or two-room cabins of primitive construction. Few families had lamps or candles; the fireplace was the only source of illumination at night, and posed a constant hazard for unattended young children. Families rented "one-mule farms," about 20 acres, and paid up to half of their annual produce in rent to the landowner, who often exploited their illiteracy by overcharging them for household provisions. Hogs and hominy were the dietary staples (Frissell and Bevier 1899). Turnover was high, and because they were renters there was little incentive to improve the property on which they resided. Conditions were no better in Alabama, where clothing was described as coarse, scanty, and ragged, and where cracks in the flooring of cabins accommodated insects and snakes. The status of a black farmer was determined mainly by the number of bales of cotton he could produce in a year. One family, miserably poor, subsisted for days at a time on nothing but corn pone. Dietary protein was deficient, although caloric consumption was generally adequate (Atwater and Woods 1897).

Literacy and Income

The earliest good evidence on the relation between child mortality and literacy or income in the United States is drawn from the Children's Bureau study. Rochester's study of Baltimore births in 1915 found no systematic relationship between mother's literacy and infant mortality, once the husband's earnings were controlled (Rochester 1923:332). Nor was the mother's ability to speak English important. In fact, among Polish mothers, those who spoke English had higher child death rates than those who didn't. Rochester notes that the mother's ability to speak English was also unrelated to her degree of contact with infant welfare agencies, except among Italian mothers (ibid.:131–32). Perhaps because its effects were so weak, literacy was dropped from consideration in Woodbury's (1925) summary of the Children's Bureau studies.

In contrast, the husband's earnings displayed a powerful effect. The infant mortality rate was 167 per 1000 live births for families in which the father's annual income was less than $450, and only 59 per 1000 for families with father's annual earnings in excess of $1250. The sample average mortality rate was 110 (Woodbury 1926:151–52). Among literate mothers, the infant mortality rate in Baltimore ranged from 161 per 1000 if the father earned less than $450 per year to only 37 per 1000 if he earned $1850 or more (Rochester 1923:332). Strong earnings effects were evident among both foreign-born and native-born mothers. Breastfeeding duration varied inversely with father's earnings, providing a partial offset to the enormous influence of this variable.

Some of the earnings effects appeared to operate through housing variables. Among infants born to native white women who survived at least two weeks, the death rate was 46 per 1000 if there were fewer than one person per room in the household. It was 86 per 1000 if there were between 1 and 2 persons per room, and 140 per 1000 if there were more than 2 persons per room (Rochester 1923:111).[4] The effect of overcrowding was also evident within families in the same earnings class, with children in overcrowded households typically having double the death rate of other children (ibid.:291). Presence of toilets and bathtubs in the household also improved the infant mortality rate, with diarrheal and intestinal diseases accounting for most of the mortality differential (ibid.:113).

Diet

Beyond the age of 6 months, children became increasingly dependent upon foods other than breast milk. While practically nothing is known about the specific food intake of American children in the late nineteenth century, it is very likely that they shared the favorable conditions that characterized the nation as a whole. Bennett and Pierce (1961) have traced changes in the American diet from 1879 to 1959. They find that the amount of calories per capita available at the retail level was about 3,700 in 1889 and 1899 (ibid.:117). This figure had declined to 3,187 by 1958. At 3,700 calories per capita per day, American food availability compared favorably with that of European countries (Atwater and Woods 1897; Wait 1909a; Fogel 1988). Approximately 27 percent of the calories were derived from wheat, 12 percent from corn, and 35 percent from animal products, of which 11 percent was in the form of milk or butter (Bennett and Pierce 1961:118).

Inquiries by the U.S. Department of Agriculture and the U.S. Bureau of Labor provide information on regional and class variation in food availability, price, and consumption. A 1901 study by the Bureau of Labor into food expenditure among 2,567 families of working men in different regions showed that the average income of the families was $827 and that an average of $237 of this income was spent on food. The percentage spent on food ranged only from 34.6 percent in the West to 40.5 percent in the North Atlantic region (U.S. Bureau of Labor 1906:187). Beef was more expensive in the North Atlantic region than elsewhere because most was shipped from the Midwest or West. At 15.4 cents per pound, fresh beef was 29 percent more expensive in the North Atlantic region than in the South Central (Holmes 1907:79). Nevertheless, the North Atlantic region consumed more beef per capita than the national average. Hog products showed very little regional price variability. The largest regional variability in the diets of working men's families related to milk products and salt pork. The North Atlantic, North Central, and Western states consumed about 50 percent more milk per family than the South, but less than half as much salt pork (U.S. Bureau of Labor 1906:189). The typical family in the South Atlantic region consumed 222 pounds of salt-hog products in 1901 and 307 pounds of fresh beef; in the South Central region, the figures were 249 and 317 pounds, respectively.

Contemporary observers believed that urban residents enjoyed a more varied diet than rural residents because markets offered a wider selection of products (Bryant 1898; Hills 1909) and because urban residents had more appliances for food preservation and preparation (Wait 1909b). Diets in poor rural areas in the South were particularly monotonous. In one study of eastern Tennessee in 1901–5, three-fourths of the diet consisted of corn meal, wheat flour, and cured pork (Wait 1909a:108). The difficulty of preserving food in the warmer South was said to be a major reason for its heavy reliance on these basics. The diet of blacks in Alabama was even more rudimentary, consisting of little but salt pork, corn meal, and molasses (Atwater and Woods 1897). This diet was recognized at the time as being deficient in protein. What was not recognized was its even more severe deficiencies in vitamins and minerals, which contributed greatly to the high morbidity from pellagra, for example (Rose 1989). The first indication of the importance of vitamins in the diet did not occur until 1906, when one "growth-enhancing" substance was hypothesized (North 1921). Blacks on the shores of the Chesapeake achieved much better diets through fishing (Frissell and Bevier 1899).

Although on average urban diets may have been better than rural, the poorest classes in cities struggled to put food on the table. A 1905 Bureau of Labor inquiry into the budgets of 19 impoverished working-class families in Washington, D.C. "carrie[d] the investigation down the scale of adversity as far as it is practicable to go" (Forman 1906:593). These families spent greater proportions of their incomes on food, ranging up to 69 percent, and were unable to accumulate any savings. Their diets showed substantially less meat than those of other working men's families (Holmes 1907), and a high percentage of their incomes was spent on bread and breadstuffs (Forman 1906:601).

Although the diets of the Washington, D.C. families were not converted into calories, another study of 25 families in the poorest part of Philadelphia showed an average daily consumption (per adult male equivalent) of 3,235 calories per person per day. Twenty-six families in the poorest part of Chicago consumed 3,425 calories per person per day. Alabama blacks consumed 3,270 calories daily (Atwater and Woods 1897:65). These figures far exceed the consumption of poorer classes in Europe, which fell below 2,300 calories in Saxony and Naples (ibid.:66). For only 10 cents, Americans could purchase 1,800 calories in the form of sweet potatoes, 5,000 calories in the form of wheat flour, 7,700 in peanuts, or 8,300 in corn meal (Holmes 1907:87). At those prices, even the poor could buy enough food to keep body and soul together.

Undoubtedly, the composition of the diet was inadequate among many groups. But this inadequacy was in part attributable to the

3. By 1900, Americans were well fed by international standards of the time or even of today. Two girls from the slums of 1890 display a giant bread loaf and pretzel.

primitive state of the nutritional sciences, which paralleled the inadequacies of medical knowledge, public-health technology, and social organization that we documented earlier in this chapter. It was not a deficiency of resources but ignorance about their most efficient deployment that was the greatest threat to child survival in the late nineteenth century.

Summary

This chapter has described a variety of social incapacities in the area of child health at the turn of the century. Theories about the etiology of infectious diseases, which were responsible for the bulk of infant and child deaths, were unsettled. The new germ theory was resisted by many physicians and health professionals, and even among adherents it had led to few innovations of practical significance for child survival. The principle of public responsibility for enhancing individual health had been accepted, but implementation of this principle was at the early stages, especially in rural areas where the majority of the population lived. Parents seemed, in general, to be highly motivated to improve their children's health, but they had relatively few means at their disposal to do so. Material resources were not the binding constraint. Even by present international standards, the United States in 1900 was a rich country (see Chapter 5), and it had an abundance of food. But it was not able to translate these material advantages into a high standard of child survival.

These are incapacities as viewed from the present. Undoubtedly, analysts a century hence will find the present level of health knowledge and technique deficient in important respects. Were we to view the situation in 1900 from the vantage point of 1850, on the other hand, it would appear very favorable. Great progress had been made in understanding the mechanisms of the transmission of infectious disease. Antiseptic surgery had become widespread, and diphtheria was being brought under control by a successful therapeutic. Many cities had mounted major efforts to improve their water supplies, and increasingly the standard of success was bacteria counts rather than odor and appearance. Although little progress had been made in improving the purity of retail milk supplies, consumers were beginning to reduce contamination in milk by heating it in the home. Standards of medical practice were improving, and the more enlightened physicians were dispensing useful advice about food purity and the need to isolate infectious family members. Most of the innovations were adopted first in cities, and as a result mortality in cities appeared to be falling faster than in rural areas.

This record of successes and failures is vital background for understanding the levels, trends, and differentials in child mortality that we describe in the next three chapters. After displaying the facts of child survival in greater precision and detail than was previously possible, we return to these broader themes in the final two chapters.

TWO

NEW ESTIMATES OF CHILD MORTALITY
DURING THE LATE NINETEENTH CENTURY

THE BASIC PURPOSE of this chapter is to use the public use sample of the 1900 census to construct improved estimates of levels of child mortality in the United States during the last decade of the nineteenth century. The 1900 census asked questions on the number of children that had been born to women and the number of those children who were still living at the time of the census. These data do not provide direct information on such conventional life table measures as the infant mortality rate or the probability of dying before age 5. Instead, these measures must be estimated indirectly from the data, using the extensive procedures that demographers have developed for this purpose and that are described in this chapter.

Our results show a close agreement between the indirect estimates of child mortality for the Death Registration Area (DRA) and the direct estimates that are available from vital registration of deaths in this Area. We also show, however, that child mortality was higher in the DRA than in the nation as a whole for whites and, especially, for blacks. Ironically, the bias in DRA measures is largely offset when both racial groups are combined because blacks represented a very small fraction of population in the DRA, so that their exceptionally high mortality was underweighted.

Previous Estimates of Mortality in the Nineteenth Century

Little is known about trends, levels, and differentials in American mortality in the nineteenth century. It is not altogether clear when or even whether mortality declined in the United States during the period. The official Death Registration Area was not formed until 1900, and even then it only covered ten states and the District of Columbia.[1] As may be seen in Table 2.1, the DRA contained only 26.3 percent of the American population in 1900 and was significantly more urban than the nation as a whole. The percentage of the DRA population that lived in urban areas with at least 2,500 inhabitants was

TABLE 2.1

Comparison of Selected Characteristics of the Original Death Registration
States with the United States as a Whole, 1900

	U.S. (%)	DRA (%)
Total population	100.0	26.3
Percentage black	11.6	1.9
Percentage urban[a]	39.7	62.9
Percentage foreign-born	13.6	22.4
Percentage of U.S. blacks	100.0	4.4
Percentage of blacks who are urban	20.5	82.0

Source: U.S. Bureau of the Census 1902a, 1975.

Note: The original Death Registration states of 1900 consisted of Maine, New Hampshire, Vermont, Massachusetts, Rhode Island, Connecticut, New York, New Jersey, Indiana, Michigan, and the District of Columbia. See note 1 in chapter 2 for more information about the DRA.

[a] Population living in incorporated areas with populations of 2,500 and over.

62.9, compared with 39.7 percent for the nation as a whole. The DRA also had a larger proportion of foreign-born residents (22.4 percent versus 13.6 percent for the entire country) and contained only 4.4 percent of the American black population. Of the black population residing in the Death Registration Area, 82 percent were urban, although in the U.S. as a whole only 20.5 percent of blacks lived in urban areas. These differences would not be important if mortality differences along these dimensions had not been pronounced; but, as we will show, there were large differences in mortality by residence, race, and nativity.[2]

Before 1900, official mortality data were limited to selected cities and states and to the imperfect mortality statistics from the decennial federal censuses from 1850 to 1890 that asked questions on household deaths in the preceding year. In 1842, Massachusetts was the first state to institute vital registration, and it is widely cited as a source of information on nineteenth-century American mortality and fertility (Gutman 1956; Vinovskis 1972, 1981). By 1860, the Massachusetts death registration data were quite good, but evidence for years before that date must be sought from other sources such as genealogies, family reconstitutions, and bills of mortality (Vinovskis 1981: app. B). The population of Massachusetts was also more urban and industrial and had a higher percentage born abroad than the population of the country as a whole. Some analysts (e.g., Coale and Zelnick 1963) have been forced to assume that Massachusetts's mortality was representative of that of the United States as a whole, but its representativeness has been seriously questioned (Vinovskis 1978).

The federal census data on mortality have the virtue that they covered the whole nation. But they only provide information on events in the year prior to the census, and they were clearly seriously incomplete in the volume of deaths recorded (see Condran and Crimmins 1979, 1980; Condran and Crimmins-Gardner 1976, 1978; Crimmins and Condran 1983; Haines 1979a; Higgs and Booth 1979; Suliman 1983).

The absence of reliable national-level data has prompted the use of roundabout methods and symptomatic data to estimate mortality trends. Operating from assumptions about the inverse relationships between mortality and income per capita and between mortality and public health adequacy, and assuming a positive relationship between mortality and urbanization, Easterlin (1977:132–40) suggested that the rising effect of income per capita probably outweighed the negative effect of urbanization, with public health playing little or no role before about 1880. He thus posited an increase in expectation of life at birth starting around 1840. This finding contrasts with that of Vinovskis (1981: ch. 2), who suggests that little change occurred in the mortality level in Massachusetts between 1790 and 1860. More recent work by Fogel (1986), using a large genealogical data base, suggests that expectation of life at birth actually declined in the half-century prior to the Civil War, despite evidence of substantial economic growth from 1840 to 1860. One possible explanation for such a decline is that increases in income per capita were accompanied by a poorer income distribution (Williamson and Lindert 1980: ch. 4; Pessen 1973), although extensive data on workers hired by the Army is inconsistent with such a deterioration (Margo and Villafor 1987). Another explanation is that urbanization more than offset the gains from higher income. Such a process can be better documented in England in the first half of the nineteenth century, where urbanization was far more widespread (Woods 1985).

More evidence exists for the postbellum era. Higgs (1973) argues that mortality began its decline in rural America in the 1870s and that the decline took place largely as a result of improvements in diet, nutrition, housing, and general levels of living and without much assistance from public health. Meeker (1972, 1974) contends that mortality improved little if at all before about 1880, and that only after about 1880 was the fall in urban death rates substantially aided by new public-health measures, especially installation of sanitary sewers and pure central water supplies. Both analysts use a variant of intercensal survival analysis—tracking the survivorship of a birth cohort from one census to the next—which produces virtually no information on mortality in early childhood. Meeker's result is supported by work with extant nineteenth-century American life tables and model life table systems, which shows little evidence of sustained mortality reduction before about 1880 (Haines 1979a). Table 2.2 compiles previous estimates of nineteenth-century mortality in the United States. The data are confined to available life table information. On the whole, the results indicate little or no decline before the 1870s, higher mortality in urban areas, and much higher mortality among blacks.

By the 1890s, it is likely that mortality was declining in both rural and urban areas, although the absence of high-quality data of national scope leaves the matter open (Condran and Crimmins 1980). Urban death rates began at a higher level but apparently fell more rapidly, probably pushed by improvements in standards of living as well as advances in public health. Mortality improvements have been linked to specific public-health initiatives in the late nineteenth and early twentieth centuries in New York (Duffy 1974), Baltimore (Howard 1924), Philadelphia (Condran and Cheney 1982), Boston (Meckel 1985), Chicago (Cain 1972, 1974, 1977), and New Orleans (Lentzner 1987). Indeed, detailed studies of individual cities furnish perhaps the best opportunity to study this complex process.

As noted in Chapter 1, several European countries in the late nineteenth century also provide several examples of more rapid mortality decline in urban than in rural areas. Kingsley Davis (1973), focussing especially on Stockholm, demonstrates that urban areas in Europe often had mortality declines that were even more rapid than the much-heralded declines in less-developed countries after World War II. The accumulating evidence calls into question, at least for urban residents, Thomas McKeown's influential studies discrediting the importance of public-health measures as a factor in the nineteenth-century mortality decline (see especially McKeown and Record 1962). Accordingly, his explanatory emphasis on rising standards of nutrition as a factor in the nineteenth-century European mortality decline also appears overdrawn (see also Szreter 1988).

Whatever the progress of the mortality decline in nineteenth-century America, accurate data on mortality levels become available for part of the country with the formation of the Death Registration Area in 1900. Table 2.3 presents data from the DRA for 1900–1902, together with data from other countries during the period 1889–1910. The life table values given are $q(1)$, the probability of dying between birth and exact age 1 (also referred to here and elsewhere as the infant mortality rate); $q(5)$, the probability of dying between birth and exact age 5; and e_o, the expectation of life at birth. The values are calculated for both sexes combined.

In 1900–1902, more than 12 percent of infants in the DRA died before reaching age 1, and more than 18 percent died before their fifth

TABLE 2.2

Estimates of Child Mortality and Expectation of Life at Birth in the United States, 1830–1910

Source	Region	Period	Sex	Child mortality[a]			e_0	e_{10}
				$q(1)$	$q(2)$	$q(5)$		
Jacobson (1957)	Massachusetts-Maryland	1850	M	.16064	.21394	.27245	40.4	47.8
			F	.13079	.18262	.24122	43.0	48.6
Meech (1898)	United States, whites	1830–60	M	.16195	.21569	.27468	41.0	48.4
			F	.13430	.18752	.24769	42.9	48.8
Elliott (1857)	Massachusetts	1855	Total				39.8	
Vinovskis (1972)	Massachusetts	1859–61	M			.22646	46.4	51.6
			F			.19193	47.3	50.1
Haines (1977)	Seven New York counties	1850–65	M	.14655	.18067	.21268	45.9	49.2
			F	.12389	.15821	.19105	48.9	51.4
			Total	.13549	.16972	.20213	47.4	50.3
Haines (1979a)	United States	1850	M	.24092		.32195	36.5	45.0
			F	.21712		.29845	38.5	46.1
		1860	M	.20210		.27361	40.7	47.1
			F	.19153		.26684	41.2	47.3
		1870	M	.19210		.26007	42.1	47.9
			F	.17724		.24531	43.7	49.0
		1880	M	.22015		.29538	38.7	46.3
			F	.22980		.31019	38.2	46.5
		1890	M	.16334		.22875	43.9	47.9
			F	.15765		.22546	44.5	48.5
		1900	M	.13356		.21252	46.3	48.3
			F	.12476		.18611	47.4	49.2

TABLE 2.2 (cont.)

Source	Region	Period	Sex	Child mortality[a]			e_0	e_{10}
				$q(1)$	$q(2)$	$q(5)$		
Haines (1979a)	United States, white	1850	M	.22829		.30697	37.7	45.5
			F	.20596		.28486	39.6	46.6
		1870	M	.18513		.25056	43.1	48.5
			F	.16633		.23114	45.1	49.7
		1880	M	.21436		.28794	39.6	46.7
			F	.21526		.29268	39.6	47.1
		1890	M	.15675		.21914	45.1	48.7
			F	.14490		.20829	46.3	49.4
		1900	M	.12784		.18497	47.6	49.2
			F	.11206		.16781	49.6	50.4
Fogel (1986)	United States	1850–60	M					46.7
Billings[b]	Massachusetts	1878–82	M	.18080	.23250	.28342	41.7	49.9
			F	.15257	.20245	.25408	43.5	50.0
Billings[b]	New Jersey	1879–80	M	.15153	.19398	.24132	45.6	51.6
			F	.13121	.16939	.21217	48.0	52.5
Glover (1921)	Massachusetts	1890	M	.16777	.20851	.25322	42.5	48.4
			F	.14755	.18738	.23415	44.5	49.6
Abbott (1899)	Massachusetts	1893–97	M	.17233	.20726	.24234	44.1	49.3
			F	.14699	.18115	.21593	46.6	50.7
Glover (1921)	DRA, total	1900–1902	M	.13574	.16614	.19452	47.9	50.4
			F	.11267	.14092	.16881	50.7	51.9
			Total	.12448	.15283	.18196	49.2	51.1

Source	Category	Period	Sex					
Glover (1921)	DRA, whites	1900–1902	M	.13345	.16331	.19136	48.2	50.6
			F	.11061	.13832	.16574	51.1	52.2
Glover (1921)	DRA, blacks	1900–1902	M	.25326	.31098	.35615	32.5	41.9
			F	.21475	.26990	.31944	35.0	43.0
Glover (1921)	DRA, urban	1900–1902	M	.15097	.18683	.22128	44.0	47.5
			F	.12545	.15883	.19195	47.9	50.3
Glover (1921)	DRA, rural	1900–1902	M	.10900	.13065	.15043	54.0	54.4
			F	.08979	.10967	.12983	55.4	54.4
Glover (1921)	DRA, total	1909–11	M	.12495	.15016	.17282	49.9	51.1
			F	.10377	.12743	.14883	53.2	53.3
			Total	.11462	.13908	.16113	51.5	52.2
Glover (1921)	DRA, whites	1909–11	M	.12326	.14799	.17028	50.2	51.3
			F	.10226	.12545	.14651	53.6	53.6
Glover (1921)	DRA, blacks	1909–11	M	.21935	.27155	.31411	34.0	40.6
			F	.18507	.23303	.27232	37.7	42.8
Glover (1921)	DRA, urban	1909–11	M	.13380	.16247	.18815	47.3	49.1
			F	.11123	.13831	.16266	51.4	52.2
Glover (1921)	DRA, rural	1909–11	M	.10326	.12105	.13777	55.1	54.5
			F	.08497	.10119	.11679	57.4	55.5
Haines (1979a)	Suffolk Co., Mass. (Boston)	1859–61	M	.18057		.31389	36.0	44.1
			F	.15970		.29893	43.5	53.5
Haines (1979a)	Suffolk Co., Mass. (Boston)	1874–76	M	.20053		.34800	34.7	45.2
			F	.18403		.32401	37.1	47.1

TABLE 2.2 (cont.)

Source	Region	Period	Sex	Child mortality[a]			e_0	e_{10}
				$q(1)$	$q(2)$	$q(5)$		
Billings[b]	Boston, whites	1879–80	M	.21739	.28518	.34218	37.0	47.5
			F	.18873	.25365	.30823	39.1	48.4
Haines (1979a)	Suffolk Co., Mass. (Boston)	1884–86	M	.20171		.32815	36.0	44.9
			F	.17732		.30309	37.9	46.0
Haines (1979a)	Suffolk Co., Mass. (Boston)	1894–96	M	.17884		.29599	37.1	44.1
			F	.15032		.26518	41.0	47.3
Glover (1921)	Boston	1900–1902	M	.15736	.19875	.24002	41.6	46.0
			F	.13548	.16983	.21017	45.1	48.5
Glover (1921)	Boston	1909–11	M	.13527	.16333	.19050	46.0	47.7
			F	.11330	.13851	.16181	50.3	50.9
Condran & Cheney (1982)	Philadelphia	1870	Total	.17400		.29121	39.6	
Condran & Cheney (1982)	Philadelphia	1880	Total	.15970		.26104	42.3	
Condran & Cheney (1982)	Philadelphia	1890	Total	.15290		.24701	43.7	
Glover (1921)	Philadelphia	1900–1902	M	.15027	.18978	.23006	42.5	46.3
			F	.12741	.16369	.20232	46.2	49.1
Glover (1921)	Philadelphia	1909–11	M	.14174	.17456	.20558	45.5	48.1
			F	.11926	.14959	.17796	49.6	51.2

Source	City	Year	Sex	$Q(1)$	$Q(2)$	$q(5)$	E_0	e_{10}
Billings[b]	New York City	1878–81	M	.26278	.35464	.42751	29.0	42.4
			F	.22411	.31513	.38744	32.8	45.3
Billings[b]	New York City, whites	1879–80	M	.23421	.32245	.38085	33.3	44.9
			F	.20427	.28527	.34167	36.8	46.9
Billings[b]	Brooklyn, whites	1879–80	M	.19477	.27036	.33101	37.5	48.1
			F	.16424	.24336	.30545	39.7	49.1
Glover (1921)	New York City	1900–1902	M	.15673	.20308	.24435	40.6	44.9
			F	.13298	.17564	.21542	44.9	48.2
Glover (1921)	New York City	1909–11	M	.13186	.16799	.19907	45.3	47.4
			F	.11405	.14762	.17708	49.5	50.9
Billings[b]	Chicago, whites	1879–80	M	.20526	.27950	.34394	38.1	50.6
			F	.15107	.22919	.29958	41.3	51.6
Glover (1921)	Chicago	1900–1902	M	.12010	.15142	.18191	46.3	47.7
			F	.09762	.12764	.15676	50.8	55.0
Glover (1921)	Chicago	1909–11	M	.13066	.16079	.18980	45.9	51.5
			F	.10431	.13196	.15959	51.7	52.4

Source: Jacobson 1957; Meech 1898; Abbott 1899; Glover 1921; Haines 1977, 1979a; Vinovskis 1972; Fogel 1986: Table 3; U.S. Bureau of the Census 1886 (Billings); Condran and Cheney 1982: Table 1; various Massachusetts vital statistics and census data (Haines 1979a).

[a] $Q(1)$ is the probability of dying before reaching age 1. It is the infant mortality rate. $Q(2)$ and $q(5)$ are the probabilities of dying before reaching ages 2 and 5, respectively. E_0 and e_{10} are the expectations of life at birth and at age 10.

[b] From U.S. Bureau of the Census 1886.

TABLE 2.3

Comparison of Published Life Table Values: U.S., 1900–1902 and 1909–11, and Selected Foreign Nations, 1889–1911

Location	Period	$q(1)$	$q(5)$	e_0
United States (DRA)	1900–1902	.124	.182	49.2
Whites	1900–1902	.122	.179	49.6
Blacks	1900–1902	.234	.338	33.8
Urban (whites)	1900–1902	.138	.207	45.9
Rural (whites)	1900–1902	.100	.140	54.7
United States (DRA)	1901–10	.117	.166	50.9
	1909–11	.115	.161	51.5
Australia	1890–1900	.110	.151	52.9
	1901–10	.088	.116	57.0
Austria	1900–1901	.230	.321	38.8
Belgium	1891–1900	.156	.224	47.0
	1900	.195	.230	46.8
Bulgaria	1899–1902	.155	.289	40.1
Czechoslovakia	1899–1902	.229	.307	40.3
Denmark	1895–1900	.134	.177	51.7
England & Wales	1891–1900	.156	.234	45.9
	1901–10	.131	.192	50.4
France	1890–92	.172	.250	43.3
	1895–97	.159	.220	46.1
	1898–1903	.150	.209	47.4
Germany	1891–1900	.217	.292	42.2
	1901–10	.187	.243	46.5
Prussia	1891–1900	.203	.282	42.8
Ireland	1890–92	.098	.157	48.8
	1900–1902	.103	.159	50.2
Italy	1891	.190	.339	38.6
	1900–1902	.167	.283	43.0
	1901–10	.160	.266	44.5
Japan	1899	.162	.246	43.4
Netherlands	1890–99	.158	.226	47.6
	1901	.116	.224	49.0
	1900–1909	.129	.186	52.2
New Zealand (whites)	1891–95	.088	.118	58.1
	1896–1900	.080	.104	59.9

TABLE 2.3 (*cont.*)

Location	Period	$q(1)$	$q(5)$	e_0
Norway	1891–1900	.096	.149	52.2
	1901–10	.074	.109	56.2
Russia (European)	1896–97	.277	.422	32.4
Scotland	1891–1900	.131	.212	46.0
Sweden	1891–1900	.102	.160	52.2
	1898–1902	.107	.154	52.7
	1901–10	.084	.126	55.7
Switzerland	1889–1900	.151	.199	47.1
	1901–10	.126	.163	50.7

Source: United States: Glover 1921. All other life tables are from the published official life tables used by Coale and Demeny 1966, except those for Belgium (1900), the Netherlands (1901), and Sweden (1898–1902), which are taken from Keyfitz and Flieger 1968; Italy (1891) and Japan (1899), which were taken from Preston, Keyfitz, and Schoen 1972; and Ireland (1890–92 and 1900–1902), which were constructed from data given in Mitchell and Deane 1971 using the Reed-Merrell method (U.S. Bureau of the Census 1971: ch. 15). Male and female life tables were combined assuming a sex ratio at birth of 105 males per 100 females.

Note: $q(1)$ is the probability of dying between birth and exact age 1. It is the infant mortality rate; $q(5)$ is the probability of dying between birth and exact age 5; e_0 is the expectation of life at birth.

birthday. Mortality in the Death Registration Area was considerably better than that achieved in central, eastern, and southern Europe (i.e., Germany, Prussia, Austria, Czechoslovakia, European Russia, Bulgaria, and Italy); but Norway, Sweden, Australia, and New Zealand had superior survivorship. DRA mortality was not greatly ahead of that of Japan, the one non-Western nation represented in Table 2.3. For the largely urban black population of the DRA, mortality was so severe that it approached levels in European Russia in 1896–97, which are the highest mortality rates presented here. The series of life tables from 1900–1902 to 1901–10 to 1909–11 for the Death Registration Area indicates that mortality fell after 1900.

Child Mortality Estimates Based upon the Census Sample

We now turn attention to estimating levels of child mortality for the nation as a whole based upon the enumerators' manuscripts from the 1900 United States Census. Estimates are made separately for the

white and black populations; Chapter 3 will describe levels of childhood mortality according to more detailed characteristics.

The Sample

The original schedules of the 1900 census asked questions on the
number of children who had been born to women who had ever been
married and the number of those children who were still living. Instructions to enumerators indicated that stillbirths were to be excluded (U.S. Bureau of the Census 1979:34). For reasons that are not
clear, the returns from these questions were never published or analyzed.[3] Several years ago, a 1-in-750 stratified random sample of
households was produced from these manuscripts at the University
of Washington (Graham 1980). The data consist of a self-weighted
sample of 27,069 households containing 100,438 individuals from all
the states and territories of the United States, including Alaska and
Hawaii.

A comparison of selected characteristics of the sample with published census data reveals that differences in age, sex, race, residence, and nativity distributions were small and insignificant. Table
2.4 provides a number of these comparisons, including calculations
of the singulate mean age at first marriage for females in various race
and nativity groups. The latter requires distributions of the population by age, sex, and marital status (Hajnal 1953). As can be seen, the
differences from published results are negligible.[4] This sample has
been used by a number of other scholars, who have, in some cases,
confirmed its representativeness (see Haines and Anderson 1988).
For the analysis presented in this chapter, a subfile was created containing a sample of all 32,866 adult women who completed question-
naire information on both children ever born and children surviving
and whose responses were legible. Other restrictions on the data analyzed in the chapter are presented below.[5]

Estimation Procedures

The indirect estimation procedures used in this chapter begin with
the recognition that the proportion dead among children ever born
to a group of women is the joint outcome of a set of age-specific
death rates and the distribution of exposure times to the risk of death
that were experienced by offspring of those women. For example, if
the probability of dying before age 5 is .30 and if all of the women's
births occurred exactly 5 years earlier, then the proportion dead
among their children should be .30. If all of their births had occurred

TABLE 2.4

Comparison of Selected Population Characteristics in the National Sample
of the 1900 U.S. Census and Published Census Results

	Sample	Published census
Total persons (N)	100,468	75,994,575
Percentage female	48.91	48.92
Percentage black	11.34	11.62
Percentage foreign-born	14.23	13.61
Percentage urban	40.52	39.69
Percentage female at ages 20–24		
Total	46.66	46.66
White	45.03	45.26
Native white	44.36	45.15
Foreign white	47.03	45.91
Black	56.61	54.68
Singulate mean age at first marriage, females		
Total	23.54	23.66
White	23.69	23.86
Native white	23.76	23.88
Foreign white	23.50	23.58
Black	22.81	22.49

Source: Sample of census enumerators' manuscripts, U.S., 1900. U.S. Bureau of the
Census 1902a, 1975. Singulate mean age at marriage calculated according to Hajnal
1953.

exactly 2 years earlier, however, then the proportion dead among
their children would be less than .30, since some child deaths occur
between ages 2 and 5. The aim of indirect estimation techniques is to
provide an adjustment for children's exposure to the risk of death
that allows the underlying probabilities of death to emerge. In particular, the procedures are based on the following identity (Sullivan
1972; Brass 1975; Trussell 1975; United Nations 1983a: ch. 3):

$$D/B = \int_0^\alpha c(a)q(a)da, \qquad (2.1)$$

where B is the cumulative number of children born to reporting
women; D is the cumulative number of deaths among those children;
$c(a)da$ is the proportion of children born to reporting women who

were born within period a to $a + da$ years before the census; $q(a)$ is the probability of death before age a for a child born to reporting women a years before the census; and α is the number of years since the birth of the first child born to reporting women.

By the mean value theorem, there must be some age A between 0 and α such that

$$D/B = q(A) \int_0^\alpha c(a)da = q(A);$$

that is, the proportion dead among children ever born to the women must equal the probability of death prior to some age A in the life table pertaining to those children. The briefer the period of the child's exposure to the risk of death, the lower will be A. Short exposure periods can be constructed, for example, by limiting data to women aged 15–19 or to women who have been married less than 5 years. Numerous simulations of mortality and fertility histories (Sullivan 1972; Trussell 1975) have established that $q(1)$ (the probability of dying before exact age 1) is best identified by proportions dead among children born to women aged 15–19, $q(2)$ is best identified by reports of women aged 20–24 or in marital duration category 0–4 years, $q(3)$ by women aged 25–29 or married 5–9 years, and so on. The complete set of these correspondences is presented in Table 2.5 below.

The correspondences are not exact, of course, and conventional estimation procedures provide adjustment factors tailored to a particular application. These adjustment factors are designed to correct the estimates according to the shape of the age-specific fertility function prevailing in the population under study, a shape that determines the time distribution of children's exposure to the risk of mortality. This shape is indexed by the ratio of cumulative average numbers of children ever born in successive age or marital-duration intervals. Clearly, the ratio involves comparisons of cumulative childbearing across cohorts; to apply the methods, it is necessary to assume that the ratios also pertained in the course of childbearing to an actual cohort, which amounts to assuming that fertility has been constant.

An alternative approach to the indirect estimation of child mortality is the surviving-children method (Preston and Palloni 1978). This method involves the backward projection of the age distribution of surviving "own-children" by various levels of mortality within a model life table system to the point where the back-projected number of births equals the number of children reported as ever born by the

group of women. A model life table is simply an empirical representation of a "typical" life table for populations at a particular level of
mortality. A model life table *system* consists of a set of model life tables that vary systematically in their level of mortality, typically indexed by life expectancy at birth. Various systems of model life tables
have been constructed that vary in their input data and in their methods of estimation. Most frequently used, by virtue of their broad data
base and careful construction, are the four regional systems of Coale
and Demeny (1966). Coale and Demeny observed four different types
of relationships among age-specific death rates that prevailed histor-
ically in (mainly) European populations and assigned labels to these
relationships that correspond roughly to the region of Europe supplying input data for a particular system.

The surviving-children procedure is based on a rearrangement of
equation (2.1):

$$B/(B - D) = \int_0^\alpha [C_s(a)/(1 - q(a)]da, \qquad (2.2)$$

where $C_s(a)da$ is the proportion of surviving children who were aged
a to $a+da$ at the time of the census. Women can be grouped into
broad age, marital-duration, or other categories to implement this approach. The census sample provides direct reports on B and D, and
$C_s(a)$ can be estimated directly from the age distribution of surviving
own-children enumerated with the mother. An "own-child" is not
simply any child in the household but one who is identified as, or is
surmised to be, the natural offspring of the mother. The matching of
mothers and children is done through an examination of information
on relationship to head of household, age, surname, place of birth,
and order of enumeration in the original census manuscripts for both
mother and child. The availability of the age distribution of these
own-children is one of the advantages of a sample of original census
returns. Given B, D, and $C_s(a)$, the analyst then locates the set of
$q(a)$'s within a model life table system that will satisfy equation (2.2).
In order that the own-children estimates of $C_s(a)$ not be biased by
children having left the home, it is necessary to confine the analysis
to younger women. The Coale and Demeny (1966) "West" model life
table system is used here to provide values of $q(a)$; and the solution
is derived by an iterative procedure built into a model life table generation program (Avery 1981).

The surviving-children method has some advantages over the
more conventional estimation procedures based on equation (2.1).

Most important, it is insensitive to recent fertility declines or to irregular patterns of fertility behavior in the past. The history of fertility is explicitly represented in the age distribution of surviving children, whereas fertility must be assumed constant in the conventional approach. Second, the method is flexible with respect to the age or marital-duration groups of women that can be included in the analysis, a feature of particular advantage in dealing with some of the small-sample problems that are encountered here. The procedure is more sensitive than the others, however, to age-selective omissions and misreporting of children's ages. Fortunately, the 1900 U.S. Census appears to have had exceptionally accurate age reporting, probably attributable to the unusual inclusion of questions on both age at last birthday and year of birth (Coale and Zelnik 1963).

Each of the estimation procedures used a set of model life tables. Under the conventional age and marital-duration procedures, these model life tables are embodied in the multipliers that take account of the shape of the fertility history in a particular application. Different sets of multipliers exist for different model life table systems (United Nations 1983a: Tables 47 and 56). In the surviving-children technique, the model life table is imposed directly by the analyst. In neither case, however, are results sensitive to the model life table system chosen. Alternative model life table systems applied to the same set of data will produce identical values of $q(a)$ at some age A^*. The age of child at which this identity pertains for a particular age or marital-duration group of reporting women is usually close to the age shown in Table 2.5. That is, it is around age 1 for women aged 15–19, around age 2 for women aged 20–24 or married 0–4 years, around age 3 for women aged 25–29 or married 5–9 years, etc. The reason that this identity applies is that any pair of solutions to equation (2.2) that are drawn from different model mortality systems must intersect somewhere in the range of ages 0 to α (Preston and Palloni 1978). If they did not intersect—that is, if one $q(a)$ function lay above the other at all ages—then they could not both be solutions. The result is that two $q(a)$ solutions drawn from different model life table systems for the ages shown in Table 2.5 are usually within 1 to 4 percent of one another. For the same reason, there is also an intersection between two solutions, one that is drawn from a model life table system and the other that has an arbitrary time trend in $q(a)$ built into the system. Results of simulations of various types of mortality decline enable the assignment of a "date" to each estimate. The date is the approximate point at which plausible time trends intersect. In this chapter we use the dating equations developed in the United Nations's *Manual X* (United Nations 1983a: ch. 3).[6]

Implementing the Estimation Equations

A number of filters were applied to the census data, particularly for the marital-duration model, to increase the accuracy of estimation.

First, for the surviving-children approach, analysis was confined to women aged 14–34 because of the potential bias resulting from migration of children away from home. In implementing the surviving-children method, we also excluded women whose oldest "own-child" was implied to have been born before the women reached age 14.

Second, when a woman's age was used as the index of her children's exposure to the risk of mortality (the "age model"), all women in the relevant age groups were used in the estimations, with the exception of those for whom an illegible or missing response was given either for children ever born or for children surviving. (As noted earlier, these women were also excluded from the other estimation approaches). Mean parity estimates by age, required for adjustment factors, are based on all women with a legible response on children ever born.

Third, when a woman's marital duration was used as the index of her children's exposure to the risk of mortality (the "marital-duration model"), we attempted to exclude women not in their first marriage, for whom the duration in their *current* marriage—the only information available in the census—would be a very imperfect indicator of their children's exposure to mortality. In particular, we selected only women currently married with husband present who reported no surviving children other than own-children present in their household; whose implied age at marriage (current age minus duration of marriage) was between 10 and 34 years; whose oldest own-child's age was not more than two years greater than duration of current marriage; and whose reported number of children ever born was not more than two greater than duration of current marriage in years.

Despite the efforts to exclude from the marital-duration model women who had borne children prior to their current marriage, it is likely that our procedures have not been completely successful. One of the main clues about remarriage in the census manuscripts (which listed only current marital status and duration of current marriage) is the age of the oldest own-child. But under high-mortality conditions, many of the early births would not have survived to the 1900 census and thus would have left no evidence of the earlier marriage. These same high-mortality conditions would also tend to produce a higher proportion of remarried women in the population because of marriages disrupted by the death of the husband. Thus, remarried women with high child mortality would tend to be located at earlier marital durations and would bias upward estimates of child mortality at early ages. This bias occurs because duration of marriage is being used as a proxy for the time that the children are exposed to the risk of death.

These problems are more acute among blacks, for whom both marital disruption and mortality were high at the turn of the century. The percentage of women who were widowed or divorced was approximately twice as high in the black population as it was in the white population. For example, at ages 35–44, the percentage of black women reported as "widowed or divorced" in the Census of 1900 was 19.6, compared with 8.1 for whites (U.S. Bureau of the Census 1902a: Table 29). This result is, of course, not conclusive, since it is remarriage that is of direct interest. But the census results by age, race, and marital status are suggestive of the higher rates of marital dissolution among the black population of the United States at the turn of the century. Further, evidence from the Death Registration Area for 1900–1902 (Table 2.2) and from other sources (e.g., Condran 1984) indicates that adult male mortality among blacks was substantially above that of black females and well above the average for white males.

Differences among results obtained from using the four different regional sets of Coale and Demeny tables (i.e., North, South, East, West) are usually very small, as expected. In choosing among them, it was noted that Model West fitted well to the 1900–1902 Death Registration Area life table for the total and the white populations (Coale and Zelnik 1963). It is less clear whether any of the Coale and Demeny models fits the age patterns of black mortality well (Zelnik 1969; Condran 1984). Model West, an "average" pattern, was chosen for the black population as a compromise.

For the surviving-children approach, equation (2.2) was solved to provide estimates for all women aged 14–34 and for the subgroups of all women aged 14–24 and 25–34. It should be recognized that what constitutes a mortality level in the surviving-children approach is simply a complete model life table. Although considerable detail by age of child is presented for this method, the estimates for any particular solution are not independent of one another but are constrained to correspond to the same model life table. Depending on the model life table family chosen, different $q(a)$ sequences may result. All of the model life table systems, when applied to women aged 14–34, however, yield very similar results at age 5 because of the tendency for solutions produced by different model life table systems—or by a model life table arbitrarily deformed by different time trends in mortality—to intersect at some age of child. For the total population, the range of $q(5)$'s indicated by the various Coale and Demeny model life table solutions is only .004, whereas it is .024 for $q(1)$ and .030 for $q(20)$ (Preston and Haines 1984). Using a formula presented in Preston and Palloni (1978:84), we estimate that the year to which this robust surviving-children estimate of $q(5)$ pertains is 1896.

Results

The results of the different estimation procedures are given in Table 2.5. The table includes the $q(a)$'s (i.e., the probabilities of death between birth and exact age a), the N's (number of children ever born) for each group, and the level of West Model life table implied by each estimate. In addition, for the age and marital-duration models, Table 2.5 presents the estimated dates to which each of the various $q(a)$ estimates pertains, expressed in terms of years prior to the census of June 1, 1900. The time reference becomes earlier for older women, whose children were, on average, exposed to mortality in more distant periods.

Perhaps the best way to begin summarizing the mass of information in Table 2.5 is by means of a graph. Figure 2.1 presents age-specific estimates of $q(a)$ for the total population, using the three main approaches and, in each instance, using Model West estimation equations. Agreement among the three approaches is close for ages 3, 5, and 10. Beyond ages 5 and 10, the surviving-children estimate is basically an extrapolation using the same model life table identified as pertaining to younger children; because estimation stops with women aged 34, the surviving-children approach contains little or no information on mortality among older children. Nevertheless, the inclusion of the complete surviving-children $q(a)$ function in Figure 2.1 is illuminating because it suggests that the child mortality experience among older women—who are represented in the other two estimation approaches—diverges systematically from Model West level 13.6, which is the surviving-children method estimate for the total U.S. population. If we make the reasonable assumption that the West model life table system pertained in the period 1880–1900 roughly as accurately as it did in 1900, then children of older women were clearly subject to higher mortality conditions than were children of younger women.

These estimates thus suggest that a substantial reduction in child mortality occurred prior to the census of 1900, an implication consistent with some of the research cited earlier in this chapter. The pace

TABLE 2.5

Estimates of Child Mortality by Race: U.S., 1900

	q(1)	q(2)	q(3)	q(5)	q(10)	q(15)	q(20)	q(25)	Level	Implied life expectancy at birth
Age group of women[a]	15–19	20–24	25–29	30–34	35–39	40–44	45–49	—		
					Age model					
q(a)										
Total	.15332	.17664	.16438	.17736	.20662	.21983	.26076	—		
White	.16168	.15176	.15109	.16705	.19512	.20920	.24755	—		
Black	.13090	.26216	.21502	.25164	.27776	.29367	.34327	—		
N's[b]										
Total	382	3,378	6,886	9,123	11,212	10,861	9,760	—		
White	288	2,620	5,740	7,995	9,681	9,534	8,421	—		
Black	93	732	1,079	1,099	1,488	1,275	1,315	—		
Implied level[c]										
Total	11.38	12.19	13.52	13.60	13.06	13.03	12.19	—		
White	10.85	13.50	14.19	14.06	13.53	13.44	12.66	—		
Black	12.88	8.11	11.13	10.45	10.26	10.26	9.28	—		
Years prior to census to which estimates apply[d]										
Total	0.9	2.1	3.9	6.0	8.5	11.2	14.2			
White	0.9	2.0	3.7	5.8	8.1	10.8	13.8			
Black	0.7	2.1	4.4	7.2	10.2	13.3	16.3			

			Marital-duration model				
Duration group of women[a]	0–4	5–9	10–14	15–19	20–24	25–29	30–34
$q(a)$							
Total	.14722	.15514	.18234	.19496	.21885	.25267	.27768
White	.12926	.13949	.17267	.19234	.21101	.24398	.26915
Black	.28021	.26441	.25096	.22168	.27879	.32477	.35960
N's[b]							
Total	2,592	6,716	9,088	9,034	8,746	7,222	6,326
White	2,261	5,868	8,120	8,224	7,796	6,462	5,744
Black	322	811	916	791	924	733	564
Implied level[c]							
Total	13.74	13.97	13.38	13.35	13.07	12.48	12.43
White	14.79	14.82	13.81	13.64	13.37	12.79	12.72
Black	7.36	8.96	10.48	12.47	10.80	9.90	9.68
Years prior to census to which estimates apply[d]							
Total	1.3	3.4	5.8	8.2	11.0	14.1	17.1
White	1.4	3.5	5.8	8.2	10.8	14.0	17.0
Black	1.3	3.2	5.8	8.8	11.8	14.8	17.5

TABLE 2.5 (cont.)

	q(1)	q(2)	q(3)	q(5)	q(10)	q(15)	q(20)	q(25)	Level	Implied life expectancy at birth
				Surviving-children method[c]						
Women ages 14–34										
Total	.12025	.14906	.16183	.17636	.19218	.20381	.22040	.24234	13.65	50.08
White	.11076	.13658	.14802	.16104	.17561	.18638	.20187	.22255	14.36	51.83
Black	.17034	.21380	.23304	.25496	.27640	.29209	.31304	.34026	10.32	41.83
Women ages 14–24										
Total	.13255	.16566	.18033	.19703	.21441	.22718	.24482	.26802	12.75	47.92
White	.11775	.14576	.15818	.17231	.18780	.19921	.21551	.23718	13.82	50.54
Black	.18525	.23237	.25325	.27701	.29983	.31647	.33853	.36706	9.44	39.68
Women ages 25–34										
Total	.11806	.14617	.15863	.17281	.18834	.19978	.21611	.23782	13.80	50.48
White	.10970	.13518	.14647	.15932	.17375	.18441	.19978	.22030	14.44	52.03
Black	.16612	.20851	.22728	.24866	.26969	.28509	.30571	.33253	10.57	42.46

Sources: Data are from a sample of census enumerators' manuscripts, U.S., 1900. The age and duration methods use equations in United Nations 1983a: ch. 3.

Note: Coale and Demeny (1966) West model life tables are used as the basis for all three methods in the table; $q(a)$ is the probability of death before exact age a. Levels calculated from life tables for both sexes assuming a sex ratio at birth of 1.05.

[a] The age and duration groups of women are those used to estimate the particular q's listed in that column.

[b] N is the number of children ever born to each group of women.

[c] The following expectations of life are associated with these levels in the Coale-Demeny West model system. The total is estimated assuming a sex ratio at birth of 1.05.

Level	Female e_0^0	Male e_0^0	Total e_0^0
7	35.00	32.48	33.71
8	37.50	34.89	36.16
9	40.00	37.30	38.62
10	42.50	39.71	41.07
11	45.00	42.12	43.52
12	47.50	44.52	45.98
13	50.00	47.11	48.52
14	52.50	49.56	50.99

[a] These numbers relate the date, expressed in terms of years prior to the census (June 1, 1900), to which each estimate, on average, applied.
[c] The numbers of children ever born, children surviving, and surviving own-children present for women ages 14–34 used to make those estimates are:

	Children ever born	Children surviving	Children present
Total	19,292	16,121	15,263
White	16,331	13,882	13,276
Black	2,838	2,156	1,917

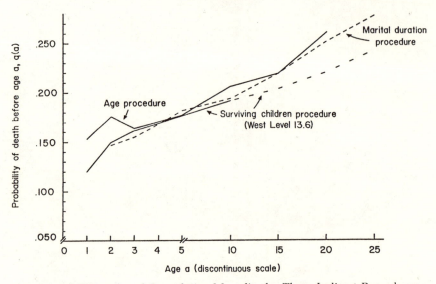

Figure 2.1 Estimates of Cumulative Mortality by Three Indirect Procedures, U.S., 1900

of this reduction can be estimated from Table 2.5. Using the marital-duration estimates, the average Model West level of mortality for marital durations 5–9 and 10–14 years was 13.68 and the average date to which these estimates pertain is 1895.9 (i.e., $1900.5 - (3.4 + 5.8)/2$). For women married 25–29 and 30–34 years, the average Model West level was 12.46 and the average date 1884.9. Thus, over the course of 11 years, the improvement in level was 1.22. These estimates translate into a decadal rate of gain in expectation of life at birth of 2.8 years between the mid-1880s and the mid-1890s.

This pace is consistent with Stolnitz's summary of changes in expectation of life at birth in western European countries between the 1880s and the 1900s, which suggested a median decadal rate of gain of 3.05 years (Stolnitz 1955: Table 6). The estimated pace of mortality decline in the U.S. depends, of course, on the suitability of the West model life table system. If post-infant mortality were much higher than assumed in the Model West pattern, some of the divergence shown in Figure 2.1 would be accounted for by this disparity in age patterns. In the extreme, if the North model were appropriate, with its very high tuberculosis death rates and relatively high mortality above age 5, then the mortality improvement over the 11-year period would be only 0.68 levels, roughly half as great as indicated by the

West model. On the other hand, if the East model is used, with its low post-infant mortality, the gain would be 1.81 levels.

Other sources, using different indirect procedures but without direct information on child mortality, have also suggested that mortality declines were occurring in the United States during this period (Higgs 1973, 1979; Meeker 1972; Haines 1979a; D. S. Smith 1983). Direct evidence from registration data (for the limited number of states and cities that had registration systems in place) also points to mortality decline for infants and for children aged 1–4 years in the 1890s (Condran and Crimmins 1980: Table 1). But the child mortality data analyzed here are the strongest evidence yet available, or likely to become available, that child mortality levels were improving for the United States as a whole in the decades before 1900.

Referring again to Figure 2.1, it can be seen that estimates of $q(1)$ and $q(2)$ are much less consistent than those at more advanced ages. In particular, the age model gives relatively high estimates of $q(1)$ and $q(2)$, and the $q(2)$ estimate exceeds all of the estimates of $q(3)$. Such an irregularity could have been produced by a sharp rise in childhood mortality in a short period before the census, but such an event seems unlikely. More plausibly, the explanation lies in data problems. As shown in Table 2.5, the age-model estimates of $q(1)$ are based on relatively few births. Also, age-model estimates of $q(1)$ and $q(2)$ are based disproportionately on first births and births to younger women, births known to be at unusually high risk of death (World Health Organization 1978). This high-risk composition of births is exacerbated by the relatively late age at marriage, with a singulate mean age at marriage of 23.66 years for females in 1900 (Table 2.4).

Before discarding age-model estimates for $q(1)$ and $q(2)$, we experimented with alternative age groupings for women. Despite the fact that the degree of age misreporting in the 1900 census was low relative to previous and subsequent censuses (Coale and Zelnik 1963), there is some indication of age heaping, particularly among blacks. The digital preference appeared largely for ages ending in 0 or 5. This pattern could create a bias if less educated or poorer women, who would also have been more likely to have experienced high mortality among their children, were also more likely to have misstated their ages. In an effort to test whether alternative age groupings would improve age-model estimates, the equations prepared by Hill, Zlotnik, and Durch (1981) were used for the age groups 18–22 (to estimate $q[2]$), 23–27 (to estimate $q[3]$), 28–32 (to estimate $q[5]$), and 33–37 (to estimate $q[10]$). The results (not presented) showed an even less regular pattern than when conventional age groupings were used. Therefore we are inclined to disregard age-model estimates of $q(1)$ and $q(2)$.

To derive a single best estimate of child mortality conditions in the United States near the turn of the century, we amalgamated the $q(3)$, $q(5)$, and $q(10)$ estimates from the three different estimation procedures. The mean West model mortality level corresponding to these variables for the age model is 13.39, and their mean date is 1893.4; for the marital-duration model, the corresponding figures are 13.57 for the date 1894.7. The surviving-children model provides a level of 13.65 and a date of approximately 1896. These are highly consistent with one another and allow for some trend of improved mortality. The grand mean is approximately a level of 13.5 for 1895. At this level of mortality in the West model life table system, $q(5)$ is .180 and the implied expectation of life at birth is 49.8 years.

The estimate of a $q(5)$ of .180 for 1895 is probably the single most robust estimate of childhood mortality that we can make based on the census sample. At this level, American child mortality compared favorably with that in most other Western countries. Among the countries shown in Table 2.3, only Australia, New Zealand, Norway, Sweden, and Ireland had lower childhood mortality in the 1890s, while Denmark's level was nearly identical. This group of countries is preponderantly rural. For the more industrialized countries of western Europe—Belgium, England, France, Germany, and the Netherlands—child mortality was 25–62 percent higher than in the United States, and in southern and eastern Europe the excess was even greater.

It should be noted that selective mortality of mothers could introduce a downward bias into our estimates of mortality for children of older mothers, and hence into estimates of trends. If women who died before 1900 experienced higher mortality among their children than women who survived, which seems likely, then the child mortality experience reported by the survivors in the census of 1900 underestimates that experienced by the cohort of women who began childbearing. Such a correlation could result from household episodes of disease that raise the death risks for both mothers and children; from shared hazards of the birth process; and from social and economic influences that affect the health of all family members.

A rough estimate of the amount of bias that might be introduced into reports of women aged 45–49 can be obtained through the following considerations:

1. The proportion of women reaching age 22 who died before age 47 in the DRA life table of 1900–1902 was 19.2 percent (Glover 1921:60–61).

2. These women can be assumed to have died about halfway through this interval, and so to have contributed about 10 percent of the cohort's births.

3. If mortality among their children was 50 percent higher than average, then child mortality in the original cohort of women would have been 5 percent higher than among the cohort of surviving women.

A differential of 50 percent is much larger than what is implied by social-class differences in child mortality described in Chapters 3 and 4. That is, the clustering of mortality by social class is unlikely to have induced a child mortality differential between living and dying mothers as large as 50 percent, even if all deaths of mothers were confined to the lowest social classes. A differential of 20 percent is more plausible. Nor could deaths of mothers and babies during childbirth create a bias as large as 5 percent. Only 1.3 percent of women surviving to age 20 died of maternal causes in the DRA life table of 1900 (Preston, Keyfitz, and Schoen 1972:727). Even if *all* of their children had died (and again assuming that they bore half as many children by age 50 as surviving women), the downward bias in the $q(5)$ of .180 (based on estimates supplied by surviving women) would only be 3.0 percent.

So 5 percent appears to be close to an upper limit on the extent of bias in child mortality resulting from the selective mortality of women before age 50. And most of our analysis is based upon younger women, among whom the forces of selection would be weaker still. We need to be aware of the potential bias from selective mortality of mothers, but it does not appear to be large enough to have seriously distorted our estimates.

Reliability of the Estimates

Before a discussion and interpretation of the mortality estimates is undertaken, it is useful to conduct tests of the reliability of the data and estimation procedures. Two tests were performed, although they were not entirely independent. The first test involved a comparison to figures contained in the 1900–1902 life tables for states in the Death Registration Area (Glover 1921). To make this comparison, we repeated the foregoing calculations for women in the 1900 census sample who resided in the states that constituted the Death Registration Area of 1900–1902. As has been mentioned above, this area comprised a minority of the population in 1900 (26.3 percent), but its mortality conditions are relatively accurately known by virtue of the

Glover life tables. Table 2.6 presents the basic results of this comparison. The various estimates are graphed in Figure 2.2. It is clear that the surviving-children approach produced a life table (West model level 13.29) in remarkably close agreement with the Glover table. It is important to note, however, that the Glover table pertains to a date some five years later than the surviving-children estimates. Nevertheless, our estimates of $q(a)$ are slightly higher, allowing the possibility of a small downtrend in mortality. Table 2.6 and Figure 2.2 are also instructive regarding the very close conformity of mortality in the DRA to the West model life table system.

As in the total American population, estimates based on the marital-duration and age models diverge systematically from the surviving-children estimates beyond age 5. This divergence occurs because the surviving-children estimates are limited to women below age 35, whereas the others are not. The indication of a downtrend in mortality—higher child mortality conditions for offspring of older women—is even clearer in Figure 2.2 than in Figure 2.1. The age model again produces high estimates for $q(1)$ and, especially, $q(2)$. The $q(a)$ sequences for both the age and duration models are less smooth and regular than for the total American population, and there are larger (but unsystematic) divergences between the two sets of estimates. Both of these traits are plausibly ascribed to the smaller number of observations available in the census sample of the DRA states. For the values believed to be most reliably estimated, $q(3)$, $q(5)$, and $q(10)$, the mean West model level is 13.03 for marital-duration-based estimates and 13.11 for age-based estimates. These levels are, respectively, 0.54 and 0.28 levels below our corresponding estimates for the total United States. The surviving-children estimate of level 13.29 is .36 levels below the estimate for the total United States in Table 2.5. Since each level represents about 2.4 years of life expectancy at birth, it appears that life expectancy at birth in the Death Registration Area was about one year lower than in the United States as a whole at the turn of the century. Note that this conclusion is not based on a comparison of data drawn from different sources but on a comparison of data for different areas from the census sample alone.

For whites, applying the surviving-children method to the census sample yields a level of mortality in the Death Registration Area very similar to that contained in the Glover 1900–1902 Death Registration Area life table: $q(3)$ in the two sources is .167 and .164, $q(5)$ is .182 and .179, and $q(10)$ is .198 and .196. The census sample data and procedures thus receive strong validation for whites and for the total population through comparison to the Glover table.

For blacks, however, there is a larger discrepancy. For $q(3)$, the cen-

TABLE 2.6

Estimates of Child Mortality by Race: U.S. Death Registration Area, 1900

	q(1)	q(2)	q(3)	q(5)	q(10)	q(15)	q(20)	q(25)	Level	Implied life expectancy at birth
	1900 Census sample using West model									
Age model										
Total	0.13010	0.17495	0.16259	0.18398	0.22284	0.24371	0.27520	—		
(N)	(56)	(675)	(1,408)	(2,156)	(2,490)	(2,729)	(2,575)	—		
White	0.13145	0.17403	0.16436	0.17947	0.21932	0.24585	0.27521	—		
(N)	(55)	(655)	(1,399)	(2,107)	(2,448)	(2,706)	(2,513)	—		
Duration model										
Total	—	0.13855	0.14707	0.19962	0.23267	0.23796	0.28059	0.30224		
(N)	—	(609)	(1,620)	(2,174)	(2,062)	(2,026)	(1,810)	(1,561)		
White	—	0.13576	0.14724	0.19472	0.23133	0.23848	0.27854	0.30215		
(N)	—	(597)	(1,599)	(2,139)	(2,037)	(2,022)	(1,784)	(1,542)		
Surviving children model women aged 14–34										
Total	0.12532	0.15577	0.16926	0.18462	0.20110	0.21318	0.23019	0.25264	13.29	49.21
White	0.12358	0.15347	0.16671	0.18179	0.19804	0.20997	0.22684	0.24912	13.41	49.51
Black	0.25814	0.32084	0.34862	0.38024	0.40824	0.42834	0.45426	0.48717	5.77	30.69
	Glover's 1900–1902 life tables for the Death Registration Area									
Total	0.12448	0.15383	0.16708	0.18196	0.19948	0.21037	0.22761	0.25232	—	49.24
White	0.12231	0.15112	0.16414	0.17886	0.19616	0.20674	0.22355	0.24785	—	49.62
Black	0.23447	0.29094	0.31561	0.33824	0.36621	0.39008	0.42135	0.45491	—	33.76

TABLE 2.6 (cont.)

	q(1)	q(2)	q(3)	q(5)	q(10)	q(15)	q(20)	q(25)	Level	Implied life expectancy at birth
				Implied level in West model life table system						
Age model										
Total	12.93	12.28	13.61	13.31	12.42	12.14	11.67	—	—	—
White	12.84	12.33	13.52	13.51	12.56	12.06	11.67	—	—	—
Duration model										
Total	—	14.24	14.40	12.65	12.04	12.35	11.47	11.60	—	—
White	—	14.40	14.40	12.85	12.09	12.33	11.55	11.60	—	—

Source: Sample of census enumerator's manuscripts, U.S., 1900. See text for estimation procedures. Death Registration Area life tables for 1900–1902 are found in Glover 1921.

Note: $q(a)$ is the probability of death before exact age a. Values of $q(a)$ for both sexes combined are derived by combining life tables for males and females assuming a sex ratio at birth of 105 males per 100 females. The value of N for the age and duration models, shown in parentheses, is the number of children ever born. For the surviving-children model, the relevant N's are:

	Children ever born	Children surviving	Children present
Total	4,261	3,533	3,344
White	4,182	3,478	3,303
Black	70	46	34

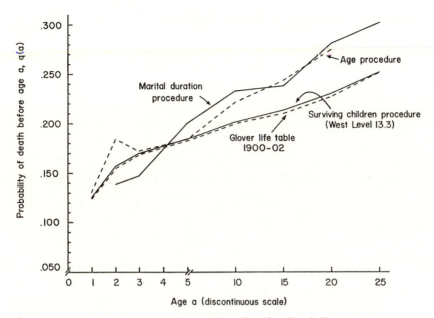

Figure 2.2 Estimates of Cumulative Mortality for Death Registration Area, U.S., 1900

sus sample gives a mortality level of .349, compared with .316 for the Glover life table. The $q(5)$ figures are .380 and .338, and $q(10)$, .408 and .366. The census sample implies even higher mortality in the DRA than does the Glover table. But the surviving-children estimates for blacks in the Death Registration Area are based on only 70 births. When such small numbers are involved, tests of significance are in order. We have assumed that death is a binomial process and that the underlying probability of death before age 5 for blacks in the DRA at this time is .33824, as in the Glover life table. With 70 observations and an "observed" $q(5)$ of .38024, the standard error of the number of deaths is $(.33824*(1 - .33824)*70)^{1/2} = 3.96$.[7] The observed number of deaths, $70*(.38024) = 26.61$, is thus within one standard error of the expected number of deaths, $70*(.33824) = 23.68$. Hence we conclude that the surviving-children approach gives a mortality level for blacks in the Death Registration Area that is not statistically significantly different from that in the 1900–1902 Glover life table for blacks.

This result is a reassuring indication that surviving—children data for blacks, at least in the Death Registration Area, are in line with other estimates believed to be accurate. It is also reassuring that our mortality estimates are slightly higher, since reporting errors in the census seem more likely to lead to an underestimate than to an overestimate of mortality.

A second test of the reliability of the census data uses a data set consisting of states and territories as the units of observation.[8] For each state or territory, a summary mortality index in the form of a ratio of actual to expected deaths was prepared using the information in the 1900 census sample on children ever born and children surviving for each geographic unit. This index, used extensively in the remainder of the book, is described in detail in Chapter 3. In addition, a death rate for children aged 0–4 was calculated from published data in the census of 1900 referring to mortality in the year prior to the census (June 1, 1899 to May 31, 1900). The census of 1900 included registration mortality data for the states of the Death Registration Area, and for cities in states outside the Death Registration Area whenever such data were available. When registration data were unavailable, responses to a census question on deaths in the household in the year prior to the census were substituted (Condran and Crimmins 1979). The registration data are known to have been more accurate than the "deaths last year" question.

The correlation between our mortality index and the published census "deaths last year" information for children 0–4 would not be expected to be perfect, since they covered different time periods and age groups. But the index was most influenced by young children, and many of those deaths had taken place in the late 1890s. The zero-order correlation between the index and the census death rate for the 45 regional aggregates (see note 8) was, in fact, .649, which is statistically significantly different from zero at a one percent confidence level. So the two independent sources of information on geographic variation in mortality are in reasonably good agreement.

Which data source, the census questions on children born and surviving (providing the "index") or the tabulations of deaths from registration and census reports (the "death rate"), is more accurate? To answer this question, a weighted least squares regression was run with a state's mortality index as the independent variable and the state's 1900 census death rate for children aged 0–4 as the dependent variable. The weights were the number of children ever born in each state. If our data are more accurate, then this simple regression fitted to *all* states and territories should produce positive residuals (i.e., actual values of the census death rate exceeding predicted values) for the DRA states and largely negative residuals (i.e., actual values of the census death rate less than predicted values) for non-DRA states and territories. That is, the death rate should be higher (relative to our index) in states in the DRA than it is in states that are not in the DRA; the regression line itself, of course, reflects the average level of incompleteness in the death rate across states both in and out of the DRA.

Exactly such a result emerges. For the ten DRA states plus the District of Columbia (also in the Death Registration Area), the mean residual was $+10.74$, and only one state, Maine, had a small negative residual (-1.28). For the other 34 states and territories (or groupings), the mean residual was -4.73, and 26 of the 34 had negative residuals. Of the states and territories in this latter group that had unexpectedly positive residuals, most had substantial registration coverage that was reflected in the census death reports.[9] Thus, the results here strongly support the superiority of the indirect mortality estimates from the census questions on children ever born and surviving relative to direct census mortality data on deaths last year.

Black Mortality

An important modification to received wisdom posed by the new figures relates to the black population. The three basic estimates of black mortality for the entire United States (from Table 2.5) are plotted in Figure 2.3. The age model and the surviving-children procedure give similar results, with the latter series basically representing a smoothed version of the former. The age model gives erratic results for the younger ages, where N's are small. The anomalous series is that pertaining to marital-duration estimates, which declines from $q(1)$ to $q(10)$ before rising sharply. A likely explanation for the irregularity is the high rate of marital disruption and nonmarital unions among the black population (Farley 1970: ch. 6). It appears that the age and surviving-children procedures afford the best estimates of black child mortality. For the whole United States, the surviving-children estimate for black women aged 14–34 is West model level 10.32. The mean West model level corresponding to the $q(3)$, $q(5)$, and $q(10)$ estimates by the age procedure is 10.61 ($e_0 = 42.46$), and the mean date to which these estimates pertain is 1893.1. The mean of the $q(5)$ values for levels 10.32 and 10.61 is .255.

The $q(5)$ figure of .255 that emerges from the census sample for blacks is far below the figure of .338 appearing in Glover's life table for blacks in the DRA. Though it is possible that errors in one or both sources account for this discrepancy, it is reassuring that the census sample for the Death Registration Area itself implies a level of mortality even higher than in the Glover table, as we have just seen. The

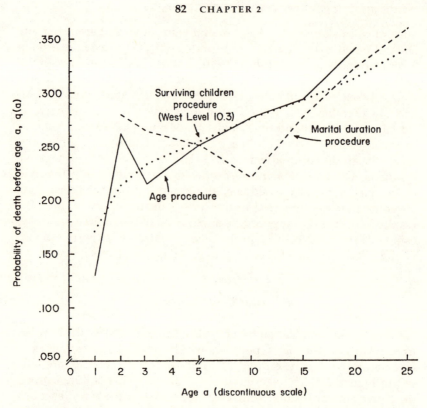

Figure 2.3 Estimates of Cumulative Mortality by Three Indirect Procedures, U.S. Blacks, 1900

most persuasive explanation of the discrepancy is that, before the extensive deployment of public-health measures aimed at communicable diseases during the twentieth century, there was a decisive rural advantage in mortality. This advantage was discussed in Chapter 1, and confirming evidence will be presented subsequently. The highly urbanized blacks in the Death Registration Area seem to have left behind a seriously distorted impression of general black mortality conditions, which has also exaggerated the black/white gap. Instead of a black/white ratio of $q(5)$'s of 1.89 from the Glover life tables (.3382/.1789), our results for the entire United States give a figure of 1.58 (.2550/.1610). Black child mortality appears to have been, both absolutely and in relation to whites, much poorer in the urban industrial states that formed the bulk of the DRA than in the more rural South. This revision of racial mortality differentials around 1900 also implies that less progress has been made during the twentieth century in narrowing the gap between black and white child mortality than is commonly assumed.

Several early warnings were sounded about the likely unrepresentativeness of Death Registration Area figures for blacks. American census officials later considered it highly probable that black mortality was better in the South than in the Death Registration Area (U.S. Bureau of the Census 1918:341). Nevertheless, most modern analysts have accepted as nationally representative the Death Registration Area mortality rates for blacks, or have even considered them too low. One reason why the DRA figures for black children appeared plausible is that *adult* black mortality for the whole United States was extraordinarily high, as revealed by one or another form of intercensal survival analysis or by stable population analysis. Demeny and Gingrich (1967), Farley (1970), and Meeker (1976) used West model life tables to combine adult mortality levels estimated from these procedures with presumed levels of child mortality. The resulting levels of expectation of life at birth for both sexes combined were 32.3 years for 1900–1910 (Demeny and Gingrich 1967), 30.2 years for 1900 (Meeker 1976), and 25.0 years for black females in 1880–1900 (Farley 1970). But the level of expectation of life at birth corresponding in the West model system to the level of black *child* mortality by the surviving-child method is 41.8 years. Coale and Rives (1973), in their reconstruction of black age distributions, used several mortality assumptions that are in the range of $e_0 = 30$ for the period; they suggested that levels of child mortality in the Death Registration Area were actually underestimates for blacks in the nation as a whole, rather than overestimates as we have shown. At a life expectancy level of 30 for 1900, $q(2)$ in the West model life table system is .328 and $q(5)$ is .388. These figures are about 50 percent higher than those which we estimate based on the census sample.

A probable key to the discrepancy is the appropriateness of the West model to black American mortality in the era. The best evidence on this matter is the age pattern of mortality in the Death Registration Area states. Zelnik (1969) has carefully studied this pattern. He demonstrated that the relation between child and adult mortality for blacks was very different from that implied by the West model between 1900–1902 and 1949–51. Mortality below age 10 was very favorable relative to mortality in the adult years, with differences in implied levels of expectation of life at birth (i.e., based on age-specific death rates in combination with West models) as large as 25 years. Moreover, the discrepancies increased as the Death Registration Area expanded to national coverage. Condran (1984) has produced similar findings for Philadelphia in the late nineteenth century. Demeny and

Gingrich (1967) argued that this trend could be explained by poor death registration for southern children, who were successively incorporated into the Death Registration Area, but the required amounts of underregistration are implausibly high. Furthermore, Zelnik introduced a life table of black Metropolitan Life Insurance clients (i.e., based on quite good data) that shows exactly the same age pattern of deviations as the entire United States life table for blacks. Although Zelnik did not speculate on reasons for the pattern of deviations, it is likely that tuberculosis played an important role. This disease was exceptionally common among American blacks (Meeker 1976; Condran 1984) and is capable of heavily distorting age patterns of mortality in the implied direction (Preston 1976).

Eblen (1974) is the only analyst to come close to what now appears to be the correct range of black child mortality. He used a more flexible model life table system that allowed the data (age distributions in successive censuses) to determine, in part, the relation between child and adult mortality. His estimate of $q(1)$ for 1890–1900 was .200, and for $q(10)$, .352. These estimates are only about 15 percent above our own.

So the previously accepted picture of extremely high black child mortality conditions around 1900 appears to have resulted from two distortions that reinforced one another: highly unrepresentative mortality conditions in the urban Northeast, the only area having an appreciable amount of direct vital registration data; and a very peculiar age pattern of mortality for blacks in the nation as a whole, with much better child mortality conditions than are implied by the levels of adult mortality that could be estimated for the nation as a whole by intercensal comparisons.

Just as the inference of child mortality levels from adult mortality levels can, and apparently did, lead to serious error, so can the extrapolation from child levels to adult levels produce distortions. Although we have presented in our tables the life-expectancy estimates corresponding to child mortality levels for blacks as a convenient metric, we caution against using them as valid estimates. They are almost certainly too high because blacks had higher adult mortality, relative to child mortality, than is implied by the West model life table system. But there is every reason to believe that the child mortality estimates for blacks that are presented here are superior to others that have been proposed.

In contrast to results for the total and white populations, the black estimates in Figure 2.3 do not suggest much of a downtrend in child mortality. Only $q(20)$ and $q(25)$ in the marital-duration model are higher than estimates implied by the surviving-children procedure (i.e., by the best-fitting West model). Even this discrepancy could be accounted for by the unusually high adult mortality in the black population relative to the West model life table system. What appears to be a mild decline could simply be the result of age distortions in the model life table used. It is always possible that higher fractions of dead children were omitted by older women and that such omissions are obscuring a true decline. The most we can say is that the census sample data are not consistent with much improvement in black child mortality in the late nineteenth century. The results do not provide much support for the possibility that black life expectancy followed a U-shaped time trend between 1860 and 1900 (Fogel, et al. 1978:78). They are, however, consistent with Ewbank's (1987) recent conclusion that black mortality rates were essentially stagnant in the late nineteenth century.

If our estimates of black child mortality are correct, they imply that the major accounts of black demographic history (e.g., Coale and Rives 1973; Farley 1970) may need revising. In particular, birth-rate estimates for the nineteenth century appear to need downward revision by approximately 8 to 10 percent, since the number of (surviving) children in censuses, on which the reconstructions are primarily based, would require fewer births to produce if child mortality were lower than previously assumed.

Mortality of Whites and of the Total Population

A similar but much smaller bias exists for the white population. Because whites in the Death Registration Area were more highly urban than in the nation as a whole (67 percent versus 43 percent), one might expect that childhood mortality for whites in the DRA was also higher than in the nation as a whole. A comparison of Tables 2.5 and 2.6 confirms this expectation. The surviving-children method applied to whites in the nation as a whole yields a $q(5)$ of .161; but for whites in the Death Registration Area, it is .182, or some 13 percent higher. It is likely that a higher proportion of foreign-born persons in the DRA (22 percent versus 14 percent for the nation as a whole) also contributed to this outcome. Since our results for whites in the Death Registration Area came very close to Glover's life table for whites in 1900–1902 ($q[5] = .179$ from Table 2.6), we conclude that the Glover life tables also give a somewhat biased view of white mortality in the entire U.S. at the turn of the century. In terms of its implication for expectation of life at birth, as shown in Tables 2.5 and 2.6, the difference between $q(5)$'s of .161 and .182 (using the surviving-children method) amounts to 2.32 years, or expectations of life at birth of 51.83 years (for the nation as a whole) versus 49.51 years (for the Death Registration Area).

Thus the Death Registration Area life tables, the most authoritative and widely cited information on American mortality rates at the turn of the century, present too pessimistic a picture of mortality conditions for whites and, especially, for blacks. Ironically, this bias is sharply attenuated among the total American population. The census sample gives a $q(5)$ of .176 for the whole United States and .185 for the Death Registration Area. The relatively small difference between these figures results from the fact that blacks contributed a much smaller proportion of births in the Death Registration Area than they did in the nation as a whole. Black births used for the surviving-children estimates were 14.7 percent of total births in the United States, but they were only 1.6 percent of births in the Death Registration Area.

Thus, the fact that the Death Registration Area life table provides reasonably good estimates of child mortality for the United States as a whole in 1900–1902 is simply the result of errors that were largely offsetting. Mortality for both blacks and whites appears to have been too high in the Death Registration Area tables, but the upward bias is largely offset by the very low proportion of blacks in the Death Registration Area.

Quantitative Summary

To summarize results of this chapter, we use the surviving-children method because it aggregates over different ages and marital durations of women and appears to work very well, especially for blacks. The basic estimates of the probability of dying before age 5, $q(5)$, are as follows (from Tables 2.2, 2.5, and 2.6):

	Census sample, *United States, 1896*	*Census sample, Death* *Registration Area, 1896*	*Vital registration,* *Death Registration* *Area, 1900–1902*
White	.161	.182	.179
Black	.255	.380*	.338
Total	.176	.185	.182

* *based upon only 70 births, insignificantly different from .338*

The summary shows clearly that mortality was substantially lower in the nation as a whole than it was in the Death Registration Area for both whites and blacks; that the census sample gives results very close to the vital statistics when confined to the states constituting the Death Registration Area; and that the bias in DRA figures is substantially offset when blacks and whites are combined because such a low percentage (1.9 percent) of the DRA population was black.

THREE

DIFFERENCES IN CHILD MORTALITY AMONG

SOCIAL, ECONOMIC, AND RESIDENTIAL GROUPS

MORTALITY is one of the most important measures of social inequality because it indicates a group's success in providing members with the most highly prized of all attributes, life itself. The sample of census enumerators' schedules from the 1900 U.S. Census affords the first opportunity to examine differences in child mortality among major social groups throughout the United States at the turn of the century.

We use this resource in the present chapter to draw a map of this largely uncharted territory. In so doing, we draw upon and extend some of the discussion in Chapter 1 about causal factors influencing mortality. Most of the effort to disentangle the influence of variables, however, is deferred until Chapters 4 and 5. The aim of the present chapter is more modest: to describe the implications for childhood mortality of membership in particular social and residential groups at the turn of the century. In a sense, the chapter constitutes a volume of the 1900 Census of Population that census officials, perhaps daunted by the difficulties of interpreting their data, and certainly lacking modern techniques for doing so, never prepared.

Sample and Methods: The Mortality Index

The underlying data source in this chapter is the nationally representative, 1-in-750 sample of enumerators' manuscripts from the U.S. Census of 1900 that was described in Chapter 2. The data set used in most of this chapter is a subset of the "woman file," consisting of 13,429 currently married women who had been in their present marriage less than 25 years and who had legible responses to the questions both on children ever born and on children surviving.

The body of indirect techniques for estimation of child mortality has been covered in detail in Chapter 2. The techniques involve calculating the proportions of children who have died to women of various intervals of ages or of marital durations and then adjusting the proportions according to the shape of the age-specific fertility schedule. This adjustment produces an estimate of a life table parameter representing child mortality. There are three advantages of indirect estimation: first, the data come from a single source (a census or survey) instead of two or more (e.g., vital statistics and census data), and are thus more consistent in coverage and in categories used; second, estimation of mortality is possible along dimensions not usually available from vital statistics (e.g., ethnicity of mother; occupation of father or mother); and third, mortality estimates can be made when vital registration is absent or defective, as was the case in the United States in the late nineteenth century.

The conventional indirect methods used in the previous chapter have several drawbacks, however, when one is attempting to study mortality levels of a large number of specific groups. Some of these groups may be quite small in size. The conventional methods produce many independent estimates for different age or duration categories, making it difficult and awkward to summarize the relative mortality of a group. Also, many of the individual age or duration intervals for smaller groups lack a sufficient number of observations to permit reliable analysis. Finally, a variable will eventually be needed that is suitable for multivariate analysis at a micro level.

Our solution to these problems was developed by Trussell and Preston (1982). An index is created that combines the child mortality experience of women with marital durations of 0–24 years. It takes the form of the ratio of actual to expected child deaths and can be calculated either for individuals or for groups. The number of actual child deaths for a woman is found, of course, directly from the difference between her reported number of children ever born and children surviving.

Expected child deaths are calculated by multiplying the number of children ever born to a woman by the expected proportion dead for her marital-duration group (that is, for marital durations 0–4, 5–9, 10–14, 15–19, and 20–24 years). The expected proportion dead is calculated from a standard model life table, in this case Coale and Demeny [1966] West model level 13, which has an expectation of life at birth of 48.5 years for both sexes combined.[1] The procedure involves taking the appropriate $q(a)$ for each duration group—$q(2)$ for women married 0–4 years, $q(3)$ for durations 5–9 years, $q(5)$ for durations 10–14 years, $q(10)$ for durations 15–19 years, and $q(15)$ for durations 20–24 years—and converting it into an expected proportion dead. This conversion is effected by rearranging the conventional estimation equations that are used to estimate $q(a)$'s from actual proportions dead and from average numbers of children ever born. The multipliers that

are normally used to convert proportions dead into $q(a)$'s now become divisors when the procedure is reversed, but continue to reflect
the pace of childbearing among the women and hence the average
exposure of children to the risk of mortality (United Nations
1983a:82). The details of construction of the mortality index are presented in Appendix C. The West model mortality pattern is chosen
because American data were used in the construction of the original
model and because, as we have shown in Chapter 2, the West model
replicates the experience of the 1900–1902 Death Registration Area
quite closely.

The index has the advantage of representing on one scale the child
mortality experience of a whole group of women of varying ages,
marital durations, and parities. It has been investigated elsewhere
and found to be robust and econometrically well-behaved when used
as a dependent variable in a regression model (Trussell and Preston
1982). The index is readily interpretable. A value of unity means that
a woman or a group of women was experiencing child mortality at
about the national average, while a value above unity means that
child mortality exceeded the national average. A disadvantage of the
index is that, if mortality was changing in the past, its value will be a
weighted average of the past mortality regimes, with the weights depending on the marital-duration composition of the group in question. Since groups may not be homogeneous with respect to marital-
duration composition, this feature can lead to some bias.[2] Because
the national mortality decline was relatively slow in the years preceding 1900—Chapter 2 suggests a rate of gain of 2.8 years in life expectancy at birth per decade—the biases in intergroup comparisons
should be minor.

Differentials in Child Mortality

The mortality indices for various categories and groups are presented
in Table 3.1, along with the numbers of women and of children ever
born that were used in calculating the index. Also presented are estimated values of $q(5)$ (the proportion of children dying before reaching age 5) and the standard error associated with the $q(5)$ values. The
$q(5)$'s were computed by multiplying the mortality index by the $q(5)$
for the standard life table used to calculate the index. That life table
is Coale and Demeny's (1966) Model west level 13.0 for both sexes
combined, which has a $q(5)$ of .19119. This value is somewhat higher
than the $q(5)$ of .180 estimated in Chapter 2 for 1895 because women's
child mortality experience is weighted by their number of births.

TABLE 3.1

Child Mortality Index in Various Social, Economic, and Residential
Categories: U.S., 1900

	Mortality index	Total women	Total children ever born	q(5)	Standard error
1. Total	1.0088	13,429	41,386	0.19287	0.00194
2. Race					
White	0.9404	11,952	35,993	0.17979	0.00202
Black	1.4650	1,410	5,211	0.28009	0.00622
Other	1.7658	67	182	0.33759	0.03505
3. Residence					
Urban	1.1263	6,302	17,292	0.21533	0.00313
Top 10 cities	1.1445	1,765	4,934	0.21881	0.00589
Other cities 25,000 +	1.2813	1,781	4,874	0.24497	0.00616
Cities 5,000–24,999	1.0994	1,408	3,763	0.21019	0.00664
Cities 1,000–4,999	0.9270	1,348	3,721	0.17724	0.00626
Rural	0.9230	7,023	23,742	0.17647	0.00247
Top 10 cities					
New York	1.2415	667	1,932	0.23735	0.00968
Chicago	1.0956	309	820	0.20947	0.01421
Philadelphia	1.1475	229	590	0.21940	0.01704
St. Louis	0.9595	106	324	0.18345	0.02150
Boston	1.3269	85	211	0.25369	0.02995
Baltimore	1.2557	101	314	0.24008	0.02410
Cleveland	0.5763	79	204	0.11019	0.02192
Buffalo	1.0304	68	195	0.19700	0.02848
San Francisco	0.9990	51	114	0.19100	0.03682
Cincinnati	1.1074	70	230	0.21172	0.02694
4. Census divisions[a]					
New England	1.1556	980	2,520	0.22094	0.00826
Middle Atlantic	1.0688	2,813	7,946	0.20434	0.00452
East North Central	0.9184	2,897	8,326	0.17559	0.00417
West North Central	0.8161	1,859	5,916	0.15603	0.00472
South Atlantic	1.0685	1,765	6,268	0.20429	0.00509
East South Central	1.0478	1,301	4,475	0.20033	0.00598
West South Central	1.1554	1,131	4,120	0.22090	0.00646
Mountain	1.1140	277	777	0.21299	0.01469
Pacific	0.8405	406	1,038	0.16070	0.01140
5. Literacy					
Wife					
Literate	0.9382	11,598	33,995	0.17937	0.00208
Illiterate	1.3467	1,571	6,683	0.25748	0.00535
Husband					
Literate	0.9545	11,562	34,732	0.18249	0.00207
Illiterate	1.3097	1,333	5,457	0.25040	0.00586
Husband and wife					
Both literate	0.9186	10,704	31,352	0.17563	0.00215
Only husband literate	1.3298	668	2,891	0.25424	0.00810
Only wife literate	1.2239	481	1,852	0.23400	0.00984
Neither literate	1.3482	830	3,532	0.25776	0.00736

TABLE 3.1 (*cont.*)

	Mortality index	Total women	Total children ever born	q(5)	Standard error
6. Ability to speak English					
Wife					
Speaks English	0.9915	12,652	38,586	0.18956	0.00200
Does not speak English	1.2667	530	2,124	0.24218	0.00930
Husband					
Speaks English	0.9928	12,618	39,139	0.18981	0.00198
Does not speak English	1.3758	285	1,078	0.26304	0.01341
Husband and Wife					
Both speak English	0.9836	12,154	37,485	0.18805	0.00202
Only husband speaks English	1.2424	265	1,131	0.23753	0.01265
Only wife speaks English	1.9579	26	88	0.37433	0.05159
Neither speaks English	1.3097	251	962	0.25040	0.01397
7. Occupation of husband[b]					
Professional, Technical	0.9450	443	943	0.18067	0.01253
Agricultural (excluding Laborers)	0.8637	4,296	15,762	0.16514	0.00296
Agricultural Laborers	1.1448	626	1,702	0.21888	0.01002
Managers, Officials, Proprietors	0.9344	899	2,341	0.17865	0.00792
Clerical & Kindred Workers	0.9121	366	712	0.17438	0.01422
Sales Workers	0.8312	398	905	0.15891	0.01215
Craftsmen, Foremen, etc.	1.1208	1,877	5,676	0.21429	0.00545
Operative & Kindred Workers	1.0458	1,301	3,916	0.19995	0.00639
Service Workers	1.0010	344	868	0.19137	0.01335
Laborers	1.2463	1,853	5,947	0.23827	0.00552
Miscellaneous & other	1.0049	221	554	0.19212	0.01674
8. Wife's labor force status					
Working	1.4149	758	2,191	0.27051	0.00949
Not working/Not in labor force	0.9865	12,671	39,195	0.18861	0.00198
9. Husband unemployed during year					
Not unemployed	0.9563	9,211	27,826	0.18283	0.00232
Unemployed at least one month during year	1.2102	1,989	6,558	0.23138	0.00521
10. Farm and Homeownership					
Own farm	0.8010	2,785	10,472	0.15314	0.00352
Rents farms	0.9688	1,814	6,292	0.18522	0.00490
Own home (non-farm)	1.0223	2,519	7,838	0.19545	0.00448
Rent home (non-farm)	1.1562	5,821	15,602	0.22105	0.00332
11. Nativity of husband & wife					
Both native-born	0.9713	9,521	28,332	0.18570	0.00231
Only husband native	1.0513	499	1,388	0.20100	0.01076
Only wife native	0.9175	887	2,694	0.17542	0.00733
Both foreign-born	1.1359	2,019	7,854	0.21717	0.00465
12. Structure of woman's household					
No unrelated individuals in household	0.9983	10,994	35,288	0.19086	0.00209
Servant(s) in household	0.8594	731	1,880	0.16431	0.00855
Boarder(s) in household	1.1702	1,371	3,690	0.22373	0.00686

TABLE 3.1 (cont.)

	Mortality index	Total women	Total children ever born	q(5)	Standard error
Woman is a servant	1.7685	40	58	0.33812	0.06212
Woman is a boarder	1.2458	173	139	0.23818	0.03613
Woman resident at an institution	1.2618	31	80	0.24124	0.04783
13. Migration status of woman					
Resident in state of birth	0.9566	7,825	23,008	0.18289	0.00255
Resident in census region of birth	1.0157	1,735	5,179	0.19419	0.00550
Born in different census region	0.9952	1,237	3,621	0.19027	0.00652
Foreign-born	1.1321	2,602	9,475	0.21645	0.00423
14. Relation of woman to household head					
Head	1.2152	151	536	0.23233	0.01824
Wife	1.0015	12,412	39,742	0.19148	0.00197
Child of head	1.0022	287	337	0.19161	0.02144
Daughter-in-law	0.9372	208	267	0.17918	0.02347
Sister	1.6863	27	32	0.32240	0.08262
Sister-in-law	1.5642	38	50	0.29906	0.06475
Niece	0.7848	14	14	0.15005	0.09544
Servant	1.7572	36	52	0.33596	0.06550
Boarder/lodger	0.9088	35	43	0.17375	0.05778
Wife of boarder/lodger	1.2127	135	87	0.23186	0.04525
15. Ethnicity (white, husband present)					
Husband & wife					
Both native	0.8660	8,157	23,220	0.16557	0.00244
Husband native, wife foreign-born	1.0513	498	1,388	0.20100	0.01076
Husband foreign-born, wife native	0.9204	881	2,684	0.17596	0.00735
Both foreign-born	1.1349	2,004	7,825	0.21697	0.00466
Wife & wife's mother					
Native white wife	0.8698	9,344	26,466	0.16630	0.00229
Native white mother	0.8656	7,245	20,417	0.16550	0.00260
British mother	0.8939	258	672	0.17090	0.01452
Irish mother	1.0189	503	1,479	0.19480	0.01030
Scandinavian mother	0.7225	83	217	0.13814	0.02342
German mother	0.8714	869	2,601	0.16659	0.00731
Other West European mother	0.5083	67	196	0.09718	0.02116
East European mother	0.5694	51	125	0.10886	0.02786
South European mother	0.2385	11	23	0.04559	0.04350
Other foreign-born mother	0.8651	257	736	0.16539	0.01369
Foreign-born wife (white)	1.1315	2,584	9,444	0.21633	0.00424
Britain	1.0993	241	822	0.21017	0.01421
Ireland	1.2883	348	1,257	0.24630	0.01215
Scandinavia	0.9408	305	1,088	0.17987	0.01164
Germany	1.1981	695	2,755	0.22906	0.00801
Other West European	0.7656	91	329	0.14637	0.01949
East Europe	1.0265	398	1,464	0.19626	0.01038
South Europe	1.1341	153	514	0.21682	0.01818
Other foreign	1.2330	353	1,215	0.23573	0.01218

Source: Sample of census enumerators' manuscripts, U.S., 1900.

Note: Sample consists of currently married women, married 0–24 years. The mortal-

TABLE 3.1 (*cont.*)

ity index is the ratio of actual to expected deaths to women in each group. For the calculation of expected child deaths, see text. $Q(5)$ is the proportion of children dying before age 5 for each group. The values for $q(5)$ are derived by multiplying the mortality index by the $q(5)$ value (.19119) for the standard life table (Model West level 13.0 for both sexes combined). The standard error assumes that the $q(5)$ value is the outcome of a binomial process with variance (p^*q/n), where q is the $q(5)$ value, $p = (1 - q)$, and $n = $ the number of children ever born.

[a] The census divisions were composed as follows: (1) New England: Maine, New Hampshire, Vermont, Massachusetts, Connecticut, Rhode Island; (2) Middle Atlantic: New York, New Jersey, Pennsylvania; (3) East North Central: Ohio, Michigan, Indiana, Illinois, Wisconsin; (4) West North Central: Minnesota, North Dakota, South Dakota, Iowa, Missouri, Nebraska, Kansas; (5) South Atlantic: Delaware, Maryland, District of Columbia, Virginia, North Carolina, South Carolina, Georgia, Florida; (6) East South Central: Kentucky, Tennessee, Alabama, Mississippi; (7) West South Central: Arkansas, Louisiana, Texas, Oklahoma Territory; (8) Mountain: Montana, Idaho, Wyoming, Colorado, Nevada, Utah, New Mexico Territory, Arizona Territory; (9) Pacific: Washington, Oregon, California, Alaska Territory, Hawaii Territory.

[b] The occupation classification system is that used for the 1950 U.S. Census.

Hence older women, whose births are more numerous than those of younger women and whose children were exposed to higher mortality conditions, receive heavier weight in the index.

The $q(5)$ life table parameter is chosen because it is likely to be least sensitive to time trends or to an error in the choice of model life tables. The standard error is computed assuming that the $q(5)$ values were generated by an underlying binomial process, which has a standard error of the square root of (pq/n), where q is $q(5)$, p is $(1 - q)$, and n is the number of "trials," i.e., children ever born.[3]

Race

As shown in Chapter 2, child mortality was considerably higher for blacks than for whites. The racial difference for the nation as a whole was, however, not as great as that in the Glover (1921) life tables for the Death Registration Area, whose base populations were concentrated in the Northeast and North Central regions. For example, the probability of dying before age 5 was 89 percent higher for blacks than whites in the Death Registration Area, but only 58 percent higher for the entire nation. Our differential of 56 percent shown in Table 3.1 (based upon a slightly more selective data set) replicates the results presented in Chapter 2. Southern rural blacks were clearly doing much better than the northern urban blacks that were over-represented in the Death Registration Area data. This fact had been suspected by the Census Bureau in 1918 (U.S. Bureau of the Census 1918:314). They conjectured that blacks in northern cities (and in cities generally) were largely migrants from the rural South and hence were subjected to many of the same mortality hazards as foreign immigrants to cities. But urban blacks were essentially beyond the pale of the social programs and settlement houses that were designed to ease the transition for immigrants to a new land (Katz 1986: 175–78).

Confirmation of the high urban mortality of blacks may be found in Table 3.2, which presents the mortality index for blacks and whites by rural/urban residence, city size, census region, race, and nativity. Rural blacks enjoyed a considerable advantage over urban blacks in both the North and the South. Black children, however, had much higher mortality than children of foreign-born white women in every residential category. Overall, northern blacks had slightly higher mortality than southern blacks in both rural and urban areas; as a whole, blacks in the North did much worse than blacks in the South, primarily because they were much more highly urbanized. It is noteworthy that blacks were slowly migrating out of the comparatively healthier rural South in the late nineteenth century for the much less salubrious urban areas of the South and North. The irony was not lost on DuBois (1899:147). Table 3.2 indicates that the urban-rural child mortality differential was higher for blacks (with 46 percent higher urban mortality) than for whites (with 29 percent higher urban mortality). Evidently, economic and social pressures in the South were sufficient to induce migration despite the much less healthy environment into which blacks were moving.

There is little evidence on which to base an assessment of the biomedical variables that may have contributed most heavily to the excess child mortality of blacks. Undoubtedly, nearly every feature of life was less conducive to a black child's survival: housing, sanitation, diet, and medical attention. As noted in Chapter 1, racial differences in breastfeeding practices were not noteworthy, although black mothers appeared to introduce (probably harmful) weaning foods at an earlier age. Black mothers were unquestionably much less likely to have had trained attendants at birth. And syphilis was undoubtedly a major threat to child survival (Rose 1989).

As noted above, these results call for further revision of views on the demographic history of blacks in the United States. Mortality among the children of southern rural blacks, who comprised a majority of the black population, was much more favorable than hitherto supposed. Contemporary claims that the black population was doomed to demographic decline because of its extravagant mortality (Hoffman 1896) were thus highly exaggerated.

TABLE 3.2
Child Mortality Index by Race, Nativity of Woman, Region, and Size of
Place: U.S., 1900

	Urban	Top 10 cities	Other cities 25,000+	Cities 5,000– 24,999	Cities 1,000– 4,999	Rural	Total
All women	1.1263	1.1445	1.2813	1.0994	.9270	.9230	1.0088
North Atlantic	1.1554	1.2145	1.2868	1.0028	.9406	.8985	1.0897
North Central	1.0094	1.0037	1.1530	1.1070	.7764	.7832	.8758
South Atlantic	1.3101	1.2557	1.2812	1.2806	1.4248	1.0020	1.0685
South Central	1.3588	—ᵃ	1.6401	1.4295	1.0550	1.0371	1.0994
West	.9432	.9990	1.1996	.7030	.7658	.9735	.9577
White	1.0709	1.1425	1.1955	1.0108	.8634	.8312	.9404
North Atlantic	1.1490	1.2124	1.2858	.9819	.9338	.8831	1.0808
North Central	.9790	.9999	1.0843	1.0657	.7680	.7746	.8579
South Atlantic	1.0750	1.2637	.9594	.8993	1.1053	.8017	.8673
South Central	1.0978	—ᵃ	1.2380	1.1619	.9262	.8993	.9472
West	.9321	1.0071	1.1996	.6308	.7658	.9236	.9216
Native white	.9732	1.1172	1.0676	.8981	.8266	.8077	.8698
North Atlantic	1.0587	1.2561	1.1690	.8088	.8725	.8386	.9808
North Central	.8760	.8961	.9438	.9541	.7576	.7455	.7919
South Atlantic	1.0481	1.1933	.9795	.8536	1.1180	.7959	.8496
South Central	1.0255	—ᵃ	1.1046	1.1693	.8733	.8769	.9109
West	.7110	.6498	.9609	.5744	.6012	.8596	.8059
Foreign-born white	1.2093	1.1641	1.3529	1.2143	.9887	.9601	1.1315
North Atlantic	1.2366	1.1822	1.3855	1.2150	1.0690	1.0827	1.2186
North Central	1.1352	1.0884	1.2448	1.2603	.8118	.8670	1.0074
South Atlantic	1.2355	1.5411	*	*	*	*	1.2312
South Central	1.7626	—ᵃ	2.0282	*	*	1.4031	1.5579
West	1.2415	1.3548	1.4650	.7396	1.0817	1.0885	1.1530
Black	1.9654	1.4208	2.4203	1.9713	1.5863	1.3382	1.4650
Northᵇ	2.1130	1.5136	2.2460	2.9116	*	1.4109	1.8726
Southᶜ	1.9238	*	2.4898	1.8010	1.6073	1.3359	1.4343
Native white with native mother	.9420	1.0942	.9928	.8991	.8703	.8306	.8656
North Atlantic	.9043	1.0741	1.0048	.7235	.8502	.8446	.8791
North Central	.9141	.9655	.9019	1.0121	.8377	.7785	.8207
South Atlantic	1.0676	1.4230	.9414	.8505	1.0951	.8024	.8521
South Central	1.0632	—ᵃ	1.2162	1.2307	.8714	.8913	.9242
West	.7854	*	.8581	.6161	.8542	.9027	.8623
Native white with foreign mother	1.0253	1.1331	1.1788	.8961	.6717	.6708	.8840
North Atlantic	1.2572	1.3671	1.3463	.9762	.9581	.7974	1.1934
North Central	.8194	.8500	1.0001	.8621	.5455	.6498	.7274
South Atlantic	.9609	.8103	1.1832	*	*	*	.8069
South Central	.8458	—ᵃ	.8828	.8666	*	.6463	.7572
West	.6054	.6589	1.2157	*	.2634	.7518	.6924

Source: Sample of census enumerators' manuscripts, U.S., 1900.

Note: The mortality index is the ratio of actual to expected child deaths to women in each group.
For the calculation of expected child deaths, see text. Sample consists of currently married women,
married 0–24 years.

ᵃ Not available.

ᵇ North is North Atlantic, North Central, and West.

ᶜ South is South Atlantic and South Central.

* Fewer than 40 children ever born for this cell.

4. Most blacks lived in the rural South and were victims of discriminatory practices that prevented their economic advance. Two black children from Georgia have just broken a trace on their goat team.

Rural/Urban Residence, Nativity, and Ethnicity

As noted in Chapter 1, urban mortality appears to have exceeded rural mortality around 1900 in the U.S. and other industrializing nations. This difference suggests that cities' efficiency in spreading communicable diseases more than offset any political or economic advantages that they may have presented for instituting health-related public works and services. But by the late nineteenth century, public-health and medical/scientific improvements had apparently begun to reduce rural/urban differentials (American Public Works Association 1976: chs. 12–13; Rosen 1958: chs. 7–8; Cassedy 1962a; Meeker 1972, 1974, 1980; Melosi 1980: chs. 1–3; Shryock 1947: ch. 15; Higgs and Booth 1979; Condran and Crimmins 1980). In England, mortality improved faster in urban areas than in rural areas after 1861 (Woods 1985:6). Watterson (1986), studying data on children ever born and surviving data from the 1911 Census of England and Wales, found that London had experienced the fastest mortality decline and rural areas the slowest. We expect that these relationships will also appear in data from the census sample.[4]

Tables 3.1 and 3.2 support the expectation that urban mortality will exceed rural. For the country as a whole, urban mortality was 22 percent higher than rural, and an excess was visible in all regions except the West, where urban mortality was exceptionally low. A clear relation also emerges between mortality and city size. Except for the group of 10 largest cities, mortality rose systematically as size of place increased. The largest cities, however, did somewhat better than the next largest group. It appears that the positive correlation between death rates and size of place that had been so characteristic of the nineteenth century was beginning to break down by the 1890s at the top of the city-size pyramid. It has now virtually disappeared (Kitagawa and Hauser 1973).

The relationship between mortality and city size varies somewhat with nativity. For native whites, the relationship is one of monotonic decline from the largest size category to the smallest, whereas the curvilinear pattern noted above holds for foreign-born whites and blacks. What appears to account for this pattern was not that native whites did particularly poorly in the largest cities, but that foreign-born whites and blacks fared relatively well in the largest cities and did *much* worse than native whites in the medium-sized cities. The relationship between nativity and race, place of residence and mortality may be summarized by indexing the child mortality index to native white rates:

	Native white	Foreign white	Black
Total	100	129	168
Rural	100	116	165
Urban	100	124	202
Top 10 cities	100	103	126
Other cities 25,000+	100	125	226
Cities 5,000–24,999	100	136	220
Cities 1,000–4,999	100	120	194

Relative to native whites, both blacks and foreign-born whites had their lowest child mortality in the largest cities.

A partial explanation for the better performance of the largest cities relative to other cities with populations greater than 25,000 may be their faster introduction of water and sewerage systems and certain medical/public-health improvements by the 1890s (Chapin 1901; Melosi 1980: chs. 1–3; Condran and Cheney 1982; Condran and Crimmins-Gardner 1978; Cain 1977). The largest cities had apparently been successful in lowering mortality in the 1890s, and public-health measures seem to have played a role (Condran and Crimmins-Gardner 1978; Weber 1899:367). The reduced penalty in the largest cities for children of foreign-born and black mothers, as opposed to the children of native white mothers, may well reflect the greater success of public-health activities in these cities in reaching the most disadvantaged groups.

Yet we also saw in Chapter 1 that public-health improvements in the large cities were fitful in the late nineteenth century, so that we must not be too facile in ascribing their superior mortality to public-health measures. Among the top 10 cities, the highest child mortality was found in the large eastern port cities of New York, Philadelphia, Boston, and Baltimore. These cities had experienced many of the consequences of the first stages of migration from Europe to the United States (Handlin 1973: chs. 3 and 6). They grew rapidly in the nineteenth century, and this growth placed strains on their antiquated water and sewerage disposal systems. Although New York had a fairly extensive sanitary water system by 1900, it was still having problems with sewage disposal (Duffy 1974:113–14). Philadelphia only began extensive water filtration after 1900, and there was frequent incidence of waterborne disease and other evidence of contamination of the water supply at the end of the nineteenth century (Condran and Cheney 1982). Baltimore had no sewerage system until after 1900, and the water supply in the late nineteenth century was subject to considerable criticism (Howard 1924:119–33). Boston, with the highest child death rate among the largest 10 cities, had a mixed record of providing public health in the form of good water and sewerage (U.S. Bureau of the Census 1902b:1xi-1xiii; Cain 1977:344–49; Meckel 1985). Thus, sanitary and public-health advances in these cities were clearly far from completely effective and allowed much room for twentieth-century improvements.

Table 3.2 shows that foreign-born white women had worse child mortality than native white women, regardless of residential category. And it is likely that differences in child mortality between native and foreign-born women were being reduced by the longer breastfeeding typical of foreign-born women. Woodbury (1925:114) shows that the excess infant mortality of foreign-born mothers in eight cities during 1911–15 increased from 30 per 1000 to 39 per 1000 when breastfeeding differences were controlled. Table 3.3 indicates that the disadvantage of foreign-born women did not pertain for all nativity groups. Irish-born women had very high mortality in urban areas above 5,000 inhabitants as well as in rural areas. Perhaps surprisingly, German-born women also did worse than average for the foreign born in all except rural areas. These two large immigrant

TABLE 3.3

Child Mortality Index by Race, Ethnicity, and Size of Place of Residence of Woman:
U.S., 1900

	Urban	Top 10 cities	Other cities 25,000+	Cities 5,000– 24,999	Cities 1,000– 4,999	Rural	Total
All women	1.1263	1.1445	1.2813	1.0994	.9270	.9230	1.0088
White	1.0709	1.1425	1.1955	1.0108	.8634	.8312	.9404
Native white	.9732	1.1172	1.0676	.8981	.8266	.8077	.8698
Native white with native mother	.9420	1.0942	.9928	.8991	.8703	.8306	.8656
Native white with foreign mother	1.0253	1.1331	1.1788	.8961	.6717	.6708	.8840
Second-generation Irish	1.1730	1.3148	1.2884	.8942	.7455	.4856	1.0189
Second-generation German	.9805	.9990	1.1827	.9277	.5485	.6791	.8714
Second-generation British	.9782	1.6296	.9592	.5056	.7763	.8033	.8939
Foreign-born white	1.2093	1.1641	1.3529	1.2143	.9887	.9601	1.1315
British	1.1105	1.0606	1.2796	1.1608	.7087	1.0856	1.0993
Irish	1.3104	1.3837	1.3495	1.2352	.7513	1.0641	1.2882
German	1.3129	1.2488	1.4006	1.2423	1.4763	.9550	1.1981
Scandinavian	.9656	1.3909	.7738	1.0171	.7071	.9166	.9408
Other West European	.8140	.6104	1.1922	.8181	*	.6945	.7656
East European	1.0779	1.0315	1.0228	1.4009	1.0495	.8993	1.0265
South European	1.2081	.9636	1.7961	*	*	.8970	1.1341
Other	1.3188	.8095	1.6924	1.3019	1.1349	1.0913	1.2469
Black	1.9654	1.4208	2.4203	1.9713	1.5863	1.3382	1.4650
Nativity of both spouses (white only)[a]							
Both native-born	.9715	1.1444	1.0512	.8940	.8452	.8064	.8650
Husband native, wife foreign	1.2933	1.3949	1.4667	.8367	1.1570	.7991	1.1146
Husband foreign, wife native	.9927	1.0354	1.1501	.9487	.6383	.8313	.9204
Both foreign-born	1.1938	1.1289	1.3277	1.2763	.9448	.9980	1.1348

Source: Sample of census enumerators' manuscripts, U.S., 1900.

Note: Sample consists of currently married women, married 0–24 years. The mortality index is the ratio of actual to expected child deaths to women in each group. For the calculation of expected child deaths, see text. In the table, unknown categories are not reported.

[a] Married women with husband present.

* Fewer than 40 children ever born for this category.

groups accounted for much of the excess child mortality of the foreign born. But British-born women did somewhat better than average for all foreign-born women in all except rural areas, while women of Scandinavian origin compared favorably to the average for all foreign-born women in all except the top 10 cities. In fact, their mortality in all urban areas combined was slightly below that of native white women. Child mortality among the immigrants from "newer" areas of origin, eastern Europe (Russia, Austria-Hungary, eastern Germany) and southern Europe (Italy), was not as high as one might have expected. Southern European mothers were about average for the foreign born in rural and urban areas, while the eastern Europeans (including many Jews) had child mortality well below the mean for foreign-born mothers, and about at the national average.

The favorable child mortality of the eastern Europeans and the relatively unfavorable experience of British and German women is inconsistent with their economic circumstances. Germans in Philadelphia in 1880 had a quite favorable male occupational structure, similar to that of native whites, while the Irish had a much higher representation in poorly paid occupations. (Hershberg et al. 1981:471). Woodbury noted that a much higher proportion of Poles and Italians than Germans had incomes below $650 in his urban sample (Woodbury 1926: Table 33). Although there are no definitive data, it does appear that migrants from southern and eastern Europe were not as successful economically as migrants from northern and western Europe in this era (Higgs 1971; Hill 1975; McGouldrick and Tannen 1977). For a slightly later period, Francine Blau found that Irish, French-Canadians, and southern and eastern Europeans had weekly wages that were 21 percent lower than those of northern and western European migrants (excluding Irish) in 1909. Much of the deficiency could be accounted for by differences in the distributions of skill, experience, and length of residence (Blau 1980: Table 1 and passim).

Ethnic differences in child mortality that were at variance with economic status may have been caused in part by differences in breast-feeding patterns among ethnic groups. Woodbury found that breast-feeding practices and economic status often offset each other, and also that Polish, Italian, and Jewish mothers tended to breastfeed more frequently and for longer periods than German women (Woodbury 1926: chs. 5 and 6). The lower-than-expected child mortality rates for eastern and southern European migrants are consistent with these behavioral differences, although Chapter 4 suggests that socioeconomic circumstances are able to account for most of the ethnic variation in child mortality.

Table 3.3 furnishes a tabulation of mortality by the nativity of both spouses for the white population. For the country as a whole and for the urban and rural populations, the most favorable conditions occurred when both spouses were native-born and the least favorable when both spouses were foreign-born. For the intermediate case, however, when one spouse was native-born and the other foreign-born, mortality was lower if the wife was a native. This relation held for the country as a whole and in urban areas, and was especially vivid in the largest cities. It may be that the foreign-born men who were able to attract native-born spouses in urban areas were unusually successful economically. In any event, it is clear that nativity of a child's mother was more important for child mortality than that of its father.

The 1900 census provides information not only about a woman's nativity, but also about the nativity of her parents. Table 3.3 presents mortality indices for native white women with native and with foreign-born mothers. Native white women of native parentage had a more favorable child mortality experience than did second-generation immigrants in large urban areas, but this difference was reversed in rural areas and in cities smaller than 5,000 inhabitants. Across all places, the mortality difference between the groups was less than 2 percent. Evidently, the assimilation process took roughly only one generation to complete in terms of child mortality, although it appears to have been somewhat arrested in the largest cities, where ethnic enclaves were perhaps most consequential (as Zunz 1982 documents effectively in Detroit).

Child Mortality of Migrants Compared to That in Countries of Origin

It is instructive to compare the child mortality levels for immigrants to levels in the countries where they were born. The latter comparison is somewhat crude because it is affected by migrant selectivity, including geographic factors that can cause migrants to be unrepresentative of the countries from which they were drawn. It should also be noted that some of the child deaths experienced by migrants may have occurred before their immigration, creating the possibility of a statistical link between mortality conditions in the country of origin and measured mortality among immigrants to the U.S.

Table 3.4 presents a comparison of $q(5)$'s, the most robustly estimated index that can be constructed from the census sample. Irish immigrants made up 15.6 percent of all the foreign born in the United States in 1900, second only to the Germans in numbers (U.S. Bureau of the Census 1975: Series C 228–295). It is apparent in Table 3.4 that, by the 1890s, Irish immigrants to the United States were experiencing significantly poorer child survival in the United States than was the case for those remaining behind in Ireland. Some of the disparity is attributable to residential differences. Ireland itself was largely rural, while Irish migrants to the U.S. settled mainly in higher mortality urban areas and had low incomes and poor housing (Hershberg et al., 1981). Of the 257 first-generation Irish women in the subsample used to calculate the mortality index, only 8 percent lived in rural areas and 74 percent lived in cities of 25,000 inhabitants and over. Of the urban dwellers, 54 percent lived in the 10 largest cities. Yet residential distributions are not the entire explanation of high Irish mortality, since Irish-born women displayed higher child mortality than average within every city-size category save one (1000–4999) in Table 3.3.

Second-generation Irish women had child mortality within 1 percent of the national average. This performance reflects the offsetting effects of an adverse residential distribution—74 percent were urban and 52 percent in places of 25,000 or more inhabitants—and unusually favorable mortality within most size-of-place categories. Only second-generation Irish women in the largest cities continued to suffer elevated mortality relative to others in their city-size group.

The largest group of the foreign born in the United States in 1900 were Germans, who comprised 25.8 percent of the foreign-born population. It appears that, in general, German immigrants (i.e., those whose birthplace was Germany, Prussia, or one of the other territories belonging to Germany in 1900) had better child mortality than German residents. Table 3.4 shows that Germany was an area of relatively high child (and overall) mortality in the late nineteenth century. It was characterized by particularly high infant mortality (Kintner 1982). It appears that duration of breastfeeding in Germany was, on average, unusually short, although there were striking regional variations that were clearly associated with infant mortality (Kintner 1985, 1987).

The probability of dying before age 5 was about 22 percent lower among offspring of German-born women who moved to the U.S. than for those who remained. Nonetheless, first-generation German immigrant women experienced mortality among their children nearly as high as among the Irish. Those living in urban areas had $q(5)$ values identical with first-generation Irish women and well above those for foreign-born white women overall. Relatively more German immigrants settled in rural areas, however; 29.6 percent of the sample of the German-born women used to calculate the mortality index lived in rural areas, as opposed to only 8.2 percent among the Irish. As a result, German immigrants had somewhat lower child mortality than immigrants from Ireland. As was the case for the Irish, there was a sharp drop in child mortality among the second-generation German migrant population, such that overall child survival ($q[5]$ = .167) was virtually identical to that for the native white population of native parentage ($q[5]$ = .164).

Another important source of emigration to the United States was Great Britain (England, Scotland, and Wales), which contributed 11.3 percent of the foreign-born population in 1900. British migrants to the United States experienced slightly more favorable childhood mor-

TABLE 3.4

Mortality among Immigrant Groups Compared to Mortality in Countries of Origin: U.S. and Europe, ca. 1900

Immigrant group	q(5)	Immigrant group	q(5)
Irish		British	
First generation in U.S.	0.246	First generation in U.S.	0.210
Urban	0.251	Urban	0.212
Rural	0.203	Rural	0.208
Second generation in U.S.	0.195	Second generation in U.S.	0.171
Urban	0.224	Urban	0.187
Rural	0.093	Rural	0.154
Ireland, 1890–92	0.157	England & Wales, 1891–1900	0.234
Ireland, 1900–1902	0.159	Scotland, 1891–1900	0.212
		Australia, 1891–1900	0.151
German		New Zealand, 1891–95	0.118
First generation in U.S.	0.229	New Zealand, 1896–1900	0.104
Urban	0.251		
Rural	0.183	Eastern European	
Second generation in U.S.	0.167	First generation in U.S.	0.196
Urban	0.187	Urban	0.206
Rural	0.130	Rural	0.172
Germany, 1891–1900	0.292	Austria, 1900–1901	0.321
Prussia, 1891–1900	0.282	Bohemia, 1899–1902	0.307
		Bulgaria, 1899–1902	0.289
Southern European		Russia, 1896–97	0.422
First generation in U.S.	0.217		

Urban	0.231
Rural	0.172
Italy, 1891	0.339
Italy, 1900–1902	0.283
Spain, 1900	0.368
Scandinavian	
First generation in U.S.	0.180
Urban	0.185
Rural	0.175
Sweden, 1891–1900	0.160
Denmark, 1895–1900	0.177
Norway, 1891–1900	0.149
Other West European	
First generation in U.S.	0.146
Urban	0.156
Rural	0.133
France, 1890–92	0.250
France, 1895–97	0.220
Belgium, 1891–1900	0.224
Netherlands, 1890–99	0.226
Switzerland, 1889–1900	0.199

Source: Sample of census enumerators' manuscripts, U.S., 1900. Specific countries: published official life tables used by Coale and Demeny 1966, except those for Ireland, which were constructed from data given in Mitchell and Deane 1971 using the Reed-Merrell method (U.S. Bureau of the Census 1971: ch. 15).

Note: Male and female life tables were combined assuming a sex ratio at birth of 105 males per 100 females.

tality than in contemporary England, Wales, or Scotland. British immigrants in the United States, however, even those living in the healthier rural areas, did not do as well as the contemporary populations of Australia and New Zealand, two areas that received a large number of migrants from the British Isles. As was the case for immigrants from Ireland and Germany, there was a substantial mortality improvement among second-generation British migrants.

Scandinavian immigrants (from Norway, Denmark, and Sweden) made up 10.4 percent of all the foreign born residing in the United States in 1900, nearly as many as the British. Scandinavia was a low-mortality area, and from the results in Table 3.4, it seems that child mortality among Scandinavians was only slightly worse in the United States than in their countries of origin. Unfortunately, there are too few cases in the sample to permit an analysis of mortality among the second-generation Scandinavian immigrant population. A favorable factor in the United States relative to other immigrant groups was the more rural character of Scandinavian settlement: 49.2 percent of women in the sample lived in rural areas, and only 31.1 percent lived in cities of 25,000 and over in population. But even among the residents of these larger cities, the child mortality index was only 1.0606 (compiled from Table 3.3), compared to a value of 1.1609 for all inhabitants of cities of 25,000 and over. Thus, the child mortality experience of northern European women in the United States seemed favorable, and some carryover of child-care practices may have occurred. Among migrant women from other areas of western Europe (i.e., France, Belgium, the Netherlands, and Switzerland), the survival rate of children was apparently rather good relative to national average child survival in the countries of origin. These nationalities, however, constituted less than 4 percent of the total foreign-born population.

Toward the end of the nineteenth century, the "new" immigration from eastern and southern Europe began to displace the "old" immigration from western and northern Europe. Although migrants from Austria, Bohemia, Hungary, Russia, Italy, and the Polish parts of Germany, Russia, and Austria made up 18.1 percent of the foreign-born population of the United States in 1900, they comprised 54.4 percent of the migration flow over the years 1895–99 (U.S. Bureau of the Census 1902a: Table 82; 1975: Series C 89–119, 228–95). As may be seen in Table 3.4, migrants from eastern and southern Europe seemed to have substantially better child survival in the United States than in their countries of origin, judging from life tables for Austria, Bohemia, European Russia, Bulgaria, and Italy.

This advantage emerged despite the fact that most of these "new" immigrants were urban dwellers in 1900. Of the women born in southern and eastern Europe making up the sample used to compute the mortality index, 79.9 percent were living in urban areas in 1900, and 62.6 percent in cities with populations of 25,000 and over. Their child mortality was not particularly good compared to that of the native white population or even to that of the native white population living in urban areas. But it was no worse than, and, in the case of eastern European women, sometimes better than, that of the total foreign-born white population, both in rural and in urban areas. As described in Chapter 1, immigrants from these areas generally breast-fed their children longer than other groups. In comparison to the ethnic stock in countries of origin, migrants from eastern Europe were disproportionately Jewish. We have no direct information on this proportion in 1900, but a tabulation by Gretchen Condran from a public use sample from the 1910 U.S. Census of Population produced at the University of Pennsylvania finds that 34 percent of reproductive-age women born in eastern Europe listed "Yiddish" as their mother tongue (Condran, personal communication). The favorable child mortality among Jewish women was noted at the time, as seen in Chapter 1, and long periods of breastfeeding by Jewish mothers may provide a partial explanation. But the surprisingly favorable child mortality of eastern Europeans was matched by favorable adult mortality as well, judging from 1910 results in Pennsylvania and New York (Dublin and Baker 1920). Their improved mortality relative to their countries of origin probably reflects their improved economic conditions, a primary goal that stimulated the migration streams in the first place.

In general, then, both first- and second-generation European migrants to the United States seemed to have had better mortality than those remaining in their country of origin, despite the fact that they concentrated heavily in larger American cities. This conclusion must be heavily qualified by the selectivity factors noted above; we cannot know what mortality conditions of the migrants themselves would have been had they remained in their countries of origin. A major exception to this conclusion applies to the Irish, who lived overwhelmingly in cities and towns in the United States, often had low-income occupations, and experienced child survival significantly worse than that in Ireland. Irish-born adults in the eastern United States also had exceptionally high mortality in 1910 from most causes of death, and especially from tuberculosis (Dublin and Baker 1920). The transplantation from highly rural Ireland to large cities in the United States seems to have exacted a special toll among the Irish.

When data are sufficiently numerous to judge, there appeared to be a convergence of the child mortality rates among the second-generation foreign born toward the more favorable patterns among the native white population of native parentage. This convergence was especially marked among the Germans, but it also occurred among the populations of Irish and British stock. Migrant populations also had uniformly better child survival than the American black population, in some cases by a wide margin.

Although migrants to the United States in general had better mortality than those in the countries they left behind (with the exception of the Irish), the nations of Australia and New Zealand, heavily populated by first- and second-generation migrants from Britain, were able to achieve child mortality rates by the 1890s that were lower than those for any immigrant group in the United States. Australia in the 1890s had a mortality rate comparable to that of rural American native whites, and New Zealand had an even lower rate. The heavily rural and agrarian character of both of these nations undoubtedly played a role in this performance, but significant medical and public-health measures had been undertaken as well. Woodbury (1926) was so impressed by the achievements of New Zealand in reducing infant mortality after 1875 that he devoted an entire chapter to discussing it in his seminal work. Infant mortality declined about 22 percent in New Zealand between 1872–74 and 1895–99 (from 105.9 to 82.7 infant deaths per 1000 live births). While pointing out that a number of conditions favored lower infant mortality in that nation, including an exceptionally favorable climate, relatively good and uncrowded housing conditions, and little or no poverty among the general population, Woodbury also noted other factors at work to promote the decline in the infant mortality rate:

> Certain influences have been operating steadily toward a decrease in infant mortality throughout the period. These influences include the gradual increase in medical knowledge of the best methods of disease prevention, the raising of the level of training in the medical profession, the improvements in public sanitation, the gradual extension of the public-health work in the Dominion as shown in the increase of powers and the improvements in methods of administration in the health department, and the gradual education of the public in methods of preventing disease and of maintaining health. These movements are difficult to trace in their individual effects upon infant mortality, but their combined influence is written plainly in the gradual and steady improvement in the rates of infant mortality from epidemic diseases and tuberculosis, as well as in the decline in infant mortality from respiratory and from gas-

tric and intestinal diseases which occurred during the period from about 1875 to 1905. (Woodbury 1926:177)

It appears that the same factors that influenced infant and child mortality were also at work in the United States, but that the extent and pace of change were slower. The United States was also more urbanized than either Australia or New Zealand, a substantial disadvantage for child mortality at the time.

Region of Residence

Geographic differences in mortality have evidently long existed in the United States (Taeuber and Taeuber 1958:282–86; Thompson and Whelpton 1933:241–42), although previous studies could not accurately trace them back to the nineteenth century. Considerable differences still existed in 1950 (Dorn 1959:468), but these largely disappeared when the rates for blacks and whites were examined separately (Bogue 1959:195–96). The South appears to have had a faster decline in mortality than the North between 1750 and 1850 (Fogel, et al., 1978), perhaps because improved drainage of swampy areas reduced the incidence of insect-borne diseases such as malaria, which were less of a threat in the North (Kunitz 1986). But in the late nineteenth century, there were few data on which a view of the relative mortality of the South could be constructed, and analysts (e.g., Fisher 1899) simply stressed the uncertainty.

Geographic differences should reflect influences of climate and prevalence of disease vectors, once other factors such as race, socioeconomic level, and rural/urban residence are controlled. Our expectation is that the South was less healthy because of a higher incidence of infectious, parasitic, and diarrheal disease related to its higher temperatures. Such a difference was evident in 1959–61, when mortality for children aged 1–14 years in the South was 16 percent higher than the national average, a difference that was partly caused by gastroenteritis and infectious and parasitic disease (Shapiro, Schlesinger, and Nesbitt 1968:205). Such a climatic affect is also evident internationally and seasonally, with summers posing special threats to child survival through most of the nineteenth and early twentieth centuries. On the other hand, the respiratory diseases that were so devastating at the time were probably spread more efficiently in the poorly ventilated conditions accompanying winters in the North.

In our sample, as Table 3.2 shows, mortality variation by region was relatively limited, with a range stretching from an index of .88 for the North Central states to 1.10 for the South Central. The North

Atlantic region, industrially the most advanced, was a close second to the South Central with an index of 1.09. Much of the disadvantage of the South Central region is traceable to the high percentage of blacks who lived and died there. Among whites, the North Atlantic region was by far the unhealthiest, with an index 15 percent higher than its nearest competitor. The North Atlantic was so unhealthy for whites that it was the only region to exceed the national average for whites by more than 1 percent. Here we can see again how the Death Registration Area, dominated by the Northeast, gave a distorted view of national mortality conditions.

The mortality problems of the Northeast were not simply a reflection of its higher degree of urbanization and large city concentration. These factors played a part; but within every residence and city-size category save one (5,000–24,999), the North Atlantic region had above-average mortality. Nor was the disadvantage principally attributable to a high percentage of foreign-born persons among North Atlantic residents; the region also had the highest mortality for native whites. Nor was it a result of below-average incomes, as we show below. Rather, settlement patterns may be the key to relatively high mortality. The Northeast not only had the highest concentration of large cities but also, as the region of earliest settlement, the most densely populated rural areas. Massachusetts and Rhode Island were the two most densely populated states in 1900, and Connecticut ranked fourth (U.S. Bureau of the Census 1975: Series A210–263). It seems plausible that density of habitation was affecting mortality in ways not fully captured by city size, a matter to which we return below.

Another anomaly associated with the North Atlantic region is that childhood mortality for native white women in the largest cities (New York, Philadelphia, Boston, and Buffalo) was *higher* than that among foreign-born white women in these cities (indices of 1.256 versus 1.182). Table 3.2 indicates that it was native white women of foreign parentage who contributed most to the higher childhood mortality among native white women in the 10 largest cities. The childhood mortality ratio for native white women who had native white mothers was only 1.074 in the largest four cities of the North Atlantic region. The ratio was 1.367 for native white women with foreign-born mothers. That this category of women did so well in rural areas suggests that selective migration patterns may have been playing a role in fashioning mortality differentials by residence among second-generation immigrants. Whatever the source, living in a large city was associated with a special health disadvantage for the children of second-generation Americans.

The North Central region had the most favorable child mortality, and its advantage carried through to rural white mothers, both native and foreign-born, and to many categories of urban population as well. The pattern of high child mortality in the Northeast and low child mortality in the North Central region arose largely from the high mortality of New England and the low mortality of the West North Central region, according to Table 3.1. An investigation of individual states reveals that Maine, Massachusetts, Rhode Island, and New Jersey were high child mortality areas in the North Atlantic region and that every state in North Central region except Illinois had below-average child mortality. Some states—Minnesota, Iowa, North Dakota, and Nebraska—had child mortality indices more than 20 percent below the national average.

The West region (Mountain and Pacific census divisions) exhibited a peculiar pattern, with much smaller rural/urban differences than prevailed in the rest of the country. A combination of favorable incomes, climate, and relatively small cities was probably instrumental in this outcome. Rural mortality was not especially advantageous in the West.

We hypothesized that the South would have above-average mortality. The mortality index was, in fact, 6–9 percent higher in the South Atlantic and South Central regions than in the nation as a whole. Combining the two regions, however, we find that child mortality was below the national average for both blacks and whites when considered separately. Its combined ranking was poor because an unusually high proportion of the population was black.

Looked at another way, however, the South did not fare so well. From Table 3.2, we can infer that overall mortality and white mortality for the combined South Atlantic and South Central regions was actually higher than the national average for each group within both rural and urban categories; the below-average child mortality rate for whites in this combined region resulted entirely from the South's disproportionately rural character. So the South's overall ranking reflected two offsetting influences: its high percentage of blacks and its rurality. Within categories of race and rural/urban residence, it appears to have had very slightly elevated mortality for whites and slightly reduced mortality for blacks.

The foreign born were subject to regional child mortality patterns similar to those of native whites, although typically at a higher level (Tables 3.3 and 3.5). The disadvantage among foreign-born women was exacerbated by their concentration in the Northeast and in larger cities. Irish mothers were concentrated in the North Atlantic region, particularly in the cities of New York, Boston, and Philadelphia. Irish

TABLE 3.5
Child Mortality Index by Region and Other Factors: U.S., 1900

	Census regions[a]					
	North Atlantic	North Central	South Atlantic	South Central	West	Total
All women	1.0897	.8758	1.0685	1.0994	.9577	1.0088
Woman's nativity and race						
White	1.0808	.8579	.8673	.9472	.9216	.9404
Native-born	.9808	.7919	.8496	.9109	.8059	.8698
Native mother	.8791	.8207	.8521	.9242	.8623	.8656
British mother	1.2875	.7500	.7163		.7470	.8939
Irish mother	1.1522	.8192	1.0831	.6770	.8092	1.0189
Scandinavian mother	*	.7963	*	*	*	.7225
German mother	1.2365	.7345	.7610	.7833	.6514	.8714
Other West European mother	*	.3577	*	*	*	.5083
East European mother	*	.6147	*	*	*	.5694
Other (including South European)	1.2951	.7118	.7358		.6440	.8468
Foreign-born	1.2186	1.0074	1.2312	1.5579	1.1530	1.1315
Britain	1.1440	.9172	*	*	1.4890	1.0993
Ireland	1.3591	.8390	1.0327		1.8326	1.2882
Scandinavia	1.2873	.8974	*	*	.8962	.9408
Germany	1.2481	1.1554	1.1627	1.8165	.9406	1.1981
Other West Europe	.6791	.9038	*	*	*	.7656
East Europe	1.0871	1.0132	.8894		.4729	1.0265
South Europe	1.0544	*	*	*	1.6896	1.1341
Other	1.3952	.8179	2.0536		1.0244	1.2469
Black	1.8364	1.8606	1.4225	1.4442	*	1.4650
Nativity of both spouses[b] (whites only)						
Both native-born	.9566	.7895	.8507	.9111	.8522	.8660
Husband native, wife foreign	1.1914	.7395	1.6684		1.7057	1.0513
Husband foreign, wife native	1.1485	.8378	.8542	.9999	.4712	.9204
Both foreign-born	1.2073	1.0433	1.2841	1.4631	1.0833	1.1348
Husband's occupation[c] (whites only)						
Professional, Technical	.9933	.9562	.7129	1.1386	.5095	.9417
Agricultural (excluding Laborers	.7399	.7098	.7383	.8835	.8398	.7714
Agricultural Laborers	.7298	.9240	.9660	1.0992	.9263	.9271
Managers, Officials, Proprietors	1.0172	.8823	.9290	1.0139	.7249	.9407
Clerical	.9365	.6254	.8634	1.2488	.9516	.8821
Sales	.8005	.9117	1.1110	.3760	.7749	.8354
Craftsmen, Foremen	1.2092	.9556	1.0640	1.2215	1.0636	1.0968
Operatives	1.0715	.8445	1.1118	1.1754	.9517	1.0028
Service Workers	1.1120	.8033	.7881	.7938	1.0103	.9457
Laborers	1.2571	1.1420	.9204	1.0448	1.0757	1.1653
Miscellaneous	1.0306	.8476	*	.6070	*	.9541
Wife working						
Total						
Works	1.1396	1.1203	1.6530	1.5123	.9726	1.4149
Not working/not in labor force	1.0883	.8686	1.0012	1.0599	.9572	.9865
White						
Works	1.0141	1.0317	1.1867	.7598	.8019	1.0024
Not working/not in labor force	1.0825	.8529	.8559	.9512	.9253	.9387
Black						
Works	2.7397		1.7432	1.6720	*	1.7416
Not working/not in labor force	1.6758	1.7616	1.3290	1.3730	*	1.3847

TABLE 3.5 (*cont.*)

	Census regions[a]					
	North Atlantic	North Central	South Atlantic	South Central	West	Total
Farm and homeownership						
Total						
Owns farm	.8313	.7090	.8113	.9037	.9152	.8010
Rents farm	.5470	.7229	1.0897	1.1603	.5703	.9688
Owns home	.9683	.9869	1.2596	1.0550	1.1079	1.0223
Rents home	1.2145	1.0092	1.1706	1.3736	.8655	1.1562
White						
Owns farm	.8285	.7078	.7067	.8488	.8356	.7617
Rents farm	.5518	.7247	.8487	.9451	.5703	.7935
Owns home	.9573	.9652	1.0652	.9423	1.0564	.9737
Rents home	1.2048	.9823	.9755	1.1523	.8451	1.0948

Source: Sample of census enumerators' manuscripts, U.S., 1900.

Note: The mortality index is the ratio of actual to expected child deaths to women in each group. For the calculation of expected child deaths, see text. Sample consists of currently married women, married 0–24 years.

[a] The census regions are: (1) North Atlantic: Maine, Vermont, New Hampshire, Massachusetts, Rhode Island, Connecticut, New York, New Jersey, Pennsylvania; (2) North Central: Ohio, Michigan, Indiana, Illinois, Wisconsin, Minnesota, Iowa, Missouri, North Dakota, South Dakota, Nebraska, Kansas; (3) South Atlantic: Delaware, Maryland, District of Columbia, Virginia, West Virginia, North Carolina, South Carolina, Georgia, Florida; (4) South Central: Kentucky, Tennessee, Alabama, Mississippi, Arkansas, Louisiana, Oklahoma Territory, Texas; (5) West: Montana, Idaho, Wyoming, Colorado, Utah, Nevada, New Mexico Territory, Arizona Territory, Washington, Oregon, California, Hawaii Territory, Alaska Territory. When combining the South Atlantic and South Central regions provides the minimum of 40 observations, the mortality index is presented for the combined group.

[b] Only for married women with husbands present.

[c] The occupational classification is that used for the 1950 census.

* Fewer than 40 children born for this cell.

mortality was much lower in the North Central region. Mothers of German birth had above-average child mortality in all except the West region, where few of them lived. Interestingly, mothers of Scandinavian origins also experienced high mortality in the urban industrial North Atlantic region, but not in the North Central region, where many of them lived on farms or in small towns.

Because of a high concentration of the group in the high-mortality North Atlantic region, second-generation Irish women also had relatively high child mortality. In fact, all second-generation foreign-born groups (largely British, Irish, and German) in that region suffered high child mortality relative to native white women with native white mothers. These second-generation immigrants were heavily concentrated in large cities, whereas the native white women of native mothers were more dispersed among rural and urban areas. But, in general, the second-generation foreign born did relatively well, with child mortality levels much below those of first-generation women and comparable to those of native whites of native parentage.

The child mortality variations by region in the late nineteenth century that we have described are presumably related to differences in the burden of sickness as well. In turn, levels of morbidity should be reflected in measures of child growth. It is now generally accepted that both child mortality and child growth are affected by the same set of circumstances, those related primarily to the adequacy of nutritional intake and the environmental "charges" made against it, especially in the form of infectious diseases (Fogel 1986:11–14; Preston and van de Walle 1978; Mosley and Chen 1984).

The census sample affords an interesting possibility for examining the correspondence between child mortality and child growth at the turn of the century through a comparison of mortality results with the average heights and weights of military recruits for the United States Army in World War I (1917–18). These latter data were collected by the Medical Department of the United States Army (Davenport and Love 1921). Unfortunately, it is not possible to standardize the mean heights and weights for the age structure or racial composition of the recruits. Of these World War I recruits, however, 78 percent were between ages 22 and 29 and probably were no longer gaining stature (Davenport and Love 1921:64). These men would have been aged 0 to 6 in 1895, the cohort whose mortality is centrally located in the census sample analysis.

We have computed the interstate correlation between estimated levels of child mortality in 1895 and the mean weight and height of World War I recruits. Because of small sample sizes, Arizona, Nevada, and New Mexico were combined into one group and Idaho, Montana, and Wyoming into another, giving 45 observations, including the District of Columbia. The correlation between our mortality index for states or groups of states and the height of recruits was only moderate ($-.294$) while that between mortality and weight was quite high ($-.649$). Weighted by the number of children ever born in the states, the correlations are $-.234$ and $-.611$, respectively. All coefficients are statistically significant at a 5 percent level.

The reason for the stronger correlation of the mortality index with weight than with height becomes apparent when it is noted that the heaviest recruits came from the Midwest and West, both of which were low child mortality areas in 1900. This pattern does not hold for stature. The tallest recruits came from the South, which was an area of high child mortality area in 1900, at least before race is controlled. It is likely that racial differences in growth patterns, and a different

5. The hazards of urban living appeared both in sharply higher child mortality and in poorer indexes of physical development. Pictured here is an obviously stunted urban youth whose family is taking advantage of free ice distribution in New York City, 1919.

6. Robust rural schoolchildren in Keota, Iowa, are playing "drop the hand-kerchief" in the early 1890s.

social composition in the two samples, are confounding the height/mortality comparison. A comparison of heights of white recruits with the mortality of whites would likely show a closer relation than when heights of both races are compared to the mortality of both races. Yet our results do attain statistical significance and suggest that the geographic differences in mortality that we have described were also reflected in differences in child morbidity and physical development.

Literacy

Years of schooling, especially among mothers, has received considerable attention in recent demographic literature on child mortality (Cochrane 1980; Caldwell 1979, 1981). A United Nations survey of mortality conditions in developing countries since 1950 found that there was a fairly regular and pronounced inverse relationship between mother's education (measured in terms of years of school completed) and child mortality. This relation was particularly evident in Latin America, which has been most extensively studied (United Nations 1982). A subsequent United Nations monograph (1985) has documented this relation in many additional countries. On the other hand, we noted in Chapter 1 that literacy of the mother had such a weak effect on infant mortality in eight American cities during 1911–15 (cf. Rochester 1923) that it was dropped from consideration in the study's final report (Woodbury 1926).

The 1900 Census of the United States collected data only on ability to read and write in any language, instead of the more useful information on years of school completed; but, as Table 3.1 shows, there is a noticeable relationship between child mortality and the literacy of either the father or the mother.[5] Child mortality was higher for the illiterate and highest when both spouses were illiterate. It was lowest when both spouses were literate. As in the case of nativity, literacy of the wife made more difference than literacy of the husband. The mortality index was 1.33 when only the husband was literate and 1.22 when only the wife was literate. For 84 percent of the couples used to calculate the index, both partners were literate, and for only 6.5 percent were both illiterate. Adult literacy was clearly widespread in the United States at the turn of the century, as in many European countries, although the minimal and ambiguous census definitions render this information somewhat difficult to interpret (see, on this subject, Graff 1979a: Introduction and app. B).

Some additional information on literacy appears in Table 3.6. Differentials in child mortality between literate and illiterate women are largest among native white women and particularly among native white women of native parentage. For this group, being illiterate

TABLE 3.6
Ratio of Child Mortality Indices of Illiterate to Literate Women: U.S., 1900

	Urban	Top 10 cities	Other cities 25,000+	Cities 5,000– 24,999	Cities 1,000– 4,999	Rural	Total
All women	1.50	1.00	1.63	1.84	1.76	1.51	1.44
White	1.33	.99	1.34	1.72	1.75	1.39	1.33
Native white	1.78	1.69	1.42	2.09	2.08	1.44	1.39
Native white, native mother	2.12	—	—	—	2.26	1.45	1.47
Native white, foreign mother	1.27	—	—	—	—	.93	1.04
Foreign-born white	1.13	.90	1.20	1.43	1.41	1.16	1.14
Black	1.18	—	1.40	1.10	.98	1.06	1.03

Source: Sample of census enumerators' manuscripts, U.S., 1900.
Note: Sample consists of currently married women, married 0–24 years.

seems to have signalled a very serious deficit that was associated with exceptionally high child mortality. Among foreign-born white women, black women, and first-generation migrants, the differentials were smaller and sometimes reversed, with illiterate women occasionally having lower child mortality.

Selectivity factors probably affect these results. Native white women were more likely to have had access to schooling. Those who did not achieve literacy must have been quite disadvantaged, perhaps being exceptionally poor or disabled. Among this group, illiteracy most likely functions mainly as an indicator of these other deficits. A larger proportion of black and foreign-born women did not have an opportunity to achieve literacy. Whereas only 5.0 percent of native white women were illiterate in the sample underlying Table 3.6, 14.8 percent of foreign-born white women and 51.4 percent of black women were unable to read and write.[6] Among these women, the measured impact of illiteracy is less likely to be inflated by its association with other deficits. There is virtually no impact of literacy on child mortality among black women, perhaps because literacy bought them very little in the way of better chances in life.

The relatively large child mortality disadvantage for a native white illiterate mother in 1900 was retained in both rural and urban areas. One might expect that literacy would have had a higher payoff in urban than rural areas because it would open more occupational doors in cities. But Table 3.6 provides no support for this proposition, nor is it supported by tabulations (not presented) involving father's literacy. In the multivariate analysis of Chapter 4, however, father's literacy emerges as an important correlate of mortality in urban areas.

The child mortality effects of mother's literacy that are presented here are larger than those revealed in the later Children's Bureau study of eight American cities. One reason for the difference may be that the Children's Bureau study was limited to infant mortality, whereas our results extend through later ages of childhood. Hobcraft et al. (1985:374) have shown that the relative influence of mother's education on child mortality in 39 developing countries conducting a World Fertility Survey increased by a factor of three as the child aged.

Table 3.1 also contains information on mortality according to the ability of the parents to speak English. As for literacy, English-language capacity was strongly inversely related to child mortality, with much higher mortality among the children of those not able to speak English at the time of the census. There were relatively few of these people, and they were likely to have been recent immigrants. The number of cases in which only one spouse could speak English is smaller still, but the evidence here suggests that English ability was more important for father than mother, perhaps reflecting its impact on his economic opportunities.

Occupation of Husband

The 1900 census contains information on the economic situation of husbands, including their occupation, unemployment status in the year prior to the census, and whether the home or farm where they lived was owned or rented. Panels 7–10 of Table 3.1 provide tabulations of mortality along these dimensions, and also according to the wife's working status. The occupational classification is based on the 1950 United States Census occupational groupings. The occupational and unemployment tabulations are, of course, only for married women with husband present.

The occupational categories reveal a rough gradient in child mortality from white-collar groups (Professional and Technical; Managers, Officials, Proprietors; Clerical and Kindred Workers; Sales Workers) to blue-collar workers (Craftsmen, Foremen, etc.; Operatives and Kindred Workers; Service Workers; Laborers). The least-skilled group (and one of the most numerous) consisted of laborers; not surprisingly, children in that group exhibited the highest mortality. Farmers (that is, the category Agricultural [excluding Laborers]), who typically lived in healthier rural areas, had very favorable child mortality conditions. Children of agricultural laborers, on the other hand, did considerably worse than average, with an index value of 1.14. Interestingly, other than farmers, the lowest mortality groups were not professionals, technical personnel, managers, proprietors, or officials. Rather, the most favorable child mortality was found among families of workers in clerical and sales occupations.

Some of the peculiarities of the occupational ranking of the mortality index are related to differences in distributions by race, nativity, and residence as shown in Table 3.7 (see also Chapter 5). The high mortality of agricultural laborers is largely attributable to the disproportionate representation in this group of blacks and foreign-born whites. For native white women whose husbands were agricultural laborers, the child mortality index, at .89, was well below average, although not as low as that for native white women married to farmers (.75). Similarly, the high child mortality for laborers was also partly caused by racial and ethnic composition. Native white wives of laborers had an index of only 1.05, but the index was 1.33 for foreign-born white wives of laborers and 1.64 for black wives in this occupational class.

Rural/urban residence also played an important role in creating oc-

TABLE 3.7
Child Mortality Index by Race and Nativity of Woman, Size of Place of Residence, and Occupation of Husband: U.S., 1900

Race and nativity of woman, occupation of husband	Urban	Top 10 cities	Other cities 25,000+	Cities 5,000– 24,999	Cities 1,000– 4,999	Rural	Total
All women	1.1263	1.1445	1.2813	1.0994	.9270	.9230	1.0088
Professional, Technical	.9903	1.2804	.7517	.9335	.9250	.8702	.9450
Agricultural (excluding Laborers)	1.0900	1.2706	1.2515	1.0851	1.0514	.8502	.8637
Agricultural Laborers	.8502	*	*	*	1.0568	1.1806	1.1448
Managers, Officials, Proprietors	.9406	.8967	1.0860	.9236	.8272	.9360	.9344
Clerical	.9154	1.0595	.9633	.8152	.3834	.8944	.9121
Sales	.8465	.8892	1.0520	.6876	.6703	.7621	.8312
Craftsmen, Foremen	1.1758	1.1900	1.3647	1.0844	.8911	.9471	1.1208
Operatives	1.0367	1.1698	1.0453	1.0721	.7684	1.0539	1.0458
Service workers	.9888	.9366	1.2334	.8943	.8396	1.0622	1.0010
Laborers	1.3630	1.2581	1.6232	1.3836	1.1479	1.0531	1.2463
Miscellaneous	1.0326	1.1736	.8433	1.0193	1.0735	.9486	1.0049
White women	1.0709	1.1425	1.1955	1.0108	.8634	.8312	.9404
Professional, Technical	.9943	1.3035	.7395	.9098	.9401	.8500	.9417
Agricultural (excluding Laborers)	1.0506	1.2706	1.2515	1.0515	.9951	.7535	.7714
Agricultural Laborers	.7778	*	*	*	.9841	.9464	.9271
Managers, Officials, Proprietors	.9443	.8990	1.0770	.9423	.8342	.9496	.9407
Clerical	.9056	1.0595	.9633	.7094	.3834	.7430	.8821
Sales	.8446	.8892	1.0520	.6738	.6703	.8032	.8354
Craftsmen, Foremen	1.1462	1.1911	1.3249	1.0314	.8507	.9342	1.0968
Operatives	1.0075	1.1738	1.0073	1.0357	.6981	.9769	1.0028
Service Workers	.9585	.9206	1.1850	.8303	.8362	.8764	.9457
Laborers	1.2345	1.2625	1.3937	1.2212	1.0004	1.0384	1.1653
Miscellaneous	.9565	1.1584	.8417	.6988	1.0863	.9752	.9541
Native white women	.9732	1.1172	1.0676	.8981	.8266	.8077	.8698
Professional, Technical	.9572	1.0972	.7590	1.0160	.9424	.8971	.9333
Agricultural (excluding Laborers)	.9699	*	*	1.2539	.8536	.7406	.7518
Agricultural Laborers	.7268	*	*	*	1.1376	.9105	.8902
Managers, Officials, Proprietors	.8632	.8016	1.0361	.7842	.7962	.9358	.8843
Clerical	.8629	1.0836	.9233	.6729	.3165	.7529	.8452
Sales	.7547	.9633	.9254	.5751	.5139	.8369	.7646
Craftsmen, Foremen	1.0507	1.1913	1.1585	.9363	.8637	.9112	1.0103
Operative	.9979	1.1971	1.0728	1.0599	.6301	.9305	.9814
Service Workers	.9752	.9116	1.2536	.6975	.9317	.7236	.9246
Laborers	1.0464	1.2927	1.0915	.9206	.9684	1.0457	1.0450
Miscellaneous	.8519	*	.7541	.4093	1.0640	.7412	.8033
Foreign white women	1.2093	1.1641	1.3529	1.2143	.9881	.9601	1.1315
Professional, Technical	1.1759	1.6665	*	*	*	*	.9915
Agricultural (exluding Laborers)	1.1939	*	1.3796	.6287	1.4081	.8364	.8867
Agricultural Laborers	*	*	*	*	*	1.1190	1.1028
Managers, Officials, Proprietors	1.1474	1.0270	1.1708	1.3946	1.1162	1.0564	1.1185
Clerical	1.0886	1.0113	*	*	*	*	1.0570
Sales	1.0254	.8182	1.3163	*	*	*	1.0278
Craftsmen, Foremen	1.2658	1.1961	1.4837	1.1900	.8071	1.0848	1.2463
Operatives	1.0144	1.1542	.8977	1.0060	.8212	1.0226	1.0182
Service Workers	.9395	.9278	1.0504	*	*	*	.9950
Laborers	1.3802	1.2515	1.5544	1.5728	1.0791	.9963	1.3292
Miscellaneous	1.0790	1.0976	.9523	*	*	*	1.1928

TABLE 3.7 (cont.)

Race and nativity of woman, occupation of husband	Urban	Top 10 cities	Other cities 25,000+	Cities 5,000– 24,999	Cities 1,000– 4,999	Rural	Total
Black women	1.9654	1.4208	2.4203	1.9713	1.5863	1.3382	1.4650
Professional, Technical	(.9524)[a]					(.7463)[a]	(.8377)[a]
Agricultural (excluding Laborers)	1.5136					1.3273	1.3259
Agricultural Laborers	1.0189					1.5328	1.4901
Managers, Offcials, Prop.							
Clerical	.9524[a]					.7463[a]	.8377[a]
Sales							
Craftsmen, Foremen	2.6411					1.0748	1.9182
Operatives	1.7369					1.5609	1.6306
Service Workers	1.2470					*	1.3644
Laborers	2.2301					1.0936	1.6428
Miscellaneous	*					*	1.5556

Source: Sample of census enumerators' manuscripts, U.S., 1900.

Note: Sample consists of currently married women, married 0–24 years. The mortality index is the ratio of actual to expected child deaths to women in each group. For the calculation of expected child deaths, see text. In this table, unknown categories are not reported. For occupational categories of husband, only women with husband present are given.

[a] Combined Professional and Technical, Managers, etc., Clerical, and Sales.

* Fewer than 40 children ever born in this category.

cupational differentials. Clearly, the two agricultural groups were favored by their residence in rural areas. As Table 3.7 shows, however, farmers in rural areas had low mortality even relative to the rural average. Native white wives of agricultural laborers in rural areas also had below-average child mortality, although it was higher than the rural average. Wives of laborers were more likely to be found in urban areas and also had relatively high mortality within those areas, especially among blacks and foreign-born spouses. Similarly, the high overall mortality among the children of craftsmen and foremen (an index of 1.12) was principally traceable to urban areas (1.18) and to families with a foreign-born white mother (1.25).

The failure of the children of the upper white-collar groups (professional, technical, managers, proprietors, officials) to have better mortality rates was only partly due to their disproportionate location in urban areas. Amazingly, within the largest 10 cities, children of professionals had higher mortality than children of any other occupational group. This disadvantage is largely traceable to the children of foreign-born women. For urban areas as a whole, however, wives of professionals had mortality that was below average (albeit only by 1 percent), as did wives of other white-collar classes. Indeed, the index was actually lower in urban areas (.86) than in rural areas (.94) for native white women with husbands in the category "Managers,

Officials, Proprietors." We explore the anomalous position of the professional class's mortality in greater detail in Chapter 5.

Urban mortality tended to be higher than rural mortality within occupational and racial/ethnic groups, and the largest cities (above 25,000 population) usually had worse conditions than smaller cities. The curvilinear pattern noted above, with the top 10 cities having lower indices than other cities of 25,000 and over, did not hold uniformly. Within occupational categories, the pattern was more visible for foreign-born women than for native white women. It is also most visible among the lowest occupational groups, service workers and laborers. These relations are additional evidence that, by the late nineteenth century, the largest cities had had some success in reaching the lower economic groups with public-health and sanitation reforms.

Mortality differentials across occupational groups within regions were similar to those for the nation as a whole. Table 3.5 shows that children in agricultural families did well relative to other groups in all regions, and children of farmers did better than children of agricultural laborers (with the exception of the North Atlantic region, where the index values were very similar). White-collar groups typically had more favorable experiences than blue-collar groups, particularly in the North Atlantic region. There is, however, considerable variability in the mortality rankings of occupations within regions, perhaps attributable to smaller sample sizes. For a particular occupational group, it was usually the case that the low-mortality region (North Central) had below-average child mortality and that the high-mortality region (South Central) had higher levels.

It must be remembered that occupation, like residence (and even literacy), is a mutable characteristic. Mortality levels are presented here only in terms of father's occupation and residence at the time of the census, whereas the child mortality estimates pertain to a period about the middle of the 1890s. Geographic and occupational mobility can intervene to obscure underlying relationships. But current residence and occupation are certainly closely related, on average, to residence and occupation in the previous decade.

Economic Activity of Mothers

Table 3.1 (panel 8) indicates that child mortality among working women (i.e., those who reported an occupation) was 43 percent higher than that of women who didn't work, confirming impressions of observers at the turn of the century. Only a small proportion of the total currently married women in this subsample were working

(5.6 percent), and this proportion was even smaller for married women with husband present (4.4 percent). Black women were much more likely to work than white women, as were women whose husbands were reported as absent (Goldin 1981; Pleck 1978). The latter case included legal separations and desertions. According to Robert Smuts: "The married women who did work away from the home were those whose husbands were permanently or temporarily unable to support their families. . . . Round the turn of the century, in short, when a married woman worked it was usually a sign that something had gone wrong" (Smuts 1959: 23, 55). That economic stress was the overwhelming factor causing women to work is also suggested by Woodbury's results for eight American cities between 1911 and 1915. Of women whose husbands earned less than $450 per year, 28 percent worked during pregnancy, compared to only 2 percent of women whose husbands earned over $1250 per year (Woodbury 1925:156–58).

Under these circumstances, it is not surprising that working wives had higher child mortality. Table 3.8 provides additional tabulations of child mortality by mother's labor force status and certain other characteristics. Excess mortality for children of working women prevailed regardless of their occupation, except that children of the few women classified as "farmers" had mortality 3 percent below the national average. Agricultural and white- collar employments were relatively favorable for the total and native white populations. This sort of work indicated some possible wealth, either as real or personal property or in the form of human capital. Overall, mothers who were laborers and service workers had very high child mortality, especially among foreign-born and black women.

Nevertheless, the detailed tabulations in Table 3.8 also pose important qualifications to the view that working per se inevitably presented a serious problem for child health. The exceptionally high mortality of children of working women was largely attributable to the very high proportion of such women who were black, and to the child mortality hazards associated with such work among both black and foreign-born women. But among native white women, those who worked actually had lower child mortality than those who didn't.

This relationship is traceable to women whose husbands were absent. An unusually high proportion of these women were employed (30.1 percent), indicating that for many the husband's absence was a long-term phenomenon that impelled them into the labor market. The unusually low child mortality among native white women whose husbands were absent is particularly surprising because children

TABLE 3.8
Child Mortality Index by Race, Nativity, and Employment of
Woman: U.S., 1900

	Total	White	Native white	Foreign white	Black
Total currently married					
women	1.0088	.9404	.8698	1.1315	1.4650
Working	1.4149	1.0024	.8026	1.4072	1.7416
Not working	.9865	.9387	.8715	1.1223	1.3847
(% Working)	(5.64)	(3.23)	(3.03)	(3.95)	(25.32)
Selected occupations[a]					
Agricultural	1.3361	.7528	.5072	1.3612	1.4801
Farmers	.9816	.8085	.4234	1.3784	1.2964
Agricultural labor	1.4315	.6706	.5907	*	1.5014
Non-agricultural	1.4594	1.0568	.8710	1.4161	2.0077
White-collar	1.0173	1.0341	.9511	*	*
Crafts, Operatives	1.2422	1.1773	1.1821	1.0460	*
(Seamstresses, Milliners)	(1.1896)	(1.1811)	(1.2259)	*	*
Service Workers	1.7769	1.2139	.6960	1.7465	2.0650
Laborers	1.5729	.8827	*	*	1.9923
Total currently married					
women, husband present	1.0034	.9386	.8708	1.1226	1.4442
Working	1.4619	1.0818	.9081	1.4510	1.7118
Not working	.9828	.9356	.8700	1.1148	1.3762
(% Working)	(4.42)	(2.27)	(2.18)	(2.60)	(22.59)
Total currently married					
women, husband absent	1.2367	1.0267	.8206	1.5053	1.9468
Working	1.2203	.7796	.4817	1.3053	1.9308
Not working	1.2494	1.1570	.9768	1.6466	1.9924
(% Working)	(40.30)	(33.42)	(30.10)	(45.68)	(69.51)

Source: Sample of census enumerators' manuscripts, U.S., 1900.

Note: Sample consists of currently married women, married 0–24 years. The mortality index is the ratio of actual to expected child deaths in each group. For the calculation of expected child deaths, see text. In this table, categories of unknowns are not reported.

[a] Non-agricultural = Total employed minus employed in agriculture; White-collar = Professional, Technical; Managers, Officials, Proprietors; Clerical; and Sales.

* Fewer than 40 children ever born in this category.

born to these women would be expected to be somewhat older than average (assuming that the husband's absence, for some women, at least, was a recent phenomenon). The number of observations for this group of native white working women with absent husbands is fairly sizable: 160 children ever born, 31.1 expected deaths and only

15 actual deaths. It is possible that the relatively low mortality of women in this group reflects their better ability, when the husband was absent, to direct resources toward purchases associated with child survival, even though there may have been fewer resources *in toto* (see Blumberg 1988 for extensive evidence of similar processes in developing countries today).

A word needs to be said concerning potential biases in child mortality statistics for working mothers. As we have seen, higher infant and child mortality among working mothers was the subject of critical comment in the late nineteenth and early twentieth centuries. One hypothesis was that care by someone other than the mother and, in particular, artificial feeding rather than breastfeeding substantially increased the risk of child loss. But it is also possible that causation may run from child death to women's working, rather than in the reverse direction. The relation may be upwardly biased because the recent death of a child, especially a first birth, may facilitate a woman's working. Unfortunately, there is no way of testing the relative importance of the two causal paths with cross-sectional data. We can, however, make some headway in addressing the self-selection via economic stress hypothesis in the next chapter when we examine the importance of mother's work controlling many other factors.

Table 3.5 shows that, for the black population, the child mortality disadvantage for working women was consistent across the North and the South. But the mortality excess was considerably greater in the North, where work may have involved a sharper disjunction between home and workplace, than in the South. The child mortality index for working black women in the North Central and North Atlantic regions, where the black population was largely urban, was 59 percent above the index for nonworking women. The excess mortality was only 31 percent in the South Atlantic region and 22 percent in the South Central region.

Other Economic Variables

Two more indicators of economic status appear in Table 3.1 (panels 9 and 10): whether the husband had been unemployed (for at least one month) at some time during the census year and whether the family owned or rented its home or farm. If the husband was unemployed for at least a month during the year preceding the census, there was a substantially increased risk of child death in the family. The mortality index for families with some unemployment for the principal wage earner (which constituted 17.8 percent of families providing this information in Table 3.1) was 26 percent higher than for families with no reported loss of work.

As shown below, this variable retains a powerful influence in multivariate analysis and emerges as one of the most important predictors of child mortality. An inquiry by the U.S. Bureau of Labor into the conditions among 19 very poor working-class families in Washington, D.C. during 1905 provides some insight into the importance of this variable. The irregularity with which men were employed was claimed to be the single most powerful cause operating to bring families down to the poverty line and keep them there. Testimony by the wage-earners themselves was said to be nearly unanimous on this point (Forman 1906:617). The wages they were paid were adequate if only sufficient work could be found, but seasonal factors, weather, and labor-market conditions often prevented continuous employment. Our results add strength to this testimony.

Although the 1900 census did not ask questions concerning income, it did ask something about wealth: whether the family owned or rented its home or farm. Table 3.1 (panel 10) indicates that farm owners had an advantage over farm renters in child mortality, and that non-farm homeowners were better off than non-farm renters. Farm renters had a child mortality index 21 percent higher than farm-owner families, and non-farm renters were 13 percent above homeowners. Regionally, however, these differences did not consistently prevail, as Table 3.5 shows. The advantage of farm owners over farm renters was largely confined to the South, where sharecropping was prevalent. In the North, it is possible that many of the owners were occupying smaller, less viable farms, whereas renters might have included a group of more progressive, innovating tenants and owners. The disadvantage of renting as compared to owning a *home* was essentially confined to the North Atlantic and the South Central region. All of the expected ownership relations are turned upside-down in the West. It must be concluded that this particular measure of economic well-being did not have a simple or predictable relationship to child mortality. It is, after all, only a partial measure of property ownership and does not indicate the value of the property nor its contribution to or drain on income.

Earlier, we described the relative mortality of international migrants to the U.S. But there was also considerable migration of native-born people *within* the United States during the period prior to the census of 1900 (Eldridge and Thomas 1964), much of it economically driven. As Table 3.1 (panel 13) shows, variation in child mortality is relatively small across groups of native-born women who were resident in their state of birth, those who were resident in their census region but not of their state of birth, and those who were resident in a census region different from that in which they were born. Women resident in their state of birth had a slight mortality advantage over migrants across state and census region boundaries, but the differences were small. Evidently, interstate migration of the native born was not associated with major hazards to child survival.

Household Relations

Table 3.1 (panels 12 and 14) provides tabulations of child mortality by household structure and the relationship of the woman to the household head. The overwhelming majority (93 percent) of women in this subsample of the 1900 census were wives of the head of household, and 82 percent lived in families with no unrelated individuals in the household. Households having servants, a sign of greater affluence and of the availability of child care, show child mortality that is 14 percent lower than in households with no unrelated individuals. Taking in boarders, however, was associated with a 17 percent increase in child mortality. Taking in boarders was often an indication that the family needed additional income, and the boarders themselves furnished an additional focus of infection for children. The economic situation of the boarders was probably below average. The child mortality of women who were enumerated as boarders or wives of boarders was about 24 percent higher than average, and it was about 6 percent higher than for women in families that took in boarders. Women who were residents of institutions had child mortality similar to that of boarders, while married women who were live-in servants (a relatively unusual circumstance in the United States in 1900) had substantially elevated mortality—almost 77 percent above the national average. Of course, the deaths of their children may have occurred before they secured places as live-in servants.

When the relationship of the woman to head of household is considered (Table 3.1, panel 14), it is apparent that female-headed households experienced elevated mortality. Although relatively infrequent among married women (as opposed to widowed and divorced women, who are not included in this analysis), the absence of a husband was often a sign of family difficulty. As we saw earlier, much of the difficulty could be overcome, at least for native white women, by working.

Daughters of household heads had the same child mortality as wives of the heads, and both groups were about at the national average. Those whose relation to head was daughter-in-law or niece actually fared better than average, whereas sisters and sisters-in-law of heads of household had very high child mortality. The United States at this time was predominantly a society of husband/wife households without lateral or vertical extension.[7] Judging from these results, based as they are on relatively few observations in the non-normative categories, vertical extension of the family was associated with fewer adverse consequences than lateral extension.

Time Trends in Child Mortality in the Late Nineteenth Century

The data available in the 1900 census provide an opportunity for us to examine time trends in child mortality for a period of 15 to 20 years before the census (United Nations 1983a: ch. 3). This examination can be made by comparing the child mortality experience of women whose children were born, on average, at different times (see Chapter 2). The longer a group of women have been married, the earlier the average date to which their children's mortality experience refers. Systematic changes in mortality should be identified through a comparison of the average model life table level pertaining to women of various marital-duration categories. This comparison captures, in a sense, the average mortality regime to which children of women of different ages or marital durations had been subjected.

Trends are analyzed separately for the total, white, native white, foreign-born white, and black populations, and also for women in various size-of-place categories. For each of the seven marital-duration categories of women per group (using quinquennial duration groups from 0–4 to 30–34 years), a corresponding $q(a)$ is computed, the probability of survival from birth to age (a) ($q[2]$, $q[3]$, $q[5]$, $q[10]$, $q[15]$, $q[20]$, and $q[25]$ respectively). This $q(a)$ was then converted into a particular "level" in the West model life table system and into the number of years prior to the census to which that particular mortality estimate applied, on average. (For the methodology, see Chapter 2 and United Nations 1983a: ch. 3.) Each higher "level" of mortality is associated with a gain of 2.45 years in life expectancy at birth.

The subsample of women used to make these calculations consisted of currently married with husband present, for whom children ever born and children surviving were known; the number of children ever born did not exceed the stated number of years of current marriage by more than two; the implied age at marriage (in the current marriage) was between 10 and 35; the inferred number of own-children present was not greater than the stated number of children surviving; and the stated number of children surviving did not exceed the stated number of children ever born. These stringent selection criteria were imposed in order to remove from the sample, as far as possible, women who had remarried. As discussed in Chapter 2, the 1900 census asked only a question about the number of years in the current marriage. If women had remarried and had children by previous marriages, then their children would have had a longer exposure to mortality risk than would be indicated by the duration of current marriage. Consequently, the implied trends in mortality would be biased by the conclusion of remarried women.

A summary of the estimated trends is provided in Table 3.9, where the "level" of mortality in the Model West life table corresponding to each marital-duration category was used as the dependent variable in a series of weighted least squares regressions. The independent variable was the negative of the number of years prior to 1900 to which that level applied. The weights are the number of children ever born in a category. The intercept term thus gives the predicted mortality "level" at the time of the census in June 1900, and the slope represents the average change in mortality "level" per year between approximately 1880 and 1900, i.e., the mortality trend. Positive values of the slope indicate improving mortality. For example, Table 3.9 shows that for the white population as a whole, the rate of mortality decline averaged .145 levels per year, which would have amounted to an improvement of about 7.1 years in expectation of life at birth over the two decades prior to 1900.

Results for the black population show a slight deterioration in mortality conditions. A variety of data problems suggests that one should be very cautious in interpreting this result. Frequency of marital disruption was high in the black population, as discussed in Chapter 2, so that marital duration is not as effective an indicator of children's exposure to mortality as it is in the white population. That the deterioration is only evident in urban areas, where marital disruption is likely to be greatest, underscores this concern. Furthermore, as a higher mortality population, a higher proportion of mothers of black children would have died before the census of 1900. Since black women who died would be expected to have had higher child mortality (see Chapters 1 and 2) and disproportionately higher marital-duration, our estimated improvements in mortality may be biased downwards. The questionable suitability of the West Model life tables for blacks (see Chapter 2) adds to the uncertainty. On the other hand, black economic conditions may have worsened during 1880–1900, in part because of problems afflicting the cotton industry (Wright 1986: 56, 115). A cautious conclusion seems in order: our

TABLE 3.9
Regression Measuring the Pace of Mortality Decline by Race, Nativity, and Place of Residence: United States, ca. 1880–1900

	All marital durations (N = 7)				
	Intercept	Slope	Significance[a]	Adj. R-square	F-ratio
Total population					
Total	14.18	0.1057	***	0.868	40.43
Urban	13.59	0.1698	***	0.895	51.95
Top 10 cities	13.83	0.2923	**	0.660	12.67
Other cities 25,000+	12.47	0.1324	—	0.251	3.01
Cities 5,000–24,999	13.09	0.1058	—	0.214	2.63
Cities 1,000–4,999	15.55	0.1473	—	0.303	3.61
Rural	14.79	0.0784	***	0.739	17.97
White population					
Total	14.94	0.1449	***	0.882	46.02
Urban	14.15	0.2099	***	0.964	160.28
Top 10 cities	13.77	0.2907	**	0.666	12.96
Other cities 25,000+	13.18	0.1830	*	0.389	4.81
Cities 5,000–24,999	14.41	0.2048	***	0.752	19.17
Cities 1,000–4,999	16.10	0.1683	**	0.643	11.82
Rural	15.81	0.1173	***	0.748	18.83
Native white population					
Total	15.18	0.1086	***	0.729	17.13
Urban	14.30	0.1268	**	0.655	12.39
Top 10 cities	13.52	0.1878	*	0.423	5.40
Other cities 25,000+	12.93	0.0659	—	0.000	0.94
Cities 5,000–24,999	14.76	0.1062	—	0.077	1.50
Cities 1,000–4,999	16.47	0.1896	**	0.662	12.74
Rural	15.91	0.1184	***	0.733	17.48
Foreign white population					
Total	13.94	0.1947	**	0.607	10.27
Urban	13.71	0.2585	***	0.815	27.44
Top 10 cities	13.83	0.3552	**	0.605	10.19
Other cities 25,000+	13.06	0.2267	—	0.240	2.89
Cities 5,000–24,999	13.48	0.3489	**	0.634	11.42
Cities 1,000–4,999	15.13	0.1096	—	0.000	1.00
Rural	15.23	0.0870	—	0.023	1.14
Black population					
Total	9.55	−0.0736	—	0.000	0.44
Urban	5.39	−0.2596	*	0.392	4.87
Rural	10.71	0.0000	—	0.000	0.00

TABLE 3.9 (*cont.*)

Source: Sample of census enumerators' manuscripts, U.S., 1900.

Note: Regressions were of the form: Level = a + b*Years, where Level = the level of the Model West life table implied by a particular $q(x)$ (where x = 2, 3, 5, 10, 15, 20, 25) and Years = the negative of the number of years prior to the census (June 1, 1900) associated with each $q(x)$. The intercept, a, is the extrapolated mortality level at the time of the census. The slope, b, is the average change in level per year between approximately 1880 and 1900. The estimation technique was weighted least squares, with the weights being the number of children ever born for each category.

[a] *** = significant at least at a 1 percent level; ** = signigicant at least at a 5 percent level; * = significant at least at a 10 percent level; — = not significant at least at a 10 percent level (two-tailed test).

data provide no evidence of an improvement in black child mortality during the last two decades of the nineteenth century.

Results for all other groups suggest that child mortality was declining. The decline occurred more than twice as rapidly in urban as in rural areas for the total population; the native white population, however, experienced comparable rates of decline in rural and urban places. Watterson (1988), using a similar approach to data from England and Wales in 1911, also finds a much faster pace of decline in urban than in rural areas. The American decline was much more rapid in the 10 largest cities than in other cities, supporting the notion that those cities were benefitting disproportionately from public-health advances in the late nineteenth century. The decline of .29 levels per year suggests that life expectancy at birth increased by some 14 years in the 10 largest cities during the two decades preceding 1900, a remarkably rapid improvement. The pattern of improvement was stronger among the foreign-born white population, as might have been inferred from Table 3.2. Some of the rapid decline for the foreign-born mothers may reflect their experience with child mortality in the countries of origin, most of which had higher mortality than the U.S. (Ireland and Scandinavia being notable exceptions). But rapid mortality decline was also characteristic of the native white population in the largest cities.

In addition, however, it is clear that rural areas and the smallest urban areas (1,000–4,999 inhabitants) had also been experiencing child mortality improvements, notably among the native white population, who constituted the dominant portion of residents in these areas. Public-health and medical advances are less likely to be responsible for mortality declines in these types of places. Mortality improvements there are more plausibly ascribed to improvements in living standards. According to Higgs (1973:187) and others that he cites, the public-health movement in the late nineteenth and early twentieth centuries almost completely bypassed the countryside (see also Chapter 1). Higgs ascribes rural mortality gains to gains in per capita food availability resulting from higher agricultural production and better transportation, as well as to improved rural housing. The evidence for these improvements is patchy, however. Bennett and Pierce's (1961) reconstructions of the average American diet show little or no change between 1880 and 1900. But it is likely that better transportation increased the variety of foods available to the typical consumer.

In sum, Table 3.9 provides evidence of decline in child mortality in both rural and urban areas and for both the native and the foreign-born white populations in the United States during the last two decades of the nineteenth century. Declines appear to have been fastest in the 10 largest cities, especially for the foreign born, but progress was being made across the board. The rapid improvements occurred in the face of a severe economic downturn between 1893 and 1897, during which unemployment averaged 14.2 percent (U.S. Bureau of the Census 1975: Series D 85-86).

The improvement in child mortality that we have depicted is roughly congruent with the scattered evidence on trends in the final heights achieved by white American males. Fogel (1986, 1988) presents a graph of final heights achieved by five-year birth cohorts and notes that the modern rise of heights probably began with children born in the 1890s (Fogel 1988:35). Final height is largely determined by growth patterns below age 3 (Fogel 1988:42). The decade of the 1880s marked the low point in heights, according to this evidence, for the entire period from 1710 to 1930. This observation raises the possibility that the mortality decline that we describe was not part of a long-term secular decline, as it was in most European countries during this era, but was a reversal of mortality increases that occurred earlier in the nineteenth century. On the other hand, Steckel (1988) finds substantially higher levels of child mortality in the 1850s than we find for the 1890s, implying that the United States was similar to England, Sweden, and other European countries in its child mortality trends.

The more rapid reductions in child mortality in the largest cities are consistent with the leadership of those cities in public-health programs and also with the notion that the direct relationship of mortality and city size, which seems to have characterized the mid-nineteenth century, was breaking down by the turn of the century. Evidently, the United States was no exception to A. F. Weber's generalization at the turn of the century, based mainly upon European experience:

> There is no inherent reason for the relatively high urban mortality except man's neglect and indifference. Recent tendencies show that the great cities are leading the way in making sanitary improvements and, in several countries, . . . the large cities now make a more favorable showing as to mortality than do other communities. This holds true even of infant mortality, which is one of the most decisive indices of a locality's healthfulness. (Weber 1899:367)

Inferences about trends in mortality according to these and other characteristics can also be drawn by comparing our results to those of Daniel Scott Smith (1978, 1983). Smith also constructed a sample from the 1900 census, but he limited it to older women, principally those aged 55 or above. His sample consists of 5,000 noninstitutionalized older persons. Because the women in his study are much older than those in ours, their child mortality experience typically refers to the 1860s and 1870s, rather than to the two more recent decades studied here.

Most of the differentials revealed in Smith's analysis were comparable in direction and magnitude to those described here. Black/white differences and native/foreign-born differences were quite similar. German-born mothers, however, appear to have done better in the earlier period. Literacy differentials were also analogous. The Midwest was a low mortality area, as in later years, but the South fared worse than in our larger and "later" sample, perhaps because of the imprint of the Civil War and Reconstruction on Smith's results. Rural/urban differences showed some tendency to widen, although this apparent result may be attributable to more migration between rural and urban areas, and hence to a blurring of the distinctions between them, among Smith's older women. The largest cities did not enjoy any advantage over the next smaller size class in Smith's sample (1983: Table 1), lending support to the suggestion of faster decline in mortality for these cities towards the end of the century.

Occupational mortality differentials in Smith's sample are much as we have described, except that clerical, sales, and service workers did not enjoy the relative advantages they had achieved later in the century, whereas skilled manual workers and operatives were in somewhat better shape. Again, occupational mobility is a more serious problem in interpreting mortality differentials in Smith's sample. Interestingly, professional occupations did not fare particularly well either in Smith's sample or in ours.

A second study to which our results can be compared matched 1,600 male-headed households in the 1850 and 1860 censuses (Steckel 1988). Mortality was inferred by the absence from the household in 1860 of a child who was present at ages 0–4 in 1850. As in our results, Steckel finds mortality to be lowest among children of farmers and to be surprisingly similar among offspring of white-collar and blue-collar workers. Urban places larger than 25,000 had significantly higher child mortality than rural places, although smaller urban places were not significantly disadvantaged. The Midwest had lower child mortality than the Northeast, as in our results, and the South's relative position was unclear. The value of real estate owned by the household was insignificantly associated with child mortality. Mother's literacy also had weak effects on child mortality. Although we report substantial effects of literacy in this chapter, it should be noted that Steckel's results are products of a multivariate analysis, and when we introduce our own multivariate analysis in the next chapter, mother's literacy loses much of its explanatory power.

In general, Steckel's (and Smith's) results are similar to our own when comparable variables can be investigated. They suggest that the mosaic of child mortality variations that we describe was largely established by the middle of the nineteenth century.

Summary

Based on one-way tabulations of the mortality index (Table 3.1), childhood mortality at the turn of the century was higher among blacks than among whites, in urban than in rural areas, and in the larger cities than in smaller ones. An exception is the category of the 10 largest cities, which appeared to have achieved lower mortality than somewhat smaller cities by making exceptionally rapid progress in the two decades before 1900, especially among the foreign born. Regionally, the highest mortality was found in the Northeast (especially in New England) and in the western part of the South. The Midwest had very favorable childhood mortality experience in 1900. Contrary to many contemporary guesses and to our own expectations, the South as a whole had below-average mortality for both whites and blacks (below, that is, the respective racial averages for the nation as a whole). The South's advantage was entirely attributable to its rurality.

Literate mothers had better child survival than illiterate ones. Their husbands's literacy also reduced child mortality, but their own literacy was more important. Being illiterate was a special disadvantage for native white wives, perhaps because of associated circumstances that the condition connoted. Similar results apply to the ability to speak English, with higher child mortality apparent among non-English speakers, especially fathers.

Child mortality varied in predictable ways according to the economic status of the family. Working wives had poorer child survival, as did husbands who had experienced some unemployment in the year prior to the census. The apparent problems faced by working wives were concentrated among blacks and the foreign born. Among women with absent husbands, those who worked had lower child mortality than those who didn't, and mortality was exceptionally low for native white women in this category. Wives whose husbands were farmers or in professional, technical, managerial, clerical, and other white-collar activities did relatively well, while wives of farm laborers, non-farm laborers, and craftsmen did poorly. White-collar/ blue-collar differences were surprisingly small, however. The lower mortality of farmers' children extended across regions and was due, in part, to their rural residence. The higher mortality of the children of agricultural laborers was partially traceable to the large numbers of blacks in this occupation in the South. Laborers tended to have high child mortality, regardless of ethnic composition, region, or rural/urban residence. Owners of homes and farms had lower mortality among their children than did renters, as did families with servants. Families with boarders, however, had elevated mortality.

Native-born white husbands and wives had lower child mortality than the foreign born, with native birth apparently being more important for wives. Generally, children of native white women with native white mothers had unusually favorable survivorship, while Irish- and German-born women did poorly. Women of Scandinavian origin (first and second generation) had relatively good child survival experience, as they did in Scandinavia itself. Foreign-born whites had higher child mortality than native whites across regions and size-of-place categories. The differences between native whites of native parentage and native whites of foreign parentage were unclear and varied from place to place, suggesting that, with regard to child mortality, the assimilation process essentially took only one generation to complete. The unfavorable child mortality experience of Irish mothers originated in urban areas of the Northeast, where they were predominantly located. The high child mortality of German mothers was especially attributable to those resident in urban areas.

We have considered it important to present these differentials in child mortality in some detail because there is no other comparable record of child mortality at the time. Discussion of mortality differences according to variables taken one or two at a time, however, inevitably raises as many questions as it answers, questions about whether the observed differences are products of other factors whose influences are not controlled. It is to these questions that we now turn.

FOUR

DISTINGUISHING THE RELATIVE
IMPORTANCE OF VARIOUS SOCIAL, ECONOMIC,
AND RESIDENTIAL FACTORS

I N CHAPTER 3, we presented information about the extent of child mortality variation among major social groupings of the American population at the turn of the century. Occasionally, we examined variation according to factors taken two or three at a time, but cell sizes often quickly became too small to produce reliable results. There was, consequently, little opportunity to consider which of the many factors reviewed are most closely associated with child mortality and which appear essentially irrelevant once other factors are taken into account. This chapter addresses these questions through multivariate analysis.

Death is a biological event, and all social influences must ultimately operate through specific biological mechanisms. Those mechanisms are not visible in the census sample, and their operations must be inferred or assumed. We are, however, able to describe relations among the socioeconomic variables contained in the data set and to see which relations appear most important and which seem to be largely by-products of differential endowments of groups with other, more important, determinants of mortality.

Analytic Strategy

The principal analytic model used in this chapter is weighted least squares multiple regression. The dependent variable in the model is the mortality index (i.e., the ratio of actual to expected child deaths) calculated for an individual woman. Each observation, however, is weighted by number of children ever born to a woman, so that women with more children in a sense contribute more observations, just as they do in the population's overall level of child mortality. Weighting by number of children ever born also reduces the problem of heteroskedasticity, the tendency for larger variance to be associated with units containing fewer observations, a tendency that violates the assumptions of ordinary least squares regression. Other research indicates that this procedure produces results that are statistically "well-behaved" and that the truncation problem at zero does not require a Tobit transformation (Trussell and Preston 1982). The independent variables are, with few exceptions, represented as sets of categories rather than as continuously valued. This representation allows us the opportunity to observe a nonlinear relation between the variable and the level of child mortality.

Initially, we pursue a sequential strategy for identifying the influence of variables on child mortality. The rationale for the sequential estimation strategy is that the values of certain variables are determined before the values of other variables, and exert an influence on those variables. If we were simply to estimate one equation that included all variables, we would have no information on these causal pathways. For example, the effect of being black on occupation, and through occupation on mortality, would not be represented; we would know only the remaining effect of being black after many of the paths through which race can affect mortality were statistically controlled. The sequential approach allows a fuller appreciation of the manifold influences on mortality, and of the relations among them.

The first equation that we estimate includes only independent variables that are inherent to a woman and cannot be affected by her behavior—her race, nativity, and age. These are background variables determined at the woman's birth. The sign of the age variable is expected to be positive. Older mothers experienced (on average) a higher child mortality level since, as shown in Chapters 2 and 3, child mortality was declining in the United States in the last two decades of the nineteenth century. Thus, mother's age acts as a partial control for the time trend in mortality.

The second equation adds variables representing a woman's literacy (in any language) and her ability to speak English. These characteristics are typically acquired in childhood or adolescence, before marriage and the birth of the woman's children. They reflect primarily conditions in the family in which she was raised. The third equation then adds similar basic characteristics of the husband that are "acquired" by the woman at marriage—his literacy and ability to speak English.[1] The expected signs of these variables were discussed in Chapter 3. We estimated a version of the third equation that included the husband's nativity, but this variable was too highly collinear with wife's nativity to allow robust estimates of the joint effects of wife's and husband's nativity.

The final equation then adds all remaining characteristics that were not permanent to either husband or wife: region of current residence, size of place of residence, property ownership, wife's labor-force activity, migration status, husband's employment, husband's age and occupation (or occupational income), and presence of servants or boarders in the household. The expected signs of most of these variables have already been discussed. Husband's age is treated differently than mother's age because it is believed to serve in part as a proxy for his income, rather than for trends in child mortality.

Some of the variables described in Chapter 3 are modified or augmented to take advantage of the greater statistical power afforded by multivariate analysis. Instead of the five census regions used in most of the tabular presentations, the regression analysis uses the nine census subregions. The property-ownership variable, whether a farm or home was owned or rented, has been supplemented with information about whether the farm or home was owned free and clear or mortgaged. Outright ownership may imply higher personal net worth, which should be reflected in lower child mortality. Wife's labor-force status was altered to add information on the availability of child care in the household: in particular, whether a servant or adult female relative (aged 16 or over) was present in the household. It is expected that availability of child care will reduce child mortality, especially for working women. The combination of information on whether a woman is working and whether she has child care available in the home produces a variable with four categories.

Two new migration-status variables have been constructed, representing the proportion of a woman's life that was lived in the United States before age 14 and the proportion lived in the U.S. after age 14. These variables are constructed from information on a woman's year of immigration to the U.S. It is expected that longer residence in the U.S. would increase social integration and reduce child mortality, since most of the immigrants came from higher mortality areas in Europe. The integration process is expected to be fastest for those arriving before age 14, so a larger coefficient is expected on this variable.

As mentioned above, the 1900 census contained no information on income, a very unfortunate omission that was not corrected until the 1940 census. We have gone to considerable lengths to fill in this gap. In particular, we have constructed two variables based upon the husband's occupation. One is the mean income of the husband's (detailed) occupation, and the other is the mean number of months unemployed during the period June 1, 1899 to May 31, 1900, for men in that occupation. Construction of these variables is described in Appendix A. We did not attempt any income assignment for farmers, since farmers' incomes depended upon weather, location, soil, farm size, and capital available, so that any income that we could assign to farmers would contain enormous measurement error.

We have also constructed an index of state income, or, more precisely, earnings levels. Construction of this variable is described in Appendix B. It is designed to be an index that is independent of the occupational composition of a state, since we already have information on the husband's occupation. We use this index in both price-adjusted and price-unadjusted form. Logarithmic transformations of income variables are used because we expect that income will show diminishing returns in its impact on child mortality, as it does in international comparisons at the turn of the century and later (Preston 1975). We experimented with polynomials to represent income, but results were not appreciably different from those where logarithms were used. Husband's age and husband's age squared were included to account for the observed curvilinear (parabolic) shape of male age/earnings profiles in this period (Appendix A).

The basic data set used in this chapter is smaller than that used in most of Chapter 3. Because we are interested in the impact of many of the husband's characteristics on child mortality, we have eliminated observations in which the husband was absent from the household. We have also deleted cases for which information was missing on key variables. Finally, we introduce the restrictions used in the analysis of trends in Chapter 3 to ensure that marital duration reflects as accurately as possible children's exposure to the risk of death. The final data set includes 10,369 currently married women with husbands present, compared to the set of 13,429 women used in most of Chapter 3.

Within a set of categories such as occupation, the selection of a particular category to be the "reference category," against which the child mortality impact of other categories is measured, is fundamentally arbitrary. It does not affect either the amount of variance explained by the set or the quantitative differences between coefficients within the set. Largely for expositional purposes, we have chosen large groups, often with extreme values of child mortality, to be the reference categories.

Results for All Groups Combined

The basic results of this chapter are presented in Table 4.1. The equations in Table 4.1 are all jointly significant at a 1 percent level, as indicated by the F-ratios. The adjusted R^2 values are not large, the highest being .051 in equation (4) in Table 4.1. It is not unusual to find this level of explanatory power in models fit to individual-level data, however, since much individual variation is idiosyncratic and unaccounted for by quantifiable variables. Grouped data yield much higher adjusted R^2 values using some of the same explanatory variables (see Chapter 5), since "random" variation tends to average out in a large group.

Race

Higher child mortality for black women is retained in multivariate analysis, as shown by the large positive and statistically significant coefficients that appear in Table 4.1. Some of the effect of being black operates through other socioeconomic variables, since the coefficient for black women is reduced when successive waves of independent variables are introduced. In equation (1) of Table 4.1, where only nativity and a woman's age are controlled, black women have 51 percent higher child mortality than white women (i.e., the coefficient for black women is .506, and highly significant). Introducing literacy and English-speaking ability of the woman in equation (2) reduces the effect of race alone by 15 percent, to .433. Additional controls for literacy, English ability, and nativity of husband in equation (3) have only a small effect, reducing the coefficient by only 6 percent. Finally, when variables representing region, size of place, property ownership, mother's labor force status, migration status, husband's unemployment and occupation, and presence of boarders and servants are introduced in equation (4), the race coefficient declines to .297. Thus, about 41 percent of the effect of race on child mortality can be accounted for by its impact on other measured variables that are also associated with mortality.

In theory, controlling for all relevant socioeconomic and demographic factors should eliminate entirely the effect of race, since there is no reason to believe that genetic differences were responsible for significantly greater biological frailty among black children, despite views of the time. But, in the present case, the selection of variables was limited and thorough controls for such factors as quality of housing, environment, water supply, sewerage disposal, clothing quality, and nutrition and food purity were not available. Moreover, many of the variables that we are including undoubtedly had a different meaning for blacks and whites. Blacks in cities were residentially segregated and fell outside the reach of most ameliorative social programs (Katz 1986). Southern rural blacks lacked the property re-

TABLE 4.1

Equations Predicting the Ratio of Actual to Expected Child Deaths for Individual Women: U.S., 1900

Independent variables	(1)		(2)		(3)		(4)	
	Coefficient	Significance	Coefficient	Significance	Coefficient	Significance	Coefficient	Significance
Intercept	0.5840	***	0.5899	***	0.5880	***	0.6280	***
Race of wife								
White	NI	NI	NI	NI	NI	NI	NI	NI
Black	0.5060	***	0.4327	***	0.4077	***	0.2968	***
Nativity of wife								
Native with native mother	NI	NI	NI	NI	NI	NI	NI	NI
Native with British mother	-0.0229	—	-0.0136	—	-0.0081	—	-0.0345	—
Native with Irish mother	0.1737	***	0.1853	***	0.1899	***	0.0562	—
Native with Scandinavian mother	-0.1981	—	-0.1869	—	-0.1809	—	0.0664	—
Native with German mother	0.0030	—	0.0142	—	0.0194	—	-0.0490	—
Native with other West European mother	-0.4059	***	-0.3888	**	-0.3903	**	-0.3055	*
Native with East European mother	-0.1855	—	-0.2020	—	-0.2034	—	-0.1479	—
Native with South European mother	-0.4914	—	-0.4782	—	-0.4723	—	-0.4353	—
British	0.2080	**	0.2120	**	0.2168	**	0.0592	—
Irish	0.3648	***	0.3678	***	0.3694	***	0.1169	—
Scandinavian	0.0810	—	0.0742	—	0.0876	—	0.1290	—
German	0.2236	***	0.2114	***	0.2162	***	0.0923	—
Other West European	-0.0838	—	-0.1059	—	-0.1264	—	-0.2089	—
East European	0.1869	***	0.0950	—	0.0860	—	-0.0779	—
South European	0.3120	***	0.1702	—	0.1482	—	-0.0816	—
Other foreign-born	0.2297	***	0.1980	***	0.1910	***	0.0443	—
Age of wife	0.0069	***	0.0063	***	0.0062	***	0.0094	***

	(1)		(2)		(3)	
Literacy of wife						
Literate	NI 0.1520	***	NI 0.1065	**	NI 0.1004	**
Illiterate						
Wife speaks English						
Yes	NI 0.1236	*	NI 0.0282	—	NI 0.0029	—
No						
Literacy of husband						
Yes			NI 0.1190	***	NI 0.1234	***
No						
Husband speaks English						
Yes			NI 0.2090	**	NI 0.1506	—
No						
Region						
New England					NI	
Middle Atlantic					−0.0557	—
East North Central					−0.0928	**
West North Central					−0.1302	***
South Atlantic					−0.2235	*
East South Central					−0.1641	—
West South Central					−0.0074	***
Mountain					0.4308	—
Pacific					−0.0615	—
Residence						
Top 10 cities					0.2954	***
Other cities 25,000 +					0.3160	***
Cities 5,000–24,999					0.2040	***
Cities 1,000–4,999					NI	NI
Rural					0.0682	—

TABLE 4.1 (cont.)

Independent variables	(1) Coefficient	Significance	(2) Coefficient	Significance	(3) Coefficient	Significance	(4) Coefficient	Significance
Property								
Owns farm clear							−0.1577	**
Owns farm mortgaged							−0.1005	—
Rents farm							−0.0634	—
Owns home clear							−0.0417	—
Owns home mortgaged							−0.1064	**
Rents home							NI	NI
Wife working								
Working—has child care							0.2139	—
Working—no child care							0.0357	—
Not working—has child care							0.0139	—
Not working—no child care							NI	NI
Migration status								
Proportion of life lived in the U.S. before age 14							−0.0266	—
Proportion of life lived in the U.S. after age 14							0.0186	—
Other dichotomous variables								
Husband unemployed							0.1586	***
Servant(s) in household							−0.0211	—
Boarder(s) in household							0.1510	***
Income								
Husband's age							−0.0006	—
Husband's age squared							−0.0000	—
Log of state income index							−0.4854	***

Husband's occupation	(1)	(2)	(3)	(4)	
Professional, Technical				−0.0652	—
Agricultural (excluding Laborers)				−0.1454	**
Agricultural Laborers				−0.0465	—
Managers, Official, Proprietors				−0.1098	*
Clerical				−0.1650	*
Sales				−0.2093	**
Craftsmen, Foremen				−0.0217	—
Operatives				−0.0904	*
Service Workers				−0.1189	—
Laborers				NI	NI
Miscellaneous				−0.1424	—
N	9,917	9,917	9,917	9,917	
Adjusted R-squared	0.0238	0.0257	0.0267	0.0505	
F-ratio	13.727 ***	12.387 ***	11.071 ***	8.875 ***	

Source: Sample of census enumerators's manuscripts, U.S. 1900.

Note: Sample consists of currently married women with husband present, married less than 25 years. The dependent variable is the ratio of actual to expected child deaths for each woman. For an explanation of its construction, and of the other variables, see text. Regressions are weighted least squares with the weights being the number of children ever born (normalized back to the original number of observations). Significance levels are: *** = significant at least at a 1 percent level; ** = significant at least at a 5 percent level; * = significant at least at a 10 percent level; — = not significant at least at a 10 percent level. NI = not included.

sources of southern rural whites, and any literacy they attained came through poorer public schools. Even though they may have overlapped with whites in the occupational distribution, blacks were typically paid less within a particular occupation (Wright 1986; Ransom and Sutch 1977). That husband's income may be a key omitted variable is suggested by Woodbury's (1925) results for eight cities during 1911–15. When income differences were controlled by standardization, the black disadvantage in infant mortality was only 9 percent (Woodbury 1925:122).

Nativity of Wife

The higher mortality of foreign-born women largely disappears in multivariate analysis. Signs of the coefficients among this group of dummy variables denote mortality levels relative to that in the reference category, native-born women with native-born mothers. In equation (1) of Table 4.1, seven of the eight categories of foreign-born women had child mortality that was higher than that of native whites of native parentage, and most differences were statistically significant. In addition, native-born women with Irish mothers also had significantly higher child mortality than native-born women of native parentage. For second-generation mothers in general, however, mortality was not significantly different from that of native born women of native parentage, and in fact it was typically somewhat lower.

As additional independent variables are added in equations (2)–(4), the importance of nativity diminishes, indicating that the effect of nativity, unlike that of race, largely operated through other measured variables. In equation (1) of Table 4.1, eight out of fifteen nativity variables are significant at least at a 5 percent level; but none of the fifteen remains significant in equation (4). Many of the coefficients also are reduced in magnitude, especially when they were large in equation (1) (e.g., women born in Ireland, Germany, or Britain). Almost none of the decline in coefficients occurs until equation (4), implying that the child mortality disadvantage of foreign-born women was not a result of literacy or English-speaking disabilities among them or their husbands, but rather of more immediate economic and residential characteristics.

The second-generation immigrants did not suffer from abnormally high mortality even before controls for current economic circumstances are instituted. When such controls are introduced, the second-generation mothers typically have child mortality levels below those of native white women of native parentage (i.e., their coefficients are generally negative in equation [4], although none of the differences is significant). In other words, whatever ethnic differences in child-care practices and breastfeeding were present among first- and second-generation mothers, they were not important enough to have left a vivid mark on child mortality levels by ethnicity, once other measured factors are controlled. In particular, breastfeeding differences that were noted at the time and that we described in Chapters 1 and 3 do not appear to have left a deep imprint on child mortality. Foreign-born mothers did have higher child mortality, but the principal causes are to be found in their economic and social circumstances rather than in unmeasured variables that ethnicity may reflect.

Probably the most important of these economic and social variables in accounting for the 12 percent higher child mortality of foreign-born mothers shown in Table 3.1 is urban residence. The distribution of the married women used to calculate the child mortality index is presented in Table 4.2. Foreign-born white women were overwhelmingly (71.8 percent) concentrated in urban areas, and, of those living in cities, 72 percent were living in the unhealthiest cities of 25,000 or more inhabitants. Indeed, 42 percent were resident in the 10 largest urban centers. In contrast, among native white women with native mothers, 64.8 percent were living in rural areas, and of those who did reside in cities, over half (58.2 percent) were living in the smaller, healthier urban areas below 25,000 in population. Child mortality of native white women of foreign parentage was intermediate between the native women of native parentage and foreign-born white women, but their residence pattern was much more similar to that of the foreign born. About two-thirds (62.2 percent) were in urban areas, and, of those, 64 percent lived in the cities of over 25,000 inhabitants. Thus, the residence patterns of first- and second-generation immigrant families placed them in a disadvantageous position vis-à-vis child survival. But once residential and socioeconomic variables are controlled, their disadvantage is essentially eliminated.

Age of Wife

The age of the wife was introduced to control for the downward trend in mortality. Older mothers bore children at earlier dates, on average, and their children would have been exposed to higher mortality conditions. The uniformly positive and significant coefficients on this variable in Tables 4.1 are consistent with the existence of such a time trend and justify the inclusion of this variable as a correction for the trend. The value of this variable of .01 in equation (4) suggests that child mortality levels were raised by about 1 percent for each

TABLE 4.2

Women and Children Ever Born in the Sample Used to Calculate the Child Mortality Index, by Race, Nativity, and Residence

	Urban	Top 10 cities	Other cities 25,000+	Cities 5,000– 24,999	Cities 1,000– 4,999	Rural	Unknown	Total
Women								
Total (*N*)	4,670	1,322	1,317	1,039	992	5,614	85	10,369
White	4,439	1,297	1,240	979	923	4,809	69	9,317
Native white	2,950	668	794	727	761	4,238	56	7,244
Native mother	1,924	292	513	519	600	3,623	47	5,594
Foreign mother	1,026	376	281	208	161	615	9	1,650
Foreign white	1,489	629	446	252	162	571	13	2,073
Black	224	21	75	60	68	770	15	1,009
Percentage of total								
Total	45.0	12.7	12.7	10.0	9.6	54.1	0.8	100.0
White	47.6	13.9	13.3	10.5	9.9	51.6	0.7	100.0
Native white	40.7	9.2	11.0	10.0	10.5	58.5	0.8	100.0
Native mother	34.4	5.2	9.2	9.3	10.7	64.8	0.8	100.0
Foreign mother	62.2	22.8	17.0	12.6	9.8	37.3	0.5	100.0
Foreign white	71.8	30.3	21.5	12.2	7.8	27.5	0.6	100.0
Black	22.2	2.1	7.4	5.9	6.7	76.3	1.5	100.0
Percentage of urban population								
Total	100.0	28.3	28.2	22.2	21.2	—	—	—
White	100.0	29.2	27.9	22.1	20.8	—	—	—
Native white	100.0	22.6	26.9	24.6	25.8	—	—	—
Native mother	100.0	15.2	26.7	27.0	31.2	—	—	—
Foreign mother	100.0	36.6	27.4	20.3	15.7	—	—	—
Foreign white	100.0	42.2	30.0	16.9	10.9	—	—	—
Black	100.0	9.4	33.5	26.8	30.4	—	—	—
Children ever born								
Total (*N*)	15,872	4,630	4,423	3,419	3,400	21,789	314	37,975
White	15,023	4,562	4,175	3,160	3,126	18,199	251	33,473
Native white	8,992	2,066	2,392	2,078	2,456	15,608	192	24,792
Native mother	5,543	809	1,427	1,392	1,915	13,325	161	19,029
Foreign mother	3,449	1,257	965	686	541	2,283	31	5,763
Foreign white	6,031	2,496	1,783	1,082	670	2,591	59	8,681
Black	831	60	243	259	269	3,452	62	4,345
Percentage of total								
Total	41.8	12.2	11.6	9.0	9.0	57.4	0.8	100.0
White	44.9	13.6	12.5	9.4	9.3	54.4	0.7	100.0
Native white	36.3	8.3	9.6	8.4	9.9	63.0	0.8	100.0
Native mother	29.1	4.3	7.5	7.3	10.1	70.0	0.8	100.0
Foreign mother	59.8	21.8	16.7	11.9	9.4	39.6	0.5	100.0
Foreign white	69.5	28.8	20.5	12.5	7.7	29.8	0.7	100.0
Black	19.1	1.4	5.6	6.0	6.2	79.4	1.4	100.0
Percentage of urban population								
Total	100.0	29.2	27.9	21.5	21.4	—	—	—
White	100.0	30.4	27.8	21.0	20.8	—	—	—

TABLE 4.2 (*cont.*)

	Urban	Top 10 cities	Other cities 25,000+	Cities 5,000– 24,999	Cities 1,000– 4,999	Rural	Unknown	Total
Native white	100.0	23.0	26.6	23.1	27.3	—	—	—
Native mother	100.0	14.6	25.7	25.1	34.5	—	—	—
Foreign mother	100.0	36.4	28.0	19.9	15.7	—	—	—
Foreign white	100.0	41.4	29.6	17.9	11.1	—	—	—
Black	100.0	7.2	29.2	31.2	32.4	—	—	—

Source: Sample of census enumerators' manuscripts, U.S., 1900. Numbers are slightly larger than those in Table 4.1, which deletes some cases with unknown values.

additional year of mother's age, once other attributes are controlled. It is likely that the age control has reduced the impact of being foreign-born, since foreign-born women were, in general, older than natives in the sample. Indeed, the nativity differences in equation (1) of Table 4.1, where only age is controlled, are generally lower than those of Chapter 3 (though many remain significant until other variables are introduced).

Literacy and English Ability of the Wife

Literacy and ability to speak English were shown to be associated with lower child mortality in Chapter 3. Multivariate analysis casts a good deal of light on the paths by which these variables operate. When it is first introduced into the regression equation at stage 2, a woman's English ability has a relatively strong effect on child mortality, with non-English speakers having about 12 percent higher mortality. Virtually all of this effect seems to operate through the type of husband a woman marries. When husband's literacy and English-speaking ability are introduced at stage 3, the woman's own English-speaking ability loses most of its ability to differentiate child mortality levels in Table 4.1. That is, a wife unable to speak English was more likely to have an illiterate and/or non-English speaking husband. Patterns of assortative mating appear to account for the initial impact of a woman's English ability on child mortality, and no significant "direct" effect remains after the characteristics of her husband that were evident at marriage are controlled.

The mother's literacy, on the other hand, does not show such a drastic change in the size of the coefficient, and its coefficient remains statistically significant, declining by about one-third as other variables are introduced. Although literacy is an imperfect measure of education, it remains a significant predictor of child mortality. The remaining differential of 10 percent between literate and illiterate mothers is not large, however, and, as we argued in Chapter 3, some of it is likely attributable to selectivity factors; illiterate women in 1900 were probably a group that had, on average, a high incidence of other debilities. Given the relatively primitive state of health knowledge and technology in the United States in 1900, it is perhaps not surprising that the payoff to literacy was relatively low. We show in Chapter 5 that the effect of literacy is considerably greater in the recent experience of developing countries.

Literacy and English Ability of the Husband

Equations (3) and (4) of Table 4.1 add the husband's literacy and capacity to speak English to the regression model. The signs of the coefficients of these variables are positive (that is, illiteracy and inability to speak English raise child mortality). The coefficient of husband's literacy remains significant and changes little in size when other socioeconomic variables are added in the fourth equation. A husband's literacy is more important than that of his wife, a finding that we subsequently show to be primarily traceable to urban areas.

The ability of the husband to speak English is not significantly related to child mortality, although the coefficient is sizable in Table 4.1. The English ability coefficient for the husband diminished considerably between equations (3) and (4), indicating that the effect of this variable largely expressed itself through the husband's present socioeconomic and residential status.

The final equation (4) of Table 4.1 introduces the last set of socioeconomic variables, those representing the current socioeconomic and residential situation of husbands and wives.

Size of Place and Region of Residence

The very large mortality differences by size of place that appeared in Chapter 3 are retained in multivariate analysis. We have chosen the reference category to be places of 1,000–4,999 inhabitants. These places were insignificantly different from rural areas in their effects on child mortality, once other variables were controlled. Relative to these very small cities, however, cities of 5,000–24,999 had mortality levels that were elevated by 20 percent, and larger cities had about 30 percent higher mortality. As in Chapter 3, there is a slight tendency for the 10 largest cities to have lower mortality than the next largest category. Unlike many of the variables studied in this chapter, each of the categories of this variable contained a substantial proportion of the population (see Table 4.2), so that size of place had both a large and a pervasive influence on mortality levels at the turn of the century. In our view, this influence reflects primarily the greater efficiency with which infectious diseases are spread in denser areas. This efficiency operates both through direct person-to-person contact and through contamination of common resources such as the water and food supply. The twentieth century witnessed major assaults on both of these modes of transmission, but the battle was just beginning, and the principal weapons for it being prepared, in the 1890s.

Regional differences in mortality are products of many factors: differences in population composition with respect to individual characteristics such as race and literacy; differences in the macroeconomic environment that affect levels of wages and income; ecological differences in climate and geography that affect the prevalence of infectious disease; and differences in the availability of health care and preventative public-health measures. As we have argued in Chapter 1, this latter factor is probably not particularly salient in the 1890s except in a few localities, because the state of medicine and public health was simply too primitive to have sharply differentiated among the mortality levels of different places. For example, it is not clear that births supervised by physicians had better outcomes than those supervised by midwives. Hospitals were clearly to be avoided except possibly in extreme emergencies.

Recall from Chapter 3 that New England and the Mountain region had relatively high mortality and the Midwest (East North Central and West North Central) had low mortality. The South was a region of unexpectedly low mortality, largely, it appeared, because of its rural character. It is now possible to see how this regional pattern is modified when particular features of these areas and their residents are controlled.

Column 1 of Table 4.3 reproduces the original interregional differences from Chapter 3 when no other variables are controlled. Column 2 presents these differences when all of the individual-level variables in equation (4) of Table 4.1 are controlled, including an individual's size of place of residence. A very different regional pattern emerges. The Midwest remains a low mortality region, but New England is no longer the region of highest mortality. Its mortality is exceeded by that of four other regions, including the three regions of the South and Southwest. New England's debilities appear to have arisen largely from the fact that it was the most highly urbanized region. Once rural/urban residence is controlled (along with other variables, such as literacy, on which New England was *not* particularly disadvantaged), its mortality does not appear exceptionally high. It

TABLE 4.3
Regional Pattern of Child Mortality with and without Control for Various
Personal and Regional Characteristics: U.S., 1900

Region	Original difference[b]	Coefficients of regional dummy variables[a]		
		No control for state economic conditions	State income controlled	State income and price level controlled
New England	NI	NI	NI	NI
Middle Atlantic	− .0868	− .0247	− .0557	− .0375
East North Central	− .2372	− .0508	− .0928	− .0512
West North Central	− .3395	− .0881	− .1302[d]	− .0835
South Atlantic	− .0871	.0117	− .2235[c]	− .1544[e]
East South Central	− .1078	.0504	− .1641[e]	− .0774
West South Central	− .0002	.1465[d]	− .0074	.0382
Mountain	− .0416	.2534[d]	.4308[c]	.3553[c]
Pacific	− .3151	− .1786[e]	− .0615	− .1221

Source: Sample of census enumerators' manuscripts, U.S., 1900.

[a] The regional dummy variables relate a region's child mortality to that of New England, controlling individual-level characteristics.

[b] The original difference in the child mortality index between the region in question and New England.

[c] Significant at a 1 percent level.

[d] Significant at a 5 percent level.

[e] Significant at a 10 percent level.

is replaced by the Mountain region, which was highly rural but which nevertheless maintained high mortality conditions.

Some indication of the conditions that may have given rise to the Mountain region's high mortality are provided by Children's Bureau study of child health in Montana in 1917 (Paradise 1919). The study describes circumstances of extreme isolation, great distances to towns and neighbors over roads that were often impassable, combined with great congestion within the largely one-room cabins. Even so, child mortality levels, though high for rural areas, were below those of each of the eight cities investigated by the Bureau. When we examine the mortality levels of specific states (not shown), those with the highest levels in the Mountain region are Arizona, Colorado, and especially New Mexico. Arizona and New Mexico had a high percentage of American Indians, and the high mortality of the region is probably traceable primarily to this group. (For a study of the very high child mortality among American Indians in the 1900 census, see Johansson and Preston 1979).

The regional pattern of mortality differences is altered once again when we control for the economic circumstances of each state. As shown in Appendix B, each of the New England states had above-average earnings levels, while the South had below-average levels (see also Wright 1986). Table 4.1 shows that (the log of) a state's income (i.e., earnings level) had a highly significant, negative impact on the child mortality level of residents. Column 3 of Table 4.3 presents the regional differences that remain after state income levels are controlled. New England again becomes a high mortality region, surpassed only by the Mountain region, an area with even higher incomes. The South once again becomes a low mortality region, significantly so in the case of the South Atlantic. In other words, New England appears to have had better mortality levels than the South once individual characteristics are controlled because it was an area of above-average income levels. Its advantage over the South, and that of the Middle Atlantic states as well, was principally economic.

A state's income level in column 3 was not adjusted for possible differences in the cost of living among states. Haines (1989a) has produced a cost of living index for states in 1890, and our final step is to see how using real income (1900 state income divided by the 1890 cost-of-living index) modifies the regional picture. Column 4 of Table 4.3 shows that New England's relatively high cost of living has overstated somewhat its economic advantage and, hence, its mortality disadvantage. It still has higher mortality than the Midwest or South, net of all other factors, but the excess is diminished. The lowest mortality region continues to be the South Atlantic, and the highest, the Mountain region. There is a 51 percent difference in child mortality levels between these regions. For all other regions the range of child mortality levels is only a modest 16 percent.[2]

To summarize, the raw differences among the child mortality levels of different regions reflect a complex array of factors. New England had the advantage of relatively high income and a low proportion of black residents, and the disadvantage of being highly urban. The South was the mirror image of New England in these respects. The outcome was a level of child mortality in the South (South Atlantic and East South Central) that was 9–11 percent lower than that of New England. When urbanization and percentage of black residents are controlled, the South had higher mortality than New England by

1–5 percent; when state income levels are additionally controlled, the South returns to having lower mortality by 8–22 percent. So when all of these characteristics are factored in, the South appears to be relatively healthy. We are surprised by this result since we expected the ecological and climatic features of the South, the effects of which should become increasingly manifest as socioeconomic characteristics are controlled, to produce above-average mortality. But it is possible that the lower population density of the South in rural areas, a factor not accounted for in our analysis, has overcome any disadvantages of climate. We return to this issue below.

The unusually favorable child mortality of the Midwest appears to be largely explicable in terms of social and economic conditions of its residents. Child mortality was 15–34 percent lower in the Midwest than in New England and the Middle Atlantic states, but after the social and economic characteristics of residents are controlled its advantage is only 3–9 percent. Undoubtedly, the rural character of the region and the high percentage of farmers were two of the main factors accounting for its lower mortality. Aggregate income differences were not significant in this regard, since the Midwest's position relative to the Northwest was largely unaffected by whether state income is controlled.

A final word is in order on the effect of state income. Since data on an individual's occupation were available in the data set, we sought a state income index that was independent of the occupational distribution in order to characterize the aggregate labor market in a state. The index pertains to 1899–1900 and is correlated with Easterlin's (1957) index of state per capita income in 1899–1900 at .810. This variable was significant in the regression equations and properly signed: a higher average annual earnings level in a state led to lower child mortality. The coefficient of −.49 in Table 4.1 implies that a 10 percent increase in annual earnings would reduce child mortality by 4.9 percent. Since annual earnings varied by a factor of 2.1 between Georgia, the lowest wage state, and Massachusetts, one of the highest, it is clear that regional variation in economic circumstances accounted for a good deal of variation in child mortality. The higher-than-average wage levels in the Northeast offset some of the disadvantage that living in this region otherwise fostered. The coefficient of state income adjusted for price levels is −.38 and is also highly significant.

Husband's Occupation and Occupational Income

For the main analysis of mortality variation by husband's occupations, we used the aggregate set of eleven occupation categories based upon the U.S. Census Bureau's 1950 classification of occupations. The reference category chosen was that of laborers, a large, low-status, high-mortality group. Results in Table 4.1 show that other occupational groups typically had lower child mortality levels than laborers. But interoccupational differences tended to be quite small. The largest disparity occurred between laborers and sales workers, but the difference in child mortality between these groups was only 20 percent. For a variable that is probably our single best indicator of socioeconomic status, this range seems very narrow. Within it, furthermore, professional and technical workers had relatively high mortality, only 7 percent below that of laborers. Farmers continued to have below-average mortality, even though their predominantly rural residence was controlled. Only farmers and sales workers had mortality that differed from that of laborers at a 5 percent significance level.

One might suspect that the occupational categories used in Table 4.1 are too coarse to capture the significant variation that existed, despite the fact that even coarser categories used in England and Wales around the same time show much larger variations in child mortality (see Chapter 5). In part to address this concern, and in part to tie occupation more closely to economic standing, we created a variable representing the predicted income of an occupational group. Incomes were assigned based on the detailed, three-digit occupational code from the 1900 census rather than the cruder categories used above. Details of the index construction are presented in Appendix A. Note that incomes of professionals, managers, and officials were generally quite a bit higher than those of laborers and other blue-collar workers, so that the negligible mortality differences between the groups just described are not attributable to anomalous economic disparities of the time (though income differentials do appear to be smaller than at present). Salesmen and merchants did well economically, on average, so that their favorable child mortality might have an economic basis. On the other hand, domestic-service employees and those in agricultural pursuits had quite low incomes, in general, which were not reflected in unusually high child mortality.

From these scattered observations, it is already clear that our predicted income variable is not likely to perform well. Nor does it. When we use this variable in place of husband's occupation in a subsample excluding farmers (for whom no income estimate was attempted), its coefficient is .023, only about 5 percent of the coefficient on state income, and it has the wrong sign. Women whose husbands had higher-income occupations had very slightly, and insignificantly, increased child mortality.

It is not likely that husband's income was unimportant for mortality. Woodbury's (1925) study for the Children's Bureau demonstrated strong income effects on infant morality in cities, and our own index of state earnings levels is strongly related to child mortality. Evidently, there is too much measurement error in the variable for it to be useful. One source of the error may be in the occupational income levels themselves, which are culled from different sources. We created an interactive variable (log of predicted income times a dummy variable that took the value of one if the source was the 1901 Cost of Living Survey and zero otherwise) to see whether source differences were important. But the coefficient of this variable is only .006 and insignificant. Another source of measurement error, probably more important, is simply that there was substantial income variance within occupations, variance not accounted for when all members of that occupational group are assigned the same mean income. With enough variance, the average income of an occupation becomes essentially meaningless. This appears to be the case.

Husband's Unemployment and Unemployment Levels in His Occupation

Unemployment in 1900 was, as now, a sensitive indicator of economic distress in the family. Indeed, it was more serious at the turn of the century, since there was little in the way of a "safety net"; unemployment insurance, welfare benefits, and private charity were meager if they existed at all (Patterson 1986: ch. 2). Table 3.1 indicated that almost 18 percent of the households with both spouses present (and for whom information was reported) experienced some unemployment in the twelve months before the census of June 1, 1900. The census year was not a year of relative economic difficulty or particularly high unemployment. Unemployed workers as a percentage of the civilian labor force were only 6.5 percent in 1899 and 5.0 percent in 1900. This level was well below the average of 14.2 percent that had prevailed during the period 1893–98 (U.S. Bureau of the Census 1975: Series D 85–86). It must be remembered that bouts of unemployment were a fact of life for many manual workers, especially those in the building trades.

A strong relation between child mortality and husband's unemployment in the census year was observed in Table 3.1. The coefficient of this variable is also large and statistically significant in Table 4.1. Unemployment of the principal income-earner in the household at some time during the year before the census was associated with a 16 percent increase in child mortality. In all likelihood, this coefficient is so large not because of the impact of unemployment in 1899–1900 per se but because unemployment in the census year is statistically associated with unemployment in previous years as well. Recall that impoverished families in Washington, D.C., in 1901 complained not so much about the level of wages that they were paid but about the irregular availability of work.

To examine whether unemployment levels in the occupation currently pursued by the husband contributed to explaining variation in mortality, over and above the contribution of the husband's own unemployment, we created an additional variable that is described in Appendix A. This variable is the average number of months unemployment for men in the husband's three-digit (i.e., detailed) occupational category. When this variable is added to equation (4) in Table 4.1 (not shown), its coefficient is $-.0074$. It is insignificant and, like occupational income, takes the wrong sign. The husband's own recent history of unemployment proves to be far more important than the level of unemployment in his occupation. Hence, our considerable efforts to use information about the husband's occupation to characterize the economic circumstances of the household have proven largely fruitless.

Wife's Labor-Force Participation

Earlier tabulations revealed a complex relationship between child mortality and the labor-force activity of the mother. The one-way comparison (Table 3.1) showed considerably higher child mortality among working mothers, but the relation did not pertain to native white women, and was reversed among households with husbands absent. The regressions in this chapter exclude women with absent husbands, and the negative "effect" of mother's work on child mortality is maintained. In Table 4.1, wife's labor-force activity was combined with a variable pertaining to child-care availability: whether there was another nonboarding female adult in the household who could potentially have provided child care. For women with child care in the home, child mortality was 20 percent higher among working than among nonworking women. But for women without child care, where the effect of working might be expected to be greatest, the differential was only 3.6 percent. None of the differences are statistically significant. Below, we show that the anomalous result involving child-care availability was confined to rural areas and that the anticipated result did pertain in urban areas.

Property Ownership

The basic relationships involving ownership variables that were observed in Tables 3.1 and 3.5 are also found in the regressions. The reference category consists of home renters, who clearly had the highest child mortality. The lowest mortality group, with mortality levels 16 percent below those of home renters, comprises those owning farms free and clear. In general, the results for this variable show the advantages both of property ownership and of farm life. If one rented, it was better to rent a farm than a nonfarm home; if one owned, it was better to own a farm than a nonfarm home. So the advantages of farm life are not entirely captured by our rural/urban variable but show up as well in occupational results (children of farmers having below-average mortality) and in farm/nonfarm residence. The more bucolic was life on any of these dimensions, the lower was mortality.

Presence of Servants or Boarders

The presence of servants is expected to be negatively associated with child mortality because it is a sign of affluence. The presence of boarders is thought to be an indicator of economic hardship in the family (Modell and Hareven 1973). Further, attending to boarders might have taken the mother's time away from child care. Both servants and boarders furnished an additional vector for introducing infectious disease into the household and may have produced more crowded conditions. Tabulations presented in Table 3.1 were consistent with these general expectations, and the regression coefficients in Table 4.1 also support them. The signs are in the expected direction (negative for servants, positive for boarders), but only the coefficient for boarders is statistically significant. The presence of boarders raised child mortality by about 15 percent, roughly equivalent to the effect of having an unemployed husband, a far more common condition.

Migration Status

The 1900 census asked a question of migrants from abroad about the year of their immigration to the United States. From this datum and current age, two variables were computed, one giving the proportion of the first 14 years of a woman's life that were lived in the United States and the other giving the proportion of years lived after age 14 that were spent in the United States. For natives, the value of both variables is 1.00. Coefficients of these variables are very small and statistically insignificant, and their signs are opposite from one another in Table 4.1. They do not prove to be helpful in understanding child mortality variation, once the nativity of the mother is taken into account.

Multivariate Relations within the Native, Foreign-Born, Rural, and Urban Populations

The relations described above are based upon a model in which effects of different variables can be added together to produce a predicted level of child mortality. This model does not include the possibility of interactions among independent variables. For example, the effect of husband's literacy may be greater in urban than in rural areas, but the effect described in Table 4.1 is an average across both types of areas.

In order to examine certain of these interactions, we have reestimated equation (4) in Table 4.1 separately for four major groups: native-born women, foreign-born women, urban women, and rural women. It would also have been useful to examine relations separately for whites and blacks, but there are too few observations for, and too little internal differentiation within, the latter group to make such an exercise worthwhile.[3] The distinctions that we explore do not exhaust the possibilities of interactions, of course, but they do capture major divisions within the American population that are suspected of conditioning the relationship between child mortality and other variables.

Results for the four groups are presented in Table 4.4. Also shown for convenience is equation (4) for all groups combined, reproduced from Table 4.1.

Race

Table 3.2 demonstrated that the child mortality disadvantage of black women was much greater in urban than in rural areas. This result is repeated in Table 4.4 when other variables are controlled. The coefficient for black women is more than twice as large in urban as in rural areas, and both coefficients are highly significant. In urban areas, black mothers had 58 percent higher child mortality than white mothers. This is the largest coefficient appearing in Table 4.4 and demonstrates again why the predominantly urban black women in the Death Registration Area presented such a distorted picture of overall black mortality conditions.

TABLE 4.4

Equations Predicting the Ratio of Actual to Expected Child Deaths for Individual Women Distinguished by Nativity and Rural/Urban Residence: U.S., 1900

Independent variables	Total Coefficient	Significance	Native-born Coefficient	Significance	Foreign-born Coefficient	Significance	Urban Coefficient	Significance	Rural Coefficient	Significance
Intercept	0.6280	***	0.6929	***	0.2131	***	0.3990	*	1.0262	***
Race of wife										
White	NI	NI	NI	NI	NI	NI	NI	NI	NI	NI
Black	0.2968	***	0.2794	***	NI	NI	0.5796	***	0.2368	***
Nativity of wife										
Native with native mother	NI	NI	NI	NI	—	—	NI	NI	NI	NI
Native with British mother	−0.0345	—	−0.0314	—	—	—	−0.0108	—	−0.0609	—
Native with Irish mother	0.0562	—	0.0447	—	—	—	0.1743	**	−0.2687	**
Native with Scandinavian mother	−0.0664	—	−0.0737	—	—	—	−0.1106	—	−0.0732	—
Native with German mother	−0.0490	—	−0.0637	—	—	—	−0.0133	—	−0.0666	—
Native with other West European mother	−0.3055	*	−0.3041	*	—	—	−0.3715	—	−0.3001	—
Native with East European mother	−0.1479	—	−0.1909	—	—	—	−0.2657	—	−0.0391	—
Native with South European mother	−0.4353	—	−0.4305	—	—	—	−0.4017	—	−0.4312	—
British	0.0592	—	—	—	−0.0565	—	0.1486	—	−0.0239	—
Irish	0.1169	—	—	—	NI	NI	0.3023	*	−0.4069	—
Scandinavian	0.1290	—	—	—	0.0232	—	0.1053	—	0.0763	—
German	0.0923	—	—	—	−0.0186	—	0.2636	*	−0.1219	—
Other West European	−0.2089	—	—	—	−0.2899	*	−0.1472	—	−0.3296	—
East European	−0.0779	—	—	—	−0.1058	—	0.0488	—	−0.1985	—
South European	−0.0816	—	—	—	−0.1163	—	0.0275	—	−0.2501	—
Other-foreign born	0.0443	—	—	—	−0.1226	—	0.1991	—	−0.1204	—

Variable	(1)	(2)	(3)	(4)	(5)
Age of wife	0.0094 ***	0.0056 **	0.0227 ***	0.0123 ***	0.0076 **
Literacy of wife					
Literate	NI	NI	NI	NI	NI
Illiterate	0.1004 **	0.1414 ***	0.0036	0.0816	0.1166 **
Wife speaks English					
Yes	NI	NI	NI	NI	NI
No	0.0029	NI	0.1123	0.0439	−0.0871
Literacy of husband					
Literate	NI	NI	NI	NI	NI
Illiterate	0.1234 ***	0.1373 ***	0.0977	0.2650 ***	0.0766
Husband speaks English					
Yes	NI	NI	NI	NI	NI
No	0.1506	NI	−0.0193	−0.0506	0.3637 **
Region					
New England	NI	NI	NI	NI	NI
Middle Atlantic	−0.0557	−0.0008	−0.1268	0.0441	−0.3618 **
East North Central	−0.0928 **	−0.0658	−0.1403	−0.0003	−0.3508 **
West North Central	−0.1302 ***	−0.0822 **	−0.3010 **	−0.0828	−0.3792 **
South Atlantic	−0.2235 *	−0.2229 *	−0.1843	0.1436	−0.5777 ***
East South Central	−0.1641	−0.1661	−0.2414	0.0738 **	−0.4812 ***
West South Central	−0.0074 ***	−0.0267	0.3875 ***	0.2734 *	−0.3263 *
Mountain	0.4308	0.4094 ***	0.4462	0.1718	0.2642
Pacific	−0.0615	−0.0090	−0.1758	−0.2565 *	−0.2225
Residence					
Top 10 cities	0.2954 ***	0.3572 ***	0.1951 *	0.2574 ***	—
Other cities 25,000 +	0.3160 ***	0.3249 ***	0.2594 **	0.2985 ***	—
Cities 5,000–24,999	0.2040 ***	0.1901 ***	0.2181 *	0.1933	—
Cities 1,000–4,999	NI	NI	NI	NI	—
Rural	0.0682	0.0440	0.1614	—	—

TABLE 4.4 (cont.)

Independent variables	Total		Native-born		Foreign-born		Urban		Rural	
	Coefficient	Significance	Coefficient	Significance	Coefficient	Significance	Coefficient	Significance	Coefficient	Significance
Property										
Owns farm clear	−0.1577	**	−0.0872	—	−0.4119	**	−0.0757	—	−0.1568	**
Owns farm mortgaged	−0.1005	—	−0.0315	—	−0.3629	**	−0.3130	—	−0.0925	—
Rents farm	−0.0634	—	0.0002	—	−0.4240	**	−0.3071	—	−0.0293	—
Owns home clear	−0.0417	—	−0.0336	—	−0.0697	—	−0.0619	—	0.0119	—
Owns home mortgaged	−0.1064	**	−0.0828	—	−0.1728	**	−0.1005	*	−0.0947	—
Rents home	NI	NI	NI	NI	NI	NI	NI	NI	NI	NI
Wife working										
Working—has child care	0.2139	—	0.2868	*	−0.5052	—	−0.1772	—	0.3436	*
Working—no child care	0.0357	—	−0.0132	—	0.2564	—	0.1506	—	−0.1039	—
Not working—has child care	0.0139	—	0.0117	—	0.0387	—	−0.0068	—	0.0335	—
Not working—no child care	NI	NI	NI	NI	NI	NI	NI	NI	NI	NI
Migration status										
Proportion of life lived in the U.S. before age 14	−0.0266	—	NI	NI	0.0138	—	0.1294	—	−0.2304	—
Proportion of life lived in the U.S. after age 14	0.0186	—	NI	NI	0.1340	—	−0.0561	—	0.1054	—
Other										
Husband unemployed	0.1586	***	0.2188	***	0.0087	—	0.1227	**	0.1788	***
Servant(s) in household	−0.0211	—	0.0138	—	−0.2120	—	−0.1132	—	0.0662	—
Boarder(s) in household	0.1510	***	0.1245	**	0.2372	***	0.1384	**	0.1718	***
Income										
Husband's age	−0.0006	—	−0.0008	—	0.0027	—	−0.0026	—	0.0009	—
Husband's age squared	0.0000	—	0.0000	—	0.0000	—	0.0000	—	0.0000	—
Log of state income index	0.4851	***	0.5589	***	−0.2846	—	0.1289	—	−0.6646	***

Husband's occupation	(1)	(2)	(3)	(4)	(5)
Professional, Technical	−0.0652 —	−0.0550 —	−0.1516 —	−0.0602 —	0.0353 —
Agricultural (excluding Laborers)	−0.1454 **	−0.1582 **	−0.1017 —	−0.0671 —	−0.0824 —
Agricultural Laborers	−0.0465 —	−0.0249 —	−0.1190 —	−0.1638 —	0.0624 —
Managers, Officials, Proprietors	−0.1098 *	−0.1258 *	−0.0808 —	−0.1315 *	−0.0150 *
Clerical	−0.1650 *	−0.1424 *	−0.2440 —	−0.2216 **	0.0875 **
Sales	−0.2093 **	−0.1898 **	−0.2335 —	−0.2330 **	−0.0539 **
Craftsmen, Foremen	−0.0217 —	−0.0099 —	−0.0726 —	−0.0355 —	0.0019 —
Operatives	−0.0904 *	−0.0324 *	−0.2442 **	−0.1370 **	0.0281 **
Service Workers	−0.1189 —	−0.0809 —	−0.2048 NI	−0.2136 **	0.1521 **
Laborers	NI NI	NI NI	NI NI	NI NI	NI NI
Miscellaneous	−0.1424 —	−0.1670 —	−0.0653 —	−0.1668 —	−0.0401 —
N	9,917	7,902	2,014	4,535	5,381
Adjusted R-squared	0.0505	0.0515	0.0480	0.0405	0.0535
F-ratio	8.875 ***	8.661 ***	2.752 ***	3.902 ***	5.905 ***

Source: Sample of census enumerators' manuscripts, U.S., 1900.

Note: Sample consists of currently married women with husband present, married less than 25 years. The dependent variable is the ratio of actual to expected child deaths for each woman. For an explanation of its construction, and of the other variables, see text. Regressions are weighted least squares with the weights being the number of children ever born (normalized back to the original number of observations).

Significance levels are: *** = significant at least at a 1 percent level; ** = significant at least at a 5 percent level; * = significant at least at a 10 percent level; — = not significant at least at a 10 percent level. NI = not included.

Nativity and Parentage

Once other factors are controlled, second-generation mothers continue to have unusually low mortality, whether the sample is limited to all native-born women, to rural women, or to urban women. Nineteen of the 21 coefficients for this group in Table 4.4 are negative, signifying child mortality levels below those of native white women of native parentage. Only the urban and rural coefficients for second-generation Irish women are significant, and these have opposite signs: women of Irish heritage did poorly in cities and quite well in rural areas. Note that this result also pertains to first-generation immigrants from Ireland, although only the coefficient for urban Irish women attained statistical significance. It is likely that migrant selectivity factors are responsible for this unusual pattern of results for Irish women. It has been suggested that rural Irish in the United States were more likely to have been Protestant and to have had some wealth when they left Ireland than the urban Irish.[4] In addition, migrants from overwhelmingly rural Ireland who settled in urban areas undoubtedly faced larger problems of adaptation than did those settling in rural areas.

Foreign-born women in general did well in rural areas and poorly in urban areas, although none of the coefficients is significant at a 5 percent level. Nevertheless, the two largest immigrant groups, German- and Irish-born women, had child mortality levels in urban areas that were 26–30 percent above those of native women with native parents, coefficients that are significant at a 10 percent level.

The literature of the era is replete with references to the crowded, dilapidated, substandard conditions in immigrant ghettos. For example, the noted social reformer Jane Addams wrote of Chicago:

> The most obvious faults were those connected with the congested housing of the immigrant population, nine-tenths of them from the country, who carried on all sorts of traditional activities in the crowded tenements. That a group of Greeks should be allowed to slaughter sheep in a basement, that Italian women should be allowed to sort over rags collected from the city dumps, not only within the city limits but in a court swarming with little children, that immigrant bakers should continue unmolested to bake bread for their neighbors in unspeakably filthy spaces under the pavement, appeared incredible to visitors accustomed to careful city regulation. . . .
>
> Many evils constantly arise in Chicago from congested housing. . . . The inevitable boarders crowded into a dark tenement already too small for the use of the immigrant family occupying it . . . The school children

who cannot find a quiet spot in which to read or study and who perforce go into the streets each evening; the tuberculosis superinduced and fostered by the inadequate rooms and breathing spaces. (Addams 1910:294, 296)

Addams reported that, during the typhoid epidemic in Chicago in the summer of 1902, approximately one-sixth of the deaths arose in one ward, which contained only one-thirty-sixth of the population. Much of the blame was attributed to poor sanitary facilities (Addams 1910:296–99).

Another noted publicist and reformer, Jacob Riis, wrote in his famous books *How the Other Half Lives* (1890) and *The Children of the Poor* (1892) of such notorious New York City neighborhoods as Hell's Kitchen, the Five Points, the Bend, and Battle Row. His photographs were equally famous. One of his descriptions concerns the infamous Gotham Court, largely populated by Irish and Italians, which had a death rate of 195 per 1000 during the last large cholera epidemic in New York City (1866). An infant mortality rate of 442 per 1000 live births had been reported in the 1860s (Riis 1890:35–36). The descriptions included common elements: small rooms, crowded conditions, poor heat in winter, few windows, deficient ventilation, and inadequate water and sewerage disposal. Oscar Handlin, in his work on immigrants to the United States, *The Uprooted* (1973), uses the technique of the "ideal type" to describe the immigrant ghetto. Some of his most lurid passages deal with the congestion of residences and the filth to be found both within the tenements and in the streets below (e.g., Handlin 1973:135–36).

Such accounts tended to focus attention on the most extreme circumstances rather than on the most typical. Immigrants had elevated mortality rates in cities, but so did natives. According to Table 4.4, native-born women living in the 10 largest cities suffered 36 percent higher child mortality than those living in cities with populations of 1,000–4,999. Apart from German and Irish immigrants, coefficients for foreign-born urban mothers in Table 4.4, though generally positive, are insignificant. Likewise, Higgs and Booth (1979) also found slight effects of nativity on mortality in the 1890s once other factors were controlled. Whatever extra hazards were present in the first generation had disappeared for all but the Irish in the second generation. Their risks pale in comparison to the 47 percent excess for the black population (from Table 3.1), very few of whom faced the stresses of tenement living. By 1900, the melting pot was already percolating, though blacks had yet to gain entrance.

7. The congested conditions of urban tenements, such as that pictured here in New York (ca. 1910), were undoubtedly related to the excessive child mortality of both natives and immigrants in cities.

Age of Mother

Consistent with earlier results, mortality was declining slightly faster for urban than for rural areas (i.e., the coefficient of mother's age was greater in the former), although the controls for other characteristics that are instituted in Table 4.4 seem to reduce the rural/urban disparity. More impressively, the foreign born had a rate-of-mortality decline that was more than three times greater than the rate among natives. This disparity may reflect in part the difficulties that some of the foreign-born women faced in their country of origin or en route to the United States, although we have controlled the length of time that they had spent in the U.S.

Literacy and English-Speaking Ability

The urban and rural coefficients for mother's literacy in Table 4.4 are similar in magnitude, though only the rural is statistically significant. Literacy did have a higher payoff among native than among immigrant women, perhaps because the census question referred to literacy in any language. Among immigrant women, ability to speak English was more important than literacy, with a coefficient similar to that of literacy among native women.

Husband's literacy and English-speaking ability are far more differentiated in their effects. Literacy was highly significant in urban areas and had more than three times the influence that it had in rural areas. It is likely that husband's literacy had a higher economic value in urban areas. It was also three times as consequential there as the wife's literacy, perhaps because the wife was rarely in the labor force. A United Nations (1985) study of 15 developing countries also found that husband's literacy makes a bigger difference for child mortality in urban than in rural areas. The husband's literacy in 1900 had smaller effects for child mortality among immigrants than among natives-born wives.

The surprising result for the husband's English-speaking ability is that it was far more consequential in rural areas than in urban. Perhaps this difference reflected a shortage of other people who could speak a foreign language and act as intermediaries with supervisors and foremen in rural areas. It may also reflect the fact that spoken discourse was more important in rural areas and written discourse in urban. These explanations may be too facile, but there is no denying the very different pattern of results in urban and rural areas: in urban areas, husband's literacy mattered a great deal for child survival and his English-speaking ability was essentially irrelevant, whereas just the opposite relations prevailed in rural areas.

Region and Size of Place

The relatively high mortality of New England, the reference category for regions of the U.S., is largely traceable to rural areas. Only rural residents of the Mountain states had worse mortality. Soil quality is relatively poor in much of New England, and since it was the earliest settled region, its rural regions were unusually densely populated. The ratio of *rural* population to land area was at least three times the national average in Connecticut, Massachusetts, and Rhode Island (U.S. Bureau of the Census 1975: Series A 195–209 and A 210–263). New England was also the most urbanized region in 1900, however, so that our sample contains only 81 women and 214 children ever born in rural New England (8.3 percent and 8.5 percent of New England observations, respectively). It is possible that this small sample has given a misleading impression of rural conditions there.

Rural South Atlantic areas had 58 percent lower mortality than rural New England once other factors were controlled, and rural areas of East South Central states were also exceptionally well off. The Mountain region is poorly situated on all regressions, while the advantages of the Midwest (East North Central and West North Central) are seen to be concentrated in rural areas and, to a lesser extent, among the foreign born. Adding to the advantages of the Midwest and South in overall rankings was their predominantly rural character.

Large cities were clearly harmful for both immigrants and natives. For each group distinguished, mortality was 20–36 percent greater in the two largest city categories than in cities of 1,000–4,999 inhabitants. The curvilinear pattern that was evident in the overall result, with the top 10 cities doing better than the next largest group, was confined to the foreign born, as suggested earlier in Table 3.2.

Economic Circumstances

We expected to find that child mortality would be highest for working mothers without people in the household who might be available for child care. That result was not found in the total sample. This result does emerge in urban areas, however, although it is not statistically significant. Women's work, and attendant child-care concerns, appear more consequential in urban areas, possibly because more of the work occurred outside of the home.

Having an unemployed husband induced positive, relatively large, and statistically significant effects in all the equations in Table 4.4 except among the foreign born. For the native population, and in both rural and urban areas, a period of unemployment by the principal income earner in the family during the census year raised the child mortality index by 12–22 percent. The coefficient is largest for the native population.

For the foreign born and in urban areas, the presence of one or more live-in servants was associated (though not significantly) with lower child mortality, while among the native born and in rural areas the effect was smaller and opposite in direction. In contrast, the presence of boarders in the household had a uniformly unfavorable and significant impact on child survival in all of the equations of Table 4.4. As mentioned earlier, a number of factors may be involved in this outcome: boarders as an indicator of economic distress in the household, as a potential source of infection, and as an additional burden on a mother's time. The effect of boarders on child mortality was about equally strong in urban and rural areas, but it was twice as strong among the foreign born as among native-born women, perhaps because the foreign born were more disadvantaged to begin with.

The final set of variables relates to income and occupation. A curvilinear relation between child mortality and husband's age was anticipated because of the curvilinear pattern of male income as a function of age, but such a pattern failed to appear in the full sample or among any of the subgroups.

State earnings levels were highly significant in the total sample. They also proved significant in rural areas and among the native population, where coefficients are even larger than in the total sample. Since both groups contained a majority of the population, they contributed the most observations to the construction of the earnings index, and it is perhaps not surprising that its variation is most clearly reflected therein. But we also expected significant and sizable coefficients in urban areas and among the foreign born, where they fail to appear. In any event, state earnings levels appear to be a good reflection of average conditions in rural areas, and to be closely associated with child mortality levels therein.

Breaking the sample down into urban and rural components sheds considerable light on the role of husband's occupation. The effects of occupation on child mortality appear greater in urban areas than in rural areas or in the country as a whole. Interoccupational mortality variation was greater, and significant coefficients more common. Relative to the low-status reference category (urban laborers), urban clerical workers, sales personnel, operatives, and service workers had significantly lower mortality. Professionals continued to do poorly in urban areas, however. Occupational mortality differentials were smaller in rural areas, and none of the rural groups had mortality that differed significantly from that of rural laborers. Occupational differentials among the foreign born, who were predominantly urban, were in general quite similar to those in urban areas as a whole.

It is possible that occupation was more closely related to income in urban areas than it was in rural areas. This situation might have arisen simply because occupational labelling is a more precise process in the more highly differentiated urban industrial establishments. Furthermore, rural workers may have changed jobs more frequently and casually, partly in response to the rhythms of the crop cycle. A less differentiated character of occupational pursuits in rural areas may partly explain why the state income level works so much more powerfully there. In any event, the relatively unstructured relations between occupation and child mortality in rural areas are reflected in the total sample, within which rural residents formed a majority. But it is reassuring to find that our expectations about occupational mortality differences—based as they inevitably are on experience in modern urbanized populations—are somewhat more clearly realized in urban areas.

The Relative Importance of Variables

The previous sections have described the degree to which child mortality was differentiated according to various characteristics, once other variables were controlled. To some extent, we were able to elucidate the paths through which characteristics that are established early affected mortality, and we tested the significance of differences between mortality levels within various categories of a variable relative to the reference category.

While these tests are illuminating, they do not tell us everything we want to know. They indicate how child mortality varied from one category of a variable to another, but not how important the *set* of categories (i.e., the variable) was relative to other sets. Of course, if there was little or no variation in mortality levels within the set, then the variable itself cannot be very helpful in explaining variation in child mortality.

To shed additional light on the issue of how important one variable was relative to others, we ask two specific questions:

1. If one knew only one piece of information about a family (e.g., husband's occupation, wife's literacy), which piece would be most helpful in predicting the family's level of child mortality?

2. If one piece of information about a family were missing, which omission would be most costly in terms of predicting the family's level of child mortality?

These questions can be translated into relatively simple statistical terms. The first question amounts to asking how much variance in child mortality can be explained by one variable acting alone, whereas the second question amounts to asking how much of the variation explained is lost when one variable is deleted from a model with all other variables included.

We would expect that variables with more categories would explain more variance even if child mortality were a purely random process, simply because more categories provide more opportunities for a spurious association to emerge. So it is useful to introduce tests of statistical significance that account for the greater degrees of freedom used up by variables with more categories.

Table 4.5 presents the appropriate statistics. The answer to the first question is very surprising. The single most valuable piece of information for predicting child mortality is the mother's race, despite the fact that the variable is a dichotomy.[5] That is to say, the value of R^2 for this variable, shown in the first column of Table 4.5, exceeds that of any other variable. The next most valuable pieces of information are size of place of residence, husband's occupation, and farm/home property ownership. But these variables have many categories, especially the first two, and when an adjustment is made for degrees of freedom, as for the F-ratio, they drop down in the hierarchy of variables. After race, the three variables with the highest F-ratios are all dichotomies: whether the husband was unemployed and whether the husband or wife was illiterate. All of the variables, however, when considered individually, are significantly related to mortality at a 1 percent level. Were we forced to consider variables one at a time, it would appear that child mortality was powerfully influenced by every factor that we can measure.

Multivariate analysis proves more discriminating. Fewer than half of the variables contribute significantly at a 1 percent level to explaining variation in child mortality when all other variables are present in the model. Once again, however, the most important variable turns out to be race. Adding race to the model increases the variance explained by .0052, or by 10 percent. Being black in 1900 denoted a set of economic and social conditions that powerfully affected child mortality and that was not adequately captured by other variables that may have been associated with race. The second most important variable is size of place, adding .0047 to variance explained. Larger cities were unhealthier, and the population was sufficiently dispersed by size of place that the variable explains a substantial amount of variance. The third most important variable was region of residence (controlling state income, among other factors), pointing again to the potential importance of environmental conditions as a factor in mortality variation. These three variables add at least twice as much explanatory power as any other variables in the model.

All three remain highly significant after accounting for degrees of freedom, but the multicategory size-of-place and region-of-residence variables are surpassed in F-ratios by more parsimonious variables: husband's unemployment, state income levels, presence of boarders in the household, and wife's age.[6]

Despite having many categories, wife's nativity and husband's occupation add only .0017 and .0014 to variance explained, amounts that are statistically insignificant. The literacy status of the wife is also insignificant at a 5 percent level. If we knew everything else about a family, we would gain no significant additional information about its

TABLE 4.5

Statistical Significance of Variables in the Multivariate Analysis of Child Mortality: U.S., 1900

Variable	Variables Alone				Full Model				
	R-square	Adjusted R-square	F-ratio	Prob>F	R-square without predictor	Adjusted R-square without predictor	Marginal R-square	F-ratio	Significance[a]
Race of wife	0.0150	0.0148	75.392	0.0001	0.0517	0.0454	0.0052	27.152	***
Nativity of wife	0.0064	0.0048	3.992	0.0001	0.0552	0.0503	0.0017	1.110	—
Age of wife	0.0015	0.0014	14.924	0.0001	0.0556	0.0493	0.0013	13.576	***
Literacy of wife	0.0096	0.0094	48.158	0.0001	0.0564	0.0501	0.0005	2.611	*
Wife speaks English	0.0024	0.0022	11.820	0.0001	0.0569	0.0507	0.0000	0.000	—
Literacy of husband	0.0086	0.0084	42.799	0.0001	0.0562	0.0499	0.0007	3.655	**
Husband speaks English	0.0027	0.0026	13.615	0.0001	0.0567	0.0505	0.0002	1.044	—
Region	0.0082	0.0074	10.256	0.0001	0.0529	0.0472	0.0040	5.222	***
Residence	0.0116	0.0111	23.239	0.0001	0.0522	0.0463	0.0047	9.817	***
Property ownership	0.0134	0.0128	22.404	0.0001	0.0557	0.0498	0.0012	2.089	*
Wife working	0.0029	0.0026	9.683	0.0001	0.0567	0.0506	0.0002	0.696	—
Husband unemployed	0.0064	0.0063	63.618	0.0001	0.0549	0.0486	0.0020	20.886	***

Servants in household	0.0010	0.0009	9.663	0.0019	0.0569	0.0506	0.0000	0.000	—
Boarders in household	0.0018	0.0017	18.079	0.0001	0.0557	0.0494	0.0012	12.532	***
Log state income index	0.0022	0.0021	22.272	0.0001	0.0553	0.0489	0.0016	16.709	***
Husband's occupation	0.0129	0.0119	12.955	0.0001	0.0555	0.0500	0.0014	1.462	—
All variables plus covariates[b]	0.0569	0.0505	8.875	0.0001					

Source: For sources and methods, see text.

Note: $N = 9,917$. Prob>F is the probability of observing the value of the F-ratio if there were no relationship between the variable and mortality.

[a] Significance levels are: *** = significant at least at a 1 percent level; ** = significant at least at a 5 percent level; * = significant at least at a 10 percent level; — = not significant at least at a 10 percent level.

[b] The covariates are age and age squared of husband and two variables on the proportion of life spent in the United States.

child mortality levels by knowing the husband's job or whether the wife was literate or what her ethnic background was. Since these variables are prominently featured in current discussions of child mortality (see Chapter 5 and United Nations 1985), these results are quite surprising.

A word of caution is necessary. As we argued earlier, both literacy and ethnic background to some extent work through other variables whose values are established later in life and which are controlled in the model. This layering of influence may also be operative to some extent for husband's occupation. All that these results convey is that little *additional* variance is explained when these variables are introduced; in the parlance of path analysis, no significant *direct* effect of these variables is evident. Furthermore, some of the explained variance is shared among variables, and the test reported in Table 4.5 allows all of that shared variance to be captured by the other variables that remain in the equation when individual variables are excluded. For example, in Table 4.1, the literacy of the wife remains a significant variable when all other variables are present because it appropriates some fraction of the explained variance that it shares with other variables. Nevertheless, the test in Table 4.5 is an appropriate way of answering the second question posed: we would lose nothing of significance in explaining child mortality variation in 1900 if we had no information on the wife's literacy or ethnicity or on her husband's occupation.

Taking variables one at a time as we have just done does not allow for the fact that several variables may be tapping into a common root. A final way to characterize variables, one that permits some cumulation of influences, is to list them according to the largest contrasts that occur between two categories within the variable, once other variables are controlled. In order of the size of mortality differences between two categories, and limiting ourselves to categories that accounted for at least 5 percent of births in the sample, the list is shown at the top of the next page (from equation [4] of Table 4.1).

Three of these variables (occupation, home/farm ownership, and size of place) are related to rurality, a pervasive influence on mortality at the time. Assuming that the influence of variables is additive, a laborer living in a city larger than 25,000 inhabitants who rented his home had mortality that was 61 percent higher than that of a farmer in a small town who owned his farm (.15 + .30 + .16). Clearly, farm living, farming occupations, and rural residence all contributed independently to the health advantages of a more pastoral life.

What about economic variables as a class? The surprising result is that little occupational variation existed in child mortality, whether

High-mortality category	Low-mortality category	Difference in mortality
Black	White	.30
City > 25,000	Town < 5,000	.30
New England	South Atlantic	.22
Husband unemployed	Husband not unemployed	.16
Rents home	Owns farm clear	.16
Boarders in household	No boarders	.15
Laborer	Farmer	.15
Husband illiterate	Husband literate	.12
Wife illiterate	Wife literate	.10
Wife speaks no English	Wife speaks English	.00

we use a set of occupational categories or indexes of occupational income and unemployment. Still, laborers had 19 percent higher mortality than clerical and sales workers, the low-mortality white-collar groups. And if we add the unemployment penalty of 16 percent and place the clerical/sales worker in a state with double the per capita income of the laborer's state, adding a mortality differential of (ln 2 x .485 = .34), we generate a contrast between rich and poor of 69 percent. Economic discrepancies are clearly associated with large variation in child mortality, although no single economic variable shows striking effects by itself. In addition, the large mortality variation by race that we have demonstrated is most plausibly ascribed to the enormous economic disparities that existed between the races at the time.

The variables that do not appear to be very important in child mortality, individually or as a group, are those which we expect to be most closely associated with child-care practices: mother's literacy, her ethnicity, her English-speaking ability, and her husband's occupation. None of these variables significantly explains variation at a 5 percent level in Table 4.5, once other variables are controlled. Whatever behavioral variation was associated with these variables seems to be swamped in its effects by broad geographic and economic factors. The seven variables that are significant at a 1 percent level in Table 4.5 include three geographic variables—size of place, region of residence, and state income levels—and three that denote individual economic circumstances—race, husband's unemployment, and presence of boarders. The seventh is the woman's age, which represents the health environment at the time when her children were young.

This list paints individuals as relatively passive victims of time, place, and labor markets. Behavioral factors were probably a key to child mortality declines during the twentieth century (Ewbank and

Preston 1989), but their mark was not highly visible at the turn of the century in variables such as literacy and occupation where we might expect their effects to be most obvious. One reason may be that too little knowledge of specific ways to enhance child survival had developed to allow individuals to escape from the circumstances imposed by broad geographic and economic forces. We develop this theme at greater length in the next chapter.

FIVE

AMERICAN CHILD MORTALITY DIFFERENTIALS

IN COMPARATIVE PERSPECTIVE

T HE PATTERNS OF child mortality differences demonstrated in Chapters 3 and 4 are the outcomes of a complex array of factors, including the relative social and economic standings of different groups, differences in child-care practices, and the disparate disease environments in which the groups were located. In order to gain insight into the importance of these factors in fashioning the observed differentials in child mortality, it is useful to compare the American circumstances that we have described to those in other societies. For comparative purposes we have chosen to focus in this chapter on child mortality differentials in England and Wales in 1911 and in a set of eleven developing countries in the 1970s. Both comparisons rely upon data comparable to what was available in the United States in 1900: census or survey responses by women to questions on the number of children they had borne and the number of those children who had survived to the time of the census or survey. The broader, systemic factors that condition child mortality levels and differentials are usefully revealed by these comparisons.

Child Mortality Differentials in England and Wales in 1911

The Census of Marriage and Fertility of England and Wales in 1911 produced very extensive tabulations of children ever born and surviving among different groups (England and Wales 1923). Equivalent to the analytic scheme of Chapter 4, tabulations of child mortality are produced for married women with husband present by duration of marriage (Preston, Haines, and Pamuk 1981; Watterson 1986, 1988). No public-use sample of these data has been prepared, precluding the use of multivariate techniques. But the extensive basic tabulations permit comparisons with the U.S. across a number of dimensions. A similar inquiry was undertaken in the 1911 Census of Ireland, although the scope of published tabulations was much more limited (Great Britain 1913a).

A basic contrast between England and Wales in 1911 and the United States in 1900 is their degrees of urbanization. While a majority of the American population was still living in rural areas in 1900, England and Wales, the first area to industrialize and urbanize, had 78 percent of its population living in urban areas by 1911 (England and Wales 1914: Table 13). Ireland was, of course, predominantly rural. As late as 1929, 73 percent of the Irish population lived in rural areas (Knodel and van de Walle 1979: Table 1). One might expect that the English results would look more like the results for the urban United States in Chapter 4 than those for the rural or total population. Recall that urban areas showed a somewhat higher degree of differentiation in child mortality by husband's occupation, as well as a larger penalty for women who worked. As occupational structures diversified and sharpened in urban areas, labor-force activities seemed to become more closely associated with child mortality levels.

This expectation is realized in the English data. Table 5-1 presents the basic results. Because many of the published English data are limited to women below age 45 at the time of the census, we have restricted our analysis to woman married 0–14 years. The singulate mean age at marriage in England and Wales was relatively high, at 27.7, so that women of marital durations beyond 15 years who were below age 45 would have constituted an increasingly selective sample.[1] We use the marital-duration approach to estimating $q(x)$'s that was described in Chapter 2 (United Nations 1983a: ch. 3). Because the analysis of U.S. data used marital durations below 25 years and the English results used durations below 15 years, the latter will apply to a date that is somewhat closer to the census than will the date in the U.S.

It should be noted that the mortality levels estimated through these indirect methods are not far out of line with the national figures supplied by England and Wales's excellent vital registration system. For example, the value of $q(5)$ for 1901–10 in the vital registration system is .192 (Table 2.3). The value of $q(5)$ for 1905 estimated from the marital-duration model based on women married 10–14 years is .174. It is likely that restriction of the marital-duration approach to women only once married with husband present has reduced census levels of mortality somewhat relative to the national average.

Rural/urban differences similar to those in the U.S. are revealed in England and Wales. Rural districts had the lowest child mortality. Urban areas as a whole had mortality that was 33 percent higher than rural areas, compared to the urban excess of 22 percent for the United States (from Table 3.1). London, however, exhibited mortality below

TABLE 5.1
Child Mortality Index in Various Social Categories: England and Wales,
1911

	Children ever born	Years before census	Child mortality index
Total	6,431,596	4.439	1.0000
Number of rooms			
1	82,676	3.728	1.8960
2	570,755	4.015	1.3457
3	1,118,101	4.301	1.1192
4	1,821,824	4.436	1.0395
5	1,274,477	4.485	.8647
6	678,053	4.467	.7866
7	231,254	4.550	.6676
8	121,379	4.654	.6185
9	64,062	4.666	.5624
10+	113,463	4.763	.5091
Residence			
London	767,314	4.334	1.0031
County boroughs	1,965.311	4.371	1.1584
Other urban districts	2,258,929	4.373	.9740
Rural districts	1,308,677	4.382	.7884
North	2,231,971	4.363	1.1562
County boroughs	1,115,206	4.365	1.2324
Other urban districts	804,464	4.354	1.1278
Rural districts	312,301	4.372	.9571
Midlands	1,991,786	4.392	.9130
County boroughs	583,428	4.393	1.1144
Other urban districts	863,158	4.393	.8820
Rural districts	545,200	4.388	.7462
South	1,614,799	4.364	.8582
London	767,314	4.334	1.0031
County boroughs	179,824	4.366	.8613
Other urban districts	358,794	4.400	.7464
Rural districts	308,957	4.392	.6257
Wales	461,675	4.318	1.0705
County boroughs	86,853	4.313	1.1192
Other urban districts	232,513	4.298	1.1362
Rural districts	142,309	4.354	.9336
Wife's labor-force status			
Not employed	5,819,178	4.394	.9704
Employed	481,053	4.188	1.3140
Textiles	122,340	3.911	1.6788

TABLE 5.1 (*cont.*)

	Children ever born	Years before census	Child mortality index
Husband's social class			
Professional/higher white-collar	490,466	4.386	.6463
Merchant/lower white-collar	914,219	4.493	.8339
Skilled manual	1,581,055	4.437	.9498
Semi-skilled manual	1,124,770	4.449	.9498
Unskilled manual	1,210,256	4.536	1.2151
Textile workers	204,912	4.415	1.2001
Miners	715,593	4.344	1.2770
Agricultural Laborers	271,928	4.484	.7929
Place of birth			
Husband: E & W			
Wife: E & W	5,862,453	4.373	.9998
London	789,962	4.346	.9497
Great towns	1,873,345	4.325	1.1394
Urban counties	1,434,366	4.377	1.0051
Mixed counties	734,093	4.421	.9089
Rural counties	1,030,687	4.729	.8426
Outside E & W	147,123	4.332	.9570
Scotland	35,071	4.279	.8776
Ireland	38,209	4.319	1.0260
Husband: Scotland	57,705	4.381	.8403
Wife: Scotland	19,693	4.575	.7677
E & W	46,346	4.349	.8889
Husband: Ireland	77,675	4.307	1.1410
Wife: Ireland	21,172	4.406	1.1394
E & W	53,287	4.273	1.1479

Source: England and Wales 1923.

Note: Based upon children ever born and surviving to currently married women below age 45 who were married 0–14 years. All calculations are made using the indirect techniques in United Nations 1983: ch. 3. Coale and Demeny (1986) Model West is used throughout. Only the marital-duration model is estimated. Years before census refers to the number of years prior to the census (April 2/3, 1911) to which the mortality estimate pertains. The index is the ratio of actual to expected child deaths to all women in a category. Social class of husband is defined as professional and higher white-collar; merchants, farmers and lower white-collar; skilled manual workers; semi-skilled manual workers; unskilled manual workers; textile workers; miners; and agricultural laborers.

the county boroughs, which included most of the other large industrial and commercial cites such as Liverpool, Birmingham, Manchester, Sheffield, Newcastle-upon-Tyne, Leeds, Leicester, and Coventry. Institutional changes in the provision of public health and sanitation appear to have been introduced sooner in London than in other large cities (Daley and Benjamin 1964; Wohl 1983:64–66; Szreter 1988). By 1906 or so, London had achieved childhood mortality levels comparable to those in small cities ("other urban districts;" Table 5.1). This achievement appears even more impressive when it is recognized that by 1911 London was the world's largest city, with a population of 7.2 million. The next largest European city was Paris, with a population of only 2.9 million. New York City had 4.8 million inhabitants by 1910. It is noteworthy that London's relative advantage was substantially greater for children of women married 0–4 years than for those of women married 10–14 years, implying an unusually rapid fall in mortality. In fact, London's level of $q(2)$, based on women married 0–4 years, was below the national average. Nevertheless, rural districts in England and Wales, as in the U.S., clearly had the best experience in child survival.

Rural/urban difference persisted within broad regions, but the levels varied considerably. The North region, which included some of the largest industrial and commercial cities (Liverpool, Manchester, Newcastle-upon-Tyne) had the least favorable childhood mortality experience in the nation (see also Woods et al. 1988). These urban areas were often tardy in implementing effective public-health improvements. For example, Wohl (1983:112) reports that "Manchester gained control of the Manchester and Salford Waterworks Co. in 1851 and yet as late as 1904 only one house in fourteen had water laid on." The Midlands, also relatively urban and industrial (with cities such as Birmingham, Leeds, Bradford, and Leicester), nevertheless showed more favorable childhood mortality, largely traced to the much better experience of rural areas and smaller cities. A clear north/south mortality gradient existed, with the more agrarian and less industrial South region (excepting, of course, London, which itself had made substantial progress) having had the best childhood mortality levels. Wales had some of the least healthy industrial centers and also a history of rural poverty and neglect. It also had high childhood mortality, very similar to the North region.

Child mortality levels were strikingly differentiated by husband's occupational level. As the husband's social class declines from professional and higher white-collar to unskilled manual workers, there is a clear monotonic rise in the mortality index. Among the special groups separately enumerated, the highly urbanized groups of miners and textile workers had considerably higher childhood mortality than the largely rural agricultural laborers.[2]

Women who were employed had dramatically higher mortality among their children than did women who did not work (see also Dyehouse 1979). Levels were especially elevated among women working in the textile industry, which tended to be concentrated in the high mortality cities of the North and Midlands. Labor-force activity among married women (with husband present) was not common in England and Wales. Only 10 percent of women married 0–14 years were employed outside the home. As in the U.S., the mortality differential may have been overstated by a process of reverse causation, whereby women with a dead child might be more likely to work.

Table 5.1 reveals a clear monotonic gradient of child mortality according to the number of rooms in the house. The effect was strong: the child mortality index for families living in one room was almost four times as great as that for couples living in accommodations with 10 or more rooms. This variable may be functioning largely as a proxy for general social standing, but it also is expected to have a direct effect on mortality through congestion and transmission of communicable diseases. It is probably one of the most important pathways by which economic circumstances influence child mortality. That it is not simply an indicator of economic status is implied by the Woodbury study of American cities. The risk of infant death for those with two or more people per room was 2.5 times that of those with fewer than one person per room, and the differential declined only to 2.0 when father's earnings were controlled (Woodbury 1925:129–30).

The 1911 English Census also presents some tabulations by place of birth of husband and wife, which is highly correlated with place of current residence. The same curvilinear pattern of mortality by city size is evident. There is an interesting hint of an intergenerational effect of being London-born. Children born to women who were themselves born in London had in all cases lower mortality than the national average, and lower mortality than children born to "current" London residents. A similar intergenerational advantage of urban birth was demonstrated in a United Nations (1985) study of contemporary developing countries.

Irish immigrants to England and Wales experienced elevated child mortality, as in the United States. Although the Irish fared badly in both the U.S. and England and Wales, they did surprisingly well in Ireland itself. Table 5.2 presents calculations of q(a) values for women of marital durations 0–4 years through 30–34 years for the whole of Ireland and for urban and rural places within Ireland. In particular,

TABLE 5.2
Child Mortality and Fertility by Marital Duration and Place of Residence: Ireland, 1911

	Marital Duration						
	0–4 years	5–9 years	10–14 years	15–19 years	20–24 years	25–29 years	30–34 years
Average Parity							
Ireland	0.9804	2.8051	4.1673	5.1981	5.8735	6.4185	6.7418
Six county boroughs	0.9545	2.6493	3.9834	5.0924	5.8436	6.4041	6.7893
Dublin	0.9468	2.6175	3.9250	4.9069	5.6053	6.0595	6.4876
Belfast	0.9350	2.5604	3.8220	4.9294	5.7272	6.2414	6.6207
Ireland less 6 boroughs	0.9887	2.8540	4.2248	5.2298	5.8816	6.4219	6.7327
	q(2)	q(3)	q(5)	q(10)	q(15)	q(20)	q(25)
Child mortality: $q(a)$							
Ireland	0.09806	0.11431	0.14147	0.16327	0.18128	0.19799	0.21264
Six county boroughs	0.13141	0.16486	0.20580	0.23478	0.26893	0.29209	0.31088
Dublin	0.12640	0.16758	0.21096	0.24521	0.27750	0.29643	0.32282
Belfast	0.12392	0.15169	0.18887	0.21190	0.25347	0.26859	0.28309
Ireland less 6 boroughs	0.08773	0.09950	0.12261	0.14260	0.15765	0.17572	0.19373
Years ago							
Ireland	1.56	3.28	5.83	8.70	11.71	14.70	17.46
Six county boroughs	1.30	3.33	5.83	8.56	11.48	14.52	17.35
Dublin	1.30	3.34	5.84	8.58	11.52	14.56	17.39
Belfast	1.58	3.36	5.87	8.62	11.57	14.64	17.47
Ireland less 6 boroughs	1.28	3.27	5.84	8.74	11.78	14.76	17.49
Implied level (Model West)							
Ireland	16.75	16.24	15.33	14.92	14.57	14.51	14.73
Six county boroughs	14.66	13.50	12.38	11.96	11.18	11.05	11.30
Dublin	14.96	13.36	12.17	11.54	10.85	10.90	10.90
Belfast	15.12	14.15	13.10	12.85	11.77	11.91	12.25
Ireland less 6 boroughs	17.44	17.12	16.32	15.89	15.62	15.43	15.45
Children ever born							
Ireland	87,489	255,500	338,609	350,240	337,156	290,932	271,485
Six county boroughs	20,567	57,718	77,004	78,962	71,829	55,748	43,791
Dublin	9,057	25,570	33,343	32,847	28,671	22,899	18,386
Belfast	9,518	25,650	34,669	36,142	33,544	24,616	18,922
Ireland less 6 boroughs	66,922	197,782	261,605	271,278	265,327	235,184	227,694

Source: Great Britain 1913a: lxiii–lxv, Table 65.

Note: $q(a)$ is the probability of dying between birth and exact age a. All calculations are made using the indirect techniques in United Nations 1983a: ch. 3. Coale and Demeny (1966) Model West is used throughout. Only the marital-duration model is estimated. Years ago refers to the number of years prior to the census (April 2/3, 1911). The six county boroughs are Dublin, Belfast, Cork, Londonderry, Limerick, and Waterford. The figures for Dublin are for the Dublin Registration Area (Dublin County Borough and Rathmines, Rathgar, Pembroke, Blackrock and Kingston Urban District).

census data are presented for Dublin, Belfast, six county boroughs (urban areas that also included Dublin and Belfast), and Ireland without these urban places (i.e., essentially rural and small-town Ireland).[3] These retrospective data from the 1911 census confirm the suggestion from Irish vital statistics (Table 2.3) that Ireland had unusually favorable child mortality. The Irish advantage was a cause of some astonishment among British analysts (Brend 1917). The advantage appears entirely attributable to Ireland's highly rural character. If the population of Ireland had been 78 percent urban, as in England and Wales, then its value of $q(5)$ would have been .187, slightly higher than England and Wales's value of .174.[4] Ireland apparently had somewhat lower rural mortality than England and Wales and somewhat higher urban mortality.

Inequality and Childhood Mortality: The United States in 1900 and England and Wales in 1911

There has been a resurgence of interest among economists, sociologists, and historians in social and economic inequality in the United States and Great Britain (see, for example, Phelps Brown 1977: ch. 1; Williamson and Lindert 1980; Lebergott 1976; Williamson 1982b, 1985; Lindert 1983). Much of the effort has been devoted to studying the causes of inequality: the distribution of income, earnings, wages, and wealth. Another approach, used in the standard-of-living debate for industrializing Britain, has studied outcomes (Taylor 1975: xvii–xviii, xxix–xxxvii). Among the outcomes, health and mortality have been used by a number of authors to characterize differences in well-being (Williamson 1982a; Fogel, Engerman, and Trussell 1982; J. R. Hollingsworth 1981; Kadin 1982; Preston, Haines, and Pamuk 1981; Pamuk 1985).

As the basic indicator of social class, special interest is attached to indexes of inequality by husband's occupation. Table 5.3 presents the mortality index for husband's occupation in United States in 1900 and England and Wales in 1911, standardized to an all-occupation index of 100 in each case. Comparisons with vital statistics show the English occupational data to be highly reliable.[5] The first panel of Table 5.3 aggregates occupations into a modified version of the scheme used for the 1950 American census, and involves a distinction between occupation and industry. The 1900 American data are presented separately by race and nativity of women. The English data were mapped onto the American categories as well as was permitted by the detailed occupations published in the 1911 census. The second

TABLE 5.3

Child Mortality Differentials by Husband's Social Class: U.S., 1990, and
England and Wales, 1911

	Total	White[a]	Native white[a]	Foreign white[a]	Black[a]	Total
			U.S., 1900			England and Wales, 1911
U.S. occupational classification, 1950: total	100	100	100	100	100	100
Professional, Technical	94	100	107	88	b	62
Agricultural (excluding Laborers)	86	82	86	79	92	65
Agricultural Laborers	114	99	102	98	103	77
Managers, Officials, Proprietors	93	100	102	100		81
Clerical	91	94	97	94	58[b]	68
Sales	83	89	88	92		89
Craftsmen, Foremen	112	117	116	111	133	98
Operatives	104	107	113	91	113	117
Service Workers	100	101	106	87	94	84
Laborers	124	124	120	118	114	124
Miscellaneous	100	102	92	106	108	81
England and Wales classification 1911: total	100	100	100	100	100	100
Professional, Higher White-Collar	87	93	98	85	58	65
Farmers & Lower White-Collar	86	84	87	82	90	83
Skilled Manual Workers	112	118	121	107	115	95
Semi-skilled Manual Workers	114	114	110	110	128	100
Unskilled Manual Workers	123	123	120	116	114	122
Textile Workers	123	135	139	118	*	120
Miners	98	96	105	74	139	128
Agricultural Laborers & Related	115	100	105	95	103	79

Source: Sample of census enumerators' manuscripts, U.S., 1900; England and Wales 1923.

Note: The sample consists of currently married women with husband present for whom an occupation class of husbands could be assigned. For the U.S., women are married 0–24 years, and in England and Wales, 0–14 years. For calculation of the mortality index, see text.

[a] Relative to the U.S. index for all groups combined of 100, the index for whites was 94, for native whites 87, for foreign-born whites 112, and for blacks 144.

[b] For U.S. blacks, the categories Professional, Technical; Managers, Officials, Proprietors; Clerical; and Sales were combined because of small cell sizes.

* Fewer than 40 children ever born.

panel of Table 5.3 presents the American and the English data aggregated into the eight categories of the English social classes used in the 1911 census. Both sets of aggregations are based upon 338 detailed occupational titles in the United States and 206 in England and Wales.

Table 5.3 suggests that social-class inequality in mortality was greater in England and Wales around 1907 than in the United States around 1895. First, using the English classification, we see that the range of mortality indexes is much greater in England and Wales than in the United States. In particular, the professional and higher white-collar group was considerably less favored with respect to child mortality in the United States than in England and Wales. The relative position of unskilled manual workers was similar in the two countries, but miners showed the highest mortality level in England and no excess whatever in the United States.

The more favorable position of miners in the U.S. can be partly attributed to the greater likelihood in England and Wales than in the United States that coal and iron miners would live in urban areas. Of males aged 10 and over who were coal and iron miners and mine workers in England and Wales in 1911, 69.8 percent lived in urban districts (England and Wales 1914: Table 13). Among coal miners and mine workers in the sample used to calculate the American mortality indices in Table 5.3, only 29.1 percent were found in urban areas. American miners in urban areas with between 5,000 and 24,999 inhabitants had a child mortality index of 1.21, while those in rural areas had an index of .90. America's predominantly rural miners appear to reflect the mortality of their locale. British miners, on the other hand, had inflated mortality relative to their place of residence since they were slightly less urbanized than the nation as a whole. The sample of American miners is small, however, and may not provide highly reliable measures of the mortality of this group.

Somewhat offsetting the indications of greater inequality in England and Wales, agricultural laborers did much better there than in the United States. Some of the excess of this group in the U.S. is traceable to the disproportionate representation therein of the black population, but American agricultural laborers did not do particularly well even within the native white population.

When the occupations for both countries are regrouped into the 1950 U.S. Census categories (first panel of Table 5.3), the greater advantage of the professional and technical group in childhood mortality in England and Wales is retained. It is possible that the census definitions of these occupations were more "upscale" at that time in England than in the United States, but a study of relevant sources does not give cause to believe that occupational descriptions were systematically different between the countries (U.S. Bureau of the Census 1979:35–36; Armstrong 1972:191–92, 203–11, 226–28). A more plausible explanation is to be found in the relative economic positions of these groups.

Table 5.4 presents, for selected detailed professional and white-collar occupations in both countries, the mortality index, the estimated average annual male earnings (in American dollars), and the percentage of members of the occupation living in urban areas.[6] Clearly,

TABLE 5.4

Index of Child Mortality, Income, and Percentage of Urban-dwellers for
Selected Occupations of Father: U.S., 1900, and England and Wales, 1911

Occupation	Child mortality index	Yearly income (dollars)	Income index (overall = 100)	Percentage of urban-dwellers[a]
United States, 1900				
Professional, Technical	0.9450	905	142	50
Teachers	0.9994	590	93	28
Clergy	0.8048	730	115	25
Physicians & Surgeons	0.9422	1,000	157	43
Clerks & Copyists	0.9208	714	112	81
Total	1.0087	636	100	37
England & Wales, 1911				
Professional, Technical	0.6181	1,500	362	82
Teachers	0.5412	785	190	79
Clergy	0.4713	1,080	261	62
Physicians & Surgeons	0.4035	1,920	464	84
Commercial & Business Clerks	0.6797	466	113	93
Total	1.0000	414	100	78

Source: See Tables 5.3 and 5.6.

Note: For the construction of the child mortality index and the income estimates, see Chapter 3, Appendix A, and Table 5.6.

[a] For the U.S., percentage of urban-dwellers is percentage of women used to calculate the index who were living in cities of 5,000 and more in population. For England and Wales, percentage of urban-dwellers was the official census definition for 1911 for the occupations in question. Urban areas included London, municipal and county boroughs, and other urban districts. These essentially were urban areas over 5,000 population.

the relative income level for the professional and technical occupations was higher in England and Wales than in the United States. While mean income for professional and technical workers was 42 percent higher than average in the U.S., it was 262 percent higher in England and Wales. Within specific groups of professionals—teachers, clergy, and physicians and surgeons—English workers also did better than their American counterparts, both relatively and (using the gold standard's currency conversion rate) absolutely. American teachers, clergy, physicians and surgeons, and professional/technical workers in general, all had relative child mortality indices in 1900 that were also substantially less favorable than their counterparts in England and Wales in 1911.

Residential patterns are also mildly implicated in the differences between the relative child mortality of professionals in the two countries. Using the urban definition of 5000+ population, professionals were more highly urbanized in the U.S. relative to the population as a whole (50 percent versus 37 percent) than in England (82 percent versus 78 percent). Among clerical workers, whose relative economic conditions were quite similar in the two countries, residential differences were probably more consequential. The fraction of clerical workers who were urban was more than double the national average in the U.S., but only 19 percent higher in England. This difference is probably reflected in the relatively high mortality of children in this group in the U.S. compared to England and Wales.

It seems likely that the comparative mortality advantage of professionals in England is in good measure attributable to their comparative economic advantage. This advantage may in turn reflect the greater success of England's professional societies in restricting access to the professions (Routh 1965). The Royal College of Physicians and Surgeons was established in the eighteenth century, and the Medical Act of 1858 had tightened licensing requirements for physicians (Woods and Woodward 1984:69). In the United States as late as 1900, however, "the ports of entry into medicine were still wide open and the unwelcome passed through in great numbers" (Starr, 1982:116). That British physicians were more effective at protecting themselves than protecting the public at large is suggested by the fact that $q(5)$ in England and Wales during 1901–10 (.192) was still higher than it was a decade earlier in the U.S. ($q[5] = .180$, from Chapter 2). The children of physicians were healthier in Britain, but children in general were healthier in the United States. Much of the advantage of American children, of course, reflected the society's rural character, which supplied more protection against disease than did the nostrums of physicians.

The relatively high status of professionals in England relative to the U.S. was not limited to physicians. In general, it can be said to reflect England's longer and more intensive experience with urban industrial society and the occupational differentiation that it fostered. English class divisions were well established and widely recognized by the middle of the nineteenth century (Briggs 1956–57) and were the model—a very atypical one—for Marx's theory of capitalist development (Rubinstein 1977). Professionals had been more successful in England in restricting access through licensing and also tended to serve a more elite clientele (e.g., teachers were more likely to serve the upper classes since education was less universal in England). In the United States, the movement to professionalize the professions—

8. The children of physicians and surgeons had mortality that was only 6 percent below the national average, reflecting both physicians' relatively lower status and the shortage of effective preventions and cures. Shown here is a Wisconsin doctor and his family.

to restrict access and assure some minimum level of expertise—was principally a product of the Progressive era and achieved momentum mainly in the first decade of the twentieth century (Kunitz 1974).

More explicit measures of inequality presented in Table 5.5 confirm that child mortality was more unequally distributed by social class in England and Wales. In this table we use both the occupation classification system of England and Wales and that of the United States. The coefficient of variation (standard deviation divided by the mean) shows greater dispersion of childhood mortality across social classes in England and Wales than in the United States, whether the coefficients weight all classes equally or whether they weight classes by the number of children ever born into them. Within the United States, inequality in child mortality was generally greater among foreign-born whites than among native whites (although the difference disappeared when using the 1911 English classes and weighting by children ever born). The greater apparent inequality within the

TABLE 5.5

Measures of Inequality in Child Mortality: England and Wales, 1911, and U.S., 1900

	United States, 1900					England and Wales, 1911
	Total	White	Native white	Foreign white	Black	Total
Coefficient of variation						
1950 U.S. classes						
Unweighted	.1328	.1219	.1077	.1203	.2321	.2431
Weighted[a]	.1537	.1717	.1447	.1586	.1336	.1974
1911 English classes						
Unweighted	.1383	.1618	.1441	.1701	.2495	.2293
Weighted[a]	.1592	.1772	.1539	.1540	.1514	.1959
Index of dissimilarity						
1950 U.S. classes	.0654	.0718	.0641	.0682	.0651	.0782
1911 English classes	.0718	.0784	.0654	.0676	.0611	.0744
Mean Deviation						
1950 U.S. classes						
Unweighted	.1177	.0800	.0824	.1114	.3529	.2285
Weighted[a]	.1331	.1353	.1112	.1537	.1512	.1710
1911 English classes						
Unweighted	.1436	.1381	.1243	.1613	.3120	.1950
Weighted[a]	.1436	.1465	.1132	.1516	.2140	.1567
Atkinson Index ($\varepsilon = 2.5$)						
Own Weights						
1950 U.S. classes	.0606	.0774	.0573	.0668	.0481	.1029
1911 English classes	.0558	.0702	.0509	.0606	.0430	.0870
Standardized to 1911 English weights						
1911 English classes	.0441	.0547	.0401	.0686	.0356	.0870
	Estimated income[b]					
Coefficient of variation						
Social classes						
1950 U.S. classes[c]						
Unweighted	.3604					.7888
Weighted[a]	.3760					.4628
1911 English classes						
Unweighted	.3666					.4487
Weighted[a]	.3738					.3436
Detailed occupation groups						
Unweighted	.3048					.9608
Weighted by children ever born	.3969					.5191
Weighted by number of income earners	.4052					.5928

Source: Table 5.3 and text.

Note: Coefficient of variation $= \dfrac{\sigma}{\bar{X}}$, where σ is the sample standard deviation and $\bar{X}$ is the sample mean.

TABLE 5.5 (*cont.*)

Index of dissimilarity: $\Delta = \frac{1}{2} \sum\limits_{i=1}^{k} |X_i - Y_i|$ where X_i and Y_i are the uncumulated proportional distributions of two distributions. In this case, the distributions are the actual and expected deaths of the social-class categories.

Mean deviation $= \sum\limits_{i=1}^{N} |X_i - \bar{X}| \bigg/ N$, where $\bar{X}$ is the population mean (and not the sample mean).

Atkinson index: $I = 1 - \left\{ \sum\limits_{j=1}^{n} [\bar{Y}_j/\bar{Y}]^{1-\epsilon} f(Y_j) \right\}^{1-\epsilon}$, where $\bar{Y}_j$ is the mean value of the jth group, $\bar{Y}$

is the overall mean, $f(Y_j)$ is the proportion in the jth group, and ϵ is some number, taken here as 2.5 (a commonly used value). See Atkinson 1970 and Williamson 1982b. $F(Y_j)$ is the distribution of children ever born.

[a] Weighted by number of children ever born.

[b] Earnings were imputed for 166 male occupational groups for England and Wales in 1911, and 93 male occupational groups for the United States in 1900. These were then aggregated into social classes. For the sources and methods, see Appendix A and text.

[c] Excluding agricultural (class 2).

American black population disappeared when the occupational groups were weighted because there were so few blacks in the more privileged classes.

The second measure of inequality, the index of dissimilarity, is calculated by taking one-half of the absolute difference between the proportions of actual and expected child deaths in each social-class group. It is inherently a weighted indicator and measures the extent of redistribution of child deaths necessary to make each group's mortality equal to the national average. This index also shows that greater inequality characterized England and Wales, although the relative size of the inequality was smaller, especially using the 1911 English categories of social class.

The third measure, the mean deviation of the mortality index from its group average, confirms the result from the coefficient of variation. In this case, native whites consistently showed less inequality than foreign-born whites and blacks in the United States. Finally, Atkinson's (1970) index of inequality, also an inherently weighted index, supports the basic finding of greater inequality in England and Wales. It does not much matter whether groups are weighted in the index by their own proportional distribution or by some standard set of weights (for instance, the distribution of population across the eight social classes of England and Wales). That is, the disparity in amounts of inequality that are shown in weighted measures does not appear to be attributed to differing distributions of births by social class in the two countries.

Clearly, there was a greater degree of dispersion of mortality rates across social classes in England and Wales than in the United States. This dispersion may reflect widening mortality differentials during the mortality decline because of an uneven distribution of the factors causing the decline. Although English child mortality was still slightly higher than in the U.S. a decade earlier, it apparently began its decline from a substantially higher level (Keyfitz and Flieger 1968:526; Mitchell and Deane 1971:36–43; Haines 1979a: Table 7; see also Chapter 2). The lower apparent inequality in the United States may also have been caused partly by the later measurement of the differentials for England and Wales across a decade critical for the development of medicine and public health in both countries (Shryock 1947: ch. 15; Benjamin 1964; see also Chapter 1 above). Access to and utilization of health care by the upper classes may have been more effective in England and Wales by 1911.

There were also differences in economic structure. Despite the rapid growth of the American economy since the Civil War, Britain had a more "mature" economy with a higher proportion of the population in urban areas and a larger percentage of the labor force in the secondary and tertiary sectors (91 percent in 1901 versus 65 percent for the United States in 1900; Kuznets 1966:107–8, 272). Although there is some evidence of worsening income distribution in both countries during the nineteenth century, no clear trend was apparent by the turn of the century (Williamson and Lindert 1980:281–85; Williamson 1982b:22–24).

As a step toward understanding the source of these differences in mortality inequality, estimation of earnings was undertaken for the various occupational groups in England and Wales to supplement the estimates for the United States made in Appendix A. Some of the basic results are presented in Table 5.6.[7]

Coefficients of income variation are calculated for these groups (weighted and unweighted) and for the detailed occupational groups (116 for England and Wales and 93 for the United States) used in the subsequent regression analysis. They are presented in the last panel of Table 5.5. The coefficients of variation for earnings were, with one exception, greater for England.[8] Greater mortality inequality in England was evidently matched by greater inequality in earnings, obviously suggesting that the two are related. Higher incomes could of course purchase better diets, clothing, sanitary facilities and water supplies, and, perhaps most important, larger and less congested housing. When income inequality is greater, it is reasonable to suppose that inequality in mortality will also be greater. The next section tests this proposition more explicitly.

TABLE 5.6
Estimated Earnings by Social Class of Father (current dollars): U.S., 1900,
and England and Wales, 1911

	United States, 1900		England and Wales, 1911	
	Income	Index	Income	Index
American occupational classification				
Professional, Technical	905	142	1,502	363
Agricultural (excluding Laborers)[a]	(436)	(68)	(247)	(60)
Agricultural Laborers	257	40	228	55
Managers, Officials, Proprietors	1,077	169	523	126
Clerical	790	124	458	111
Sales	710	112	—	—
Craftsmen, Foremen	695	109	435	105
Operatives	580	91	389	94
Service Workers	618	97	330	80
Laborers	438	69	283	68
England and Wales classification				
Professional, Higher White-Collar	942	148	839	203
Lower White-Collar	780	122	358	86
Skilled Manual Workers	680	107	422	102
Semi-Skilled Manual Workers	611	96	360	87
Unskilled Manual Workers	421	66	298	72
Textile Workers	523	82	362	88
Miners	482	76	420	101
Agricultural Laborers	257	40	228	55
Total	636	100	414	100

Source: U.S. Commissioner of Labor 1903:264–82; Lebergott 1964: passim; Douglas 1930: passim; Routh 1965: ch. 2; Williamson 1982b; Great Britain 1909–13.

Note: Earnings were imputed to the 1900 American census sample by assigning to each of the occupational codes (using the 1900 coding system) average annual incomes based primarily on the United States Commissioner of Labor 1901 cost-of-living survey, but augmented by work by Lebergott and Douglas. No estimates were made for farmers. Estimates for groups were aggregated up from the sample.

For England and Wales in 1911, several sources were used. These included the Board of Trade, Routh and Williamson. In this case, most earnings were available on a weekly basis. Following the practice of Routh and Williamson, the results were simply multiplied by 52 to obtain full-time equivalent annual earnings. In that sense, these results are not strictly equivalent to the American estimates. Since no estimates of unemployment were available, it was felt that this was best. The estimates were made for 116 occupational groups or aggregations. Any reaggregations (e.g., into social classes) were made from these 116 groups. Among the groups for whom earnings were lacking were, notably, farmers and proprietors of a number of types (e.g., retail merchants).

The English estimates apply to a period roughly 1901–11. They were converted to American dollars at an exchange rate of 1£ = $4.85. The American estimates apply to a period approximately 1899–1901.

[a] Based on few cases (e.g., shepherds, farm managers, market gardeners).

Regression Analysis of Comparative Occupational Mortality Differences in England and Wales and the United States

The difference between patterns of differential mortality by occupation in the United States and England may reflect differences in the attributes of an occupation (e.g., income or proportion urban) or differences in the manner in which those attributes are translated into mortality. In order to see which of these two processes is principally at work, we have estimated two basic models for each country:

(1) $M_i = a_1 + b_1 ln Y_i + c_1 U_i + \xi_{i1}$
(2) $M_i = a_2 + b_2 ln Y_i + c_2 U_i + \sum_j d_j D_{ij} + \xi_{i2}$,
   where
   M_i = child mortality index for occupation i;
   Y_i = mean earnings in occupation i;
   U_i = percentage urban of persons in occupation i;
   D_{ij} = dummy variable indicating whether occupation i is a component of social class j (using English social-class categories);
   ξ_{ij} = error term, assumed to be normally distributed and uncorrelated with $ln Y_i$, U_i, and D_i .

These models are estimated using weighted least squares regression, where the weights are the number of children ever born in occupation group i. There are 93 specific occupational groups used in the United States and 116 in England and Wales. Note that the child mortality index is multiplied by 1000 to create the dependent variable in each case. Results are shown in Table 5.7.

Results from Model 1 (equations [1] and [2]) suggest that the mortality payoff to the earnings of an occupation was quite similar in the U.S. and in Britain. The coefficients of the earnings variable are -275 and -321, respectively. A 1 percent increase in earnings is associated with a reduction in the (untransformed) mortality indexes of 0.27 percent and 0.32 percent. Both coefficients are highly significant. The somewhat higher coefficient in England is consistent with the country's lower level of national income, since we expect to observe diminishing returns in the mortality effects of income gains, an effect not entirely captured by using a logarithmic transformation of income (Preston 1975). Since earnings were more unequally distributed in England and Wales, the similarity of coefficients implies that some of the greater inequality in child mortality in England resulted from the greater inequality of earnings.

Urban location exacted about twice as high a penalty in England as in the United States, which is roughly consistent with results of individual-level analysis. The amount of inequality in the urban/rural

TABLE 5.7

Regression Equations Predicting Child Mortality within Specific Occupational Groups: U.S., 1900, and England and Wales, 1911

	Model 1						Model 2					
	(1) U.S., 1900		(2) England and Wales, 1911		(3) U.S., 1900		(4) U.S., 1900		(5) England and Wales, 1911		(6) England and Wales, 1911	
Independent variables	Coefficient	Signifi-cance	Coefficient	Signifi-cance	Coefficient	Signifi-ficance	Coefficient	Signifi-cance	Coefficient	Signifi-cance	Coefficient	Signifi-cance
Constant	2,699.66	***	2,588.22	***	899.21	***	1,237.71	*	632.98	***	354.18	—
Percentage urban	2.63	***	5.27	***			1.12	—			5.39	***
Log husband's earnings (US$)	−274.72	***	−320.96	***			−59.27	—			−42.44	—
Husband's Social Class[a]												
Professional & Higher White-Collar					NI	NI	NI	NI	NI	NI	NI	NI
Lower White-Collar					62.90	—	25.19	—	228.82	***	242.50	***
Skilled Manual					243.50	***	217.53	***	353.94	***	362.78	***
Semi-skilled Manual					194.45	***	170.39	**	448.05	***	434.71	***
Unskilled Manual					318.00	***	282.56	***	647.63	***	637.96	***
Textile Workers					96.24	—	42.46	—	628.29	***	558.80	***
Miners/Mine Workers					70.26	—	80.21	—	718.92	***	808.09	***
Agricultural Laborers					245.59	***	233.14	—	184.48	***	603.96	***
N	93		116		93		93		116		116	
Adjusted R-Squared	0.175		0.210		0.261		0.252		0.723		0.813	
F-ratio	10.76	***	16.28	***	5.64	***	4.43	***	43.96	***	56.71	***

Source: See Tables 5.3, 5.6, and text. Also England and Wales 1914: tables 7, 8, 13, 15.

Note: Sample consists of married women with husband present. The dependent variable is 1000 times the child mortality index. The weights for the regressions are the number of children ever born for each observation. The observations are (husband's) occupational groups. For the U.S. sample, all women married 0–24 years were used to calculate the index. For England and Wales, all women married 0–14 years were used to calculate the index. The significance levels are: *** = significant at least at a 1 percent level; ** = significant at least at a 5 percent level; * = significant at least at a 10 percent level; — = not significant at least at a 10 percent level; NI = not included.

[a] 1911 English social classes.

distribution, however, was similar in the two countries. Inequality is at a maximum on a dichotomous categorical variable when the population is equally distributed between the two categories, and England and the U.S. were roughly equal distances from equality in their urban/rural distribution when comparable urban definitions are used.[9] Therefore, the disparity in coefficients of proportion urban contributes little to explaining inequality in mortality.[10]

Most of the variation in occupational mortality levels in either country is unexplained by Model 1, so earnings and urbanization differences are not the keys to understanding the international differences in occupational inequality in mortality. Furthermore, when social-class categories are introduced in Model 2 (equations [3]–[6]), the coefficients of earnings in both countries drop considerably in size, remain negative and similar to one another, and become statistically insignificant. The simple eight–category class variable constructed by the Registrar General of England and Wales conveys more information about mortality than do the earnings of the 100-odd detailed occupations. There is a spectacular difference in the amount of variance in occupational mortality explained by social class in England compared to the U.S. Model 2 (including all variables) explains 81 percent of the variance in England and 25 percent in the U.S. In addition, coefficients are much larger in England. Class variation in mortality remains greater even if the outlying "professional and higher white-collar" group is omitted.

It is possible that the British class variables work so much better in England because they were tailored to British circumstances (Szreter 1984). To examine this possibility, we repeated the analysis using the occupational categories in the United States for both countries. Results were scarcely altered: occupational class was far more significant in explaining mortality variation in England, and class variations themselves were much larger there.

Thus, it does not appear that wider disparities in earnings per se were responsible for most of the greater mortality inequality in England. Model 1 explains little of the variation in occupational mortality in either country, but Model 2, which introduces social class, explains the bulk of variation in England. Evidently, social class in England connoted a constellation of factors related to mortality: earnings, education, style of life, housing, security, residential amenities, privilege, empowerment, and so forth. English society was apparently far more stratified and differentiated along these lines than was American society at the time.

One factor that we are not able to measure adequately may have contributed to the larger social-class differentials in England: a greater degree of residential segregation by occupational class. We saw in Chapter 4 the importance of residential factors even when measured in such gross categories as size of place and region of residence. Public services such as water and sewer systems varied substantially within cities as well as across cities (Condran and Crimmins-Gardner 1978; Condran and Cheney 1982; Condran, Williams and Cheney 1984). Yet the dominant basis of segregation in Detroit (and probably other American cities) in the 1890s was still ethnicity rather than occupation (Zunz 1982). In other words, there was still a substantial mixture of social classes within smaller areas of the city, a mixture that would later disappear. It is likely that the more highly differentiated social-class system in England had manifested itself in residential distinctions as well. Ashby's monograph on infant mortality in England argues that "one of the reasons why infant mortality is so much higher in crowded industrial districts is that the people are all of one class, and that often the most ignorant. . . . In the towns there is not enough mixing of the classes for the very poorest to derive the benefit of contact with richer neighbors" (Ashby 1922:40). There were also important class divisions *across* cities, with the commercial elite and the professionals that served them heavily concentrated in London and the industrial activities concentrated in the North (Rubinstein 1977). In this context it is noteworthy that London had 13–25 percent lower mortality than did urban areas of the North (Table 5.1).

We are left without a wholly persuasive explanation of why British mortality differentials by social class were so much larger than those in the United States. Undoubtedly, the greater inequality of income in England was playing a role, but our set of occupational classes is far more predictive of mortality than is the income of detailed occupations. A higher degree of residential segregation by occupation in England, combined with residentially differentiated public service and weak diffusion of information and practices across places, may also be part of the explanation. In any event, we should beware of treating England's differentials as the norm. Matthiesson's (1972) study of social-class differences in child mortality in Copenhagen in the 1870s—the only other area that appears to have comparable historical data—shows them to be more similar to those in the United States than to those in Britain. For example, "teachers and clerks" had a value of $q(5)$ that was 88 percent of the value for Copenhagen as a whole, compared to values for the two groups (from Table 5.4) of 1.00 and .92 in the U.S. and .54 and .68 in England and Wales. As a city, Copenhagen would be expected to have larger occupational mortality differentials, as we demonstrated in Chapter 4. As Rubin-stein's study of social classes in Britain concludes,

> In so many ways Britain is an anomalous country: the first with a bour-geois revolution, the last with an aristocracy; the earliest with a modern working class . . . the earliest with industrialization, yet the last among the advanced countries to witness a merger of finance and industry, and so on. Britain is always an exceptional case, and too often its being first has been confused with its being the norm. Marx himself, one suspects, would have been better employed in the Library of Congress than in the British Museum. (Rubinstein 1977:126).

The contrast between the more rigid and hierarchical British class system and the more fluid, permeable, egalitarian American class system has become almost a cliché. Such a contrast could hardly be more vividly revealed than in patterns of class differences in child mortality at the turn of the century. Because of the long tradition of solid data on the subject in Britain, it has become a model for our understanding of these relations (e.g., Antonovsky 1967). Clearly, the model needs drastic alteration if it is to comprehend the Ameri-can situation. Yet we must not forget that a major dimension of strat-ification was operative in the United States and absent in England: race. As we showed in Chapter 4, even though there is relatively little statistical variation in this dichotomous variable, race was the single most important factor in predicting child mortality levels.[11] To a major extent, what occupational class was to England, race was to the United States.

Comparative Mortality Differentials in the United States in 1900, and Contemporary Developing Countries

The range of circumstances under which mortality differentials are compared can be greatly expanded by introducing data from contem-porary developing countries. England and the United States at the turn of the century were, after all, not too dissimilar in income levels, and they shared a common, and by modern standards rather primi-tive, base of health knowledge. Contemporary developing countries offer a sharp contrast on both of these dimensions. The scheme that underlines the analysis can be illustrated as shown in Table 5.8.

Obviously, both income and health knowledge are distributed along a continuum rather than dichotomously. But by choosing the two relatively discordant circumstances represented by cases B and C, we expect to be able to illuminate the important role of both sets

TABLE 5.8
Analytic Scheme For Comparing American Child Mortality in the Late
Nineteenth Century to That of Third World Countries Today

Level of economic development	Level of technical knowledge about health	
	Low	High
Low	(A) Third World countries in the nineteenth century	(B) Third World countries today
High	(C) United States in the late nineteenth century	(D) Developed countries today

of factors under varying circumstances. That the United States in the late nineteenth century was a relatively rich country is shown by the following data. According to the National Bureau of Economic Research's series of GNP estimates, per capita GNP in the United States in 1929 dollars rose from $415 to $497 between 1890 and 1900 (U.S. Bureau of the Census 1966: Series A11). Converted into 1982 dollars, the range is from $2,148 to $2,572. This places the United States in the period 1890–1900 in a range with Hungary, Portugal, Romania, Argentina, and Chile today (World Bank 1984:219). But while these latter countries have a life expectancy at birth of 70–71 years (ibid.), the United States in 1895–1900 had a life expectancy of only 49–51 years, as shown above.

The United States in 1890–1900 was also relatively well educated. Of youths aged 5–17, 78–79 percent were enrolled in school, although the average pupil appears to have attended school only the equivalent of about four months per year (U.S. Bureau of the Census 1966: Series B 36–39). In 1910, the median adult had attended school an average of 8.1 years (ibid.: Series B 40), and a prior absence of trend in school enrollment figures suggests that the figure was not much lower twenty years earlier. In the 1900 United States Census, 87.8 percent of ever-married women were literate, as were 89.0 percent of their husbands. Like income, these are also very high levels relative to most developing countries today.

Why didn't these high levels of literacy and income translate into higher levels of life expectancy? Our answer—tautologically correct in view of the universality of goals to improve health—is that the United States in this period simply did not know how to effect this conversion. As discussed in Chapter 1, the germ theory of disease still met with opposition or indifference in many circles as late as

1900. The filth or miasmatic theory of disease had occasionally led to effective public-health interventions, especially when combined with sensible empiricism. Where accepted, the germ theory added impetus and appropriate direction to these efforts. Urban residents had awakened to the importance of clean water and proper sewage disposal, but most were living without either. On the other hand, they appeared relatively indifferent to the cleanliness of the milk supply. Physicians and hospitals had few tools at their disposal to arrest the progress of disease, and home remedies enjoyed immense popularity. The most enlightened public-health officials, such as Charles Chapin and Herman Biggs, saw clearly the implications of germ theory for preventive health care, but they despaired at the difficulties of getting the word across to physicians, let alone parents.

By modern standards, ignorance about both preventive and curative health care was widespread in the United States at the turn of the century. As a result, we expect to observe a different pattern of mortality differentials than the pattern that prevails today in the developing world. In particular, there should have been much less payoff to increasing amounts of schooling in turn-of-the century America than in today's developing nations. Schooling effects should reflect only the accretion of material resources that result from the increased earnings opportunities; the additional portion of the effect that would reflect closer connection to good health knowledge and practice among the well-educated should be largely inoperative in a situation where education "buys" one little knowledge. Indeed, for similar reasons, the size of *all* social-class differentials in mortality should be smaller in the United States in the period 1890–1900.

In order to compare differentials in the U.S. in 1900 to those in developing countries today, we draw upon a study conducted by Barbara Mensch, Harold Lentzner, and Samuel Preston at the University of Pennsylvania (United Nations 1985). This study uses data on children ever born and surviving to study child mortality differentials in fifteen developing countries. The same analytic strategy was employed as in the present study, focussing on the ratio of the number of dead children to the expected number of dead children. For present purposes, four of the countries are excluded: Sierra Leone, Sudan, and Jamaica because of small sample size and/or severe regional restrictions in the sample, and Liberia because husbands could not be linked with wives.

Child mortality differentials by mother's educational attainment for the remaining eleven countries are converted into literacy differentials in Table 5.9. No other variables are controlled in this table. Lacking direct data on literacy in most of the developing countries, we

TABLE 5.9

Comparison of Relative Mortality Levels in Modern Developing Countries
and in the United States, 1900

	Literate/illiterate ratio[a]		Urban/rural ratio[b]
U.S., 1900	.697		1.279
	Series 1[c]	Series 2[d]	
Ghana, 1971	.495	.361	.732
Kenya, 1978	.666	.613	.809
Lesotho, 1977	.851	.861	1.055
Southern Nigeria, 1972	.609	.611	.816
Indonesia, 1971	.631	—	831
Nepal, 1976	.483	.313	.519
S. Korea, 1976	—	.714	.873
Sri Lanka, 1975	.634	—	.875
Thailand, 1975	.319	—	.580
Chile, 1970	.699	.583	.782
Peru, 1978	.357	.264	.604
Mean developing countries	.574	.540	.770

Source: Table 3.1, United Nations 1985.

[a] Ratio of child mortality among literate mothers to child mortality among illiterate mothers.

[b] Ratio of child mortality among urban mothers to child mortality among rural mothers.

[c] Assuming women with 4+ years of education are literate.

[d] Assuming women with 7+ years of education are literate.

have presented two series, one assuming that literacy is achieved with four years of schooling, and the other that it is achieved after seven years of schooling. In either series, the difference from the United States is appreciable. Of the eleven countries examined, only Lesotho and South Korea (and Chile in one series) show a lower payoff to literacy than did the United States in 1900.

Multivariate results show the contrast even more vividly, although the absence of identical variables in the different countries means that exact comparability in specification cannot be achieved. Nevertheless, such standard factors as educational attainment (or literacy) of mother and father, occupation of father, and urban/rural residence are available in all of the developing-country data sets as well as in the U.S. A well-known result is that mothers' education or literacy tends to retain a powerful effect in developing countries even after all other socioeconomic variables are controlled (e.g., Cochrane 1980; Clelland and van Ginneken 1988). Such a result is also observed in the developing countries examined here. The United Nations study (1985:56), which also uses weighted least squares regression of a woman's child mortality index, finds that the average coefficient for mothers' years of schooling in these countries, once all other variables are controlled, is about .034. If the illiterate have an average of one year of schooling and the literate an average of eight—reasonable figures in the United States in 1900—such a coefficient would imply that the literate should have about 25 percent lower mortality. But the coefficient on mothers' illiteracy in the United States reported in the final equation in Table 4-1 and in all the equations in Table 4.4 ranges between .06 and .14, only a quarter to a half of the expected effect for developing nations in the later twentieth century. Some of the literacy coefficients in the United States are also statistically insignificant, notably those for the urban and for the foreign-born populations. Literacy thus appears to matter least in the areas of greatest risk, namely the unhealthy urban environments.

The Children's Bureau study of eight American cities during 1911–15 included income data as well as literacy and many other variables. Literacy was dropped from the final report (Woodbury 1925), perhaps, as noted above, because preliminary results showed it to be unimportant. But a separate report on the largest city studied, Baltimore, presented a cross-tabulation of infant mortality by fathers' income and mothers' literacy (Rochester 1923). It is reproduced here as Table 5.10. Clearly, literacy has relatively little, if any, explanatory power after income is controlled, contrary to results observed in today's developing world.

Table 5.9 also shows very different relations between mortality and urban/rural residence in the United States and in today's developing countries. Urban residents (defined as living in places of 5,000+ residents to be more consistent with developing country definitions) had 28 percent *higher* mortality in the United States in 1900, compared to an average of 23 percent *lower* mortality in developing countries today. Multivariate results are also quite different for the two populations. In most of the developing countries examined, urban/rural residence loses its significance when other variables are introduced, and rural areas often have higher mortality than urban areas (United Nations 1985: ch. 11). The lower mortality of urban residents in developing countries as shown in Table 5.9 is thus primarily attrib-

TABLE 5.10

Infant Mortality Rate (per 1000 Births) by Literacy of Mother and Earnings of Father: Baltimore, 1915

Annual earnings of father	Literate mothers		Illiterate mothers	
	Infant mortality rate	Births(N)	Infant mortality rate	Births (N)
Under $450	161	1,193	143	349
$450–549	120	1,206	108	241
$550–649	107	1,314	126	174
$650 and above	79	5,660	86	233

Source: Rochester 1923:332.

utable to their higher social standing. But in the United States in 1900, urban residence loses no power when other variables are introduced; in some instances, the higher social status of urban residents actually served to mask some of the disadvantages of urban life. For example, the unvariate tabulations in Table 3.1 showed that residents in the 10 largest cities in 1900 had child mortality that was 23 percent higher than residents of cities with populations of 1,000–4,999. But when all other variables were controlled in equation (4) of Table 4.1, the differential increased to 30 percent. Cities posed a threat to life in the U.S. in 1900 that is simply no longer operative in developing countries.

Table 5.11 shows that occupational mortality differentials in the United States in 1900 are also much smaller than those observed in developing countries today. In particular, the professional/managerial/clerical classes had mortality levels only 7 percent lower than the national average, compared to the 35 percent advantage that this group enjoys, on average, in developing countries today. None of the eleven contemporary countries examined shows less than a 21 percent advantage for this group.

The other large discrepancy occurs for the agricultural group (farmers and farm laborers). This group had mortality 11 percent below average in the United States in the 1890s, but it shows mortality 21 percent above average in developing countries today. The comparison between professionals and agricultural classes is therefore particularly striking. Agricultural classes have mortality 85 percent *higher* than professional classes in the sample of LDCs today, but 5 percent *lower* mortality in the United States in 1890–1900.

TABE 5.11

Comparison of Relative Mortality in Different Occupational Classes: U.S., 1900, and Developing Countries in the 1970s

	Father's occupational category									
	Professional/ managerial/ clerical		Sales		Service		Agricultural		Production workers	
	Rel. mort.	Exp. deaths (N)	Rel. mort.	Exp. deaths (N)	Rel. mort.	Exp. deaths (N)	Rel. mort.	Exp. deaths (N)	Rel. mort.	Exp. deaths (N)
U.S., 1900	.933	769	.831	173	1.001	165	.890	3,375	1.150	2,967
Mean of eleven developing countries	.652		.913		.841		1.206		1.007	
Ghana, 1971	.621	2,948	.775	874	.665	1,179	1.128	30,446	.802	5,081
Kenya, 1978	.652	425	.887	388	.665	1,179	1.059	1,943	1.051	1,203
Lesotho, 1977	.743	66	1.343	35	.984	85	1.197	66	1.006	1,705
Southern Nigeria, 1972	.726	536	.933	252	.910	111	1.195	10,481	1.052	421
Indonesia, 1971	.789	11,721	1.033	6,850	1.002	2,402	1.000	43,467	1.028	3,965
Nepal, 1976	.784	187	.844	173	.760	148	.995	3,884	1.253	423
S. Korea, 1971	.673	101	.883	613	—	—	.956	1,266	1.088	491
Sri Lanka, 1975	.556	225	.868	242	.767	189	1.141	1,288	.938	771
Thailand, 1975	.606	132	.519	108	1.061	72	1.123	1,378	.881	278
Chile, 1970	.629	455	1.128	196	.866	135	1.213	685	1.059	1,444
Peru, 1978	.401	491	.828	406	.732	209	1.304	2,197	.921	1,242

Source: United Nations 1985 and sample of census enumerators' manuscripts, United States 1900.

Note: The relative mortality is the ratio of deaths to expected deaths among children ever born. Expected deaths are based upon the average child mortality level in a particular country.

The explanation for the poor performance of professional classes in the United States at the turn of the century is not to be found in a peculiar composition of the group. The subgroup that we can label the intelligentsia—those whom we expect to be best apprised of good hygienic practices—shares the unexpectedly high mortality of the professional classes. The combined group of physicians and surgeons, clergymen, teachers, lawyers, and pharmacists had a mortality index of .853 (Table 5.4; Preston 1985).[12] Preliminary tabulations from the U.S. Census of 1910, prepared at the University of Pennsylvania, continue to show only slight differences from national mortality levels for children of physicians or teachers.

Taking the figures in Table 5.11 one step farther, we can estimate the absolute (rather than the relative) mortality of children born into the different classes in the United States during 1890–1900 and in a composite of LDCs today. The composite is formed in the following way. The level of life expectancy at birth in LDCs in 1975–1980, as estimated by the United Nations (1983b), was 54.8 years. This corresponds to level 15.6 in the Coale-Demeny West model life tables. At that level, the probability of dying before age 5 ($q[5]$) is .137. The mean of relative mortality levels for a particular class in Table 5.11 for our eleven LDCs is then applied to this figure to produce the values in Table 5.12. This procedure assumes that the average relationship observed among the eleven countries is representative of the average of all LDCs. "West" mortality levels are in fact relatively close: an average level of 14.9 for our eleven countries, versus 15.6 for LDCs as an aggregate. The United States 1900 West level is estimated to be

TABLE 5.12
Estimated Probability of Dying before Age 5 in Two Populations

Father's occupational category	U.S., 1900	Composite of developing countries, 1975–80	Ratio
Professional, Managerial, Clerical	.165	.089	.539
Sales	.146	.125	.856
Service	.176	.115	.653
Agricultural	.157	.165	1.051
Production Workers	.202	.138	.683
All classes	.176	.137	.778

Source: Table 5.11 and Chapter 2.

13.65 (see Chapter 2), and relative mortalities in Table 5.11 are applied to the $q(5)$ of .176 that corresponds to that level. There is good reason to suppose that the multiplicative property of $q(x)$ that is implicit in our procedure is valid to a close approximation (Trussell and Preston 1982).

Table 5.12 shows that the United States in 1900 had much higher child mortality than today's developing world in every occupational class except agricultural workers. Its disadvantage was particularly great among the professional/managerial classes. The United States professional classes in 1900, in fact, had no better child mortality than agricultural workers in developing countries today, who are by every account a seriously disadvantaged group. The combination of high national income, high national literacy, and high relative social status in 1900 produced the same mortality level as is observed in the most disadvantaged large social group in the world today. Clearly, the manner in which material resources are converted into mortality levels has changed dramatically (see also Preston 1975, 1980).

So the failure to achieve satisfactory mortality conditions in the United States at this time was widespread. It extended to the literate, to professionals, and especially to urban residents. In our view, it principally reflected the shortage of specific techniques that could be used to reduce the incidence and severity of infectious diseases as well as a failure to implement some of the techniques that had recently become available. In developing countries today, the mother's education or literacy appears to retain such a high degree of explanatory power because it is associated with such health behaviors as vaccination of children, maintenance of hygienic conditions in the home, and receipt of professional health care for maternity and for child illness (Clelland and van Ginneken 1988; Rutstein, et al. 1988). But vaccines existed only against smallpox in 1900, and the care that women and children received from physicians or midwives was often misguided and uninformed. Perhaps most important, there was still only a dim appreciation that the transmission of the major childhood diseases could be blunted by simple preventative public and private measures involving milk, water, food, handwashing, isolation, and the like. A growing recognition of the value of these measures is likely to be a major source of rapid declines in American child mortality in the first three decades of the twentieth century (Ewbank and Preston 1989).

Admittedly, the relatively high mortality levels seen in the professional classes reflected in part the lower standards of admission into these classes at the time. But in the case of physicians, the most telling of our categories, the low standards for practice were associated with the shortage of medical knowledge of certifiable accuracy. The ascendance of the germ theory and of demonstrably effective diphtheria antitoxin was the major impetus for the reform of medical standards in 1910 (Kunitz 1974). In a sense, then, the low admission standards were simply another reflection of how little specialized knowledge the professions controlled.

The high levels of mortality also reflect a failure to activate fully the political institutions that were capable of preventing the spread of disease. C.E.A. Winslow argued that, in assigning responsibility for rapid health progress, the discovery of the possibility of widespread social organization to combat disease could almost be placed alongside the discovery of the germ theory in importance (Shryock 1957:56). The excess mortality among urban residents in 1900 (and in England in 1911), now averted in poor and rich countries alike, is clear evidence that political institutions were far from realizing their potential for improving health conditions.

Those who consider the death rate to be a relatively simple function of economic resources in the family or in society at large can find little support in these results. Undoubtedly, economic factors were important in differentiating among mortality levels at the turn of the century—perhaps even more important than at present—but they were merely variations on a theme of ignorance and incapacity that principally distinguishes that era from the present. Advances in science, diffusion of knowledge of preventive measures, and improvements in social organization, rather than economic growth per se, appear primarily responsible for the dramatic successes that were to come, both in the U.S. and in much poorer countries.

SIX

YESTERDAY AND TODAY: RESTATEMENT OF A

MAIN THEME

IN 1900, the United States was the richest country in the world (Cole and Deane 1965: Table IV). Its population was also highly literate and exceptionally well-fed. On the scale of per capita income, literacy, and food consumption, it would rank in the top quarter of countries were it somehow transplanted to the present. Yet 18 percent of its children were dying before age 5, a figure that would rank in the bottom quarter of contemporary countries.

Why couldn't the United States translate its economic and social advantages into better levels of child survival? Our explanation is that infectious disease processes, those principally responsible for the foreshortening of life, were still poorly understood by public officials, by most physicians, and by individual parents; that few effective technologies based upon the new understandings had been developed; that those technologies which were developed had been slow to diffuse; and that the assumption of public responsibility for such private matters as child death was still incomplete and often ineffective.

The high level of mortality that existed amidst the relatively affluent American population casts further doubt on explanations of twentieth-century mortality decline that emphasize improvements in material resources. Thomas McKeown (e.g., 1976) has been the most influential spokesman for such a position. By process-of-elimination reasoning and without any direct evidence for his well-known claims, McKeown argues that improvements in diet were responsible for most of the British mortality improvements between 1848 and 1972. Such an explanation appears highly implausible in the United States, where food was abundant and relatively inexpensive by the turn of the century. Since American mortality has closely paralleled British mortality from the late nineteenth century to the present, our results also cast doubt on the British explanation, which in addition suffers from internal inconsistencies and evidentiary shortcomings (e.g., Szreter 1988).

We believe that McKeown is correct that the mortality decline since the middle of the nineteenth century owes little to specific drugs and medicines. In fact, McKinlay and McKinlay (1977) have replicated McKeown's demonstrations in the United States during the twentieth century. But the new understanding of infectious disease processes led to many other forms of innovation besides medicines. Public-health officials had new and vastly improved criteria to use in cleaning up water and milk supplies, and a much stronger rationale for their work. And individual parents had access to many new, or newly justified, methods for reducing death risks in the home: boiling milk and sterilizing bottles, methods first introduced in the 1890s; washing hands before preparing meals; protecting food from flies and other sources of contamination; isolating sick family members; and so on. They also had access to physicians who were better equipped to deal with the hazards of the birth process and to render sensible advice on health maintenance. Parenthood became more arduous than when the principal sources of disease were seen to lay outside the home; but the new procedures undoubtedly contributed to twentieth-century advances in survival.

Further evidence that lack of know-how rather than lack of resources was principally responsible for foreshortening life in the United States in the 1890s is the pattern of social-class differences in child mortality. Those classes which we expect to have had superior mortality because of better awareness of good hygienic practices and closer connection to networks of professional expertise simply did not enjoy a substantial mortality advantage in the late nineteenth century. Professionals did not have child mortality levels that were very different from those of other groups, and literate classes enjoyed less of an advantage than they do today. Particularly telling is the mortality of offspring of doctors, which was only 6 percent below the national average. Undoubtedly, the relative affluence of the American population and the relatively small inequalities in income helped to protect the poorest groups from some of the most damaging incursions of poverty, which were much more evident in England. But the upper classes appear to have added little in the way of behavioral advantages to their intrinsic material advantages. It is noteworthy that, by 1925, teachers and physicians had relative levels of child mortality that were 64 percent and 66 percent of the national average, respectively compared to their values of 100 percent and 94 percent in 1895 (Ewbank and Preston 1989).

In place of a sharp differentiation now commonly associated with behavioral differences among classes were important variations in mortality according to factors over which individuals had little or no control. The single most important variable in predicting child morality levels, whether in the presence or in the absence of other variables, was race. Race was a caste-like status in 1900, and the degraded social and economic circumstances of blacks, who had virtually no chance of entering the mainstream of American life, is undoubtedly reflected in their exceptionally high mortality. The importance of economic circumstances is also reflected in the role played by husband's unemployment and level of state income in explaining variation in child mortality levels, as shown in Chapter 4.

To clarify: we are not arguing that economic factors are unimportant in establishing levels of mortality in 1900 or today. We presented evidence of their importance in Chapter 4, and Woodbury's (1925) study of urban infant mortality two decades later makes even clearer the critical role of father's income. But we *are* arguing that the growth of income during the twentieth century could not have been the principal factor causing mortality to *decline*. Developing countries, and social classes within countries, that have today achieved income levels no better than those in the United States in 1900 have child mortality levels only a quarter of that in the United States at that time. Even if the special economic and social afflictions of the black population in 1900 could be eliminated so that blacks achieved the same mortality level as whites, the black child mortality level would still have been higher than India's in the 1980s, and more than twice that of China.

After race, the variable whose absence would be most costly to our ability to explain variation in child mortality levels is size of place. Larger cities had higher child mortality in the late nineteenth century, despite having administrative structures that facilitated the introduction of public-health measures. People furthest from the reach of the modern state—and furthest from one another—enjoyed the best health conditions. The excess child mortality of city residents, now averted in poor and rich countries alike, is simply another indication of the extent to which people remained in the grip of natural forces. Our evidence on mortality trends in Chapter 3 suggests that this grip was beginning to weaken in cities. But a satisfactory escape would await the technical and social triumphs of the twentieth century.

APPENDIX A

ASSIGNING INCOME AND UNEMPLOYMENT ESTIMATES TO INDIVIDUALS IN THE NATIONAL SAMPLE OF THE 1900 UNITED STATES CENSUS

T HE AVAILABLE economic data in the manuscripts of the 1900 United States Census of Population are rather limited. The manuscripts of the censuses of agriculture and manufactures for 1900 appear to have been destroyed, eliminating the possibilities of linked data from those sources. The census provided information on the occupation of the individual. Each person aged 10 years or over who was occupied in gainful labor was asked for the profession, trade, or branch of work in which he or she was engaged "ordinarily" during the "larger part of the time." This was stated even if the person was, or had been, unemployed. The number of months unemployed during the previous year was also asked. Finally, information was collected concerning whether the home or farm was owned or rented and, if owned, whether owned free or mortgaged. No data on income or wages were collected (U.S. Bureau of the Census 1979:32–37).

In order to measure the impact of income on child mortality, a procedure was developed to impute average incomes to various occupations. The procedure used the list of occupations from the 1900 sample coded according to the 1900 occupational coding system and assigned to each an average annual income for a date close to the census. The major sources used were Stanley Lebergott's historical study of American labor (Lebergott 1964), which provided data for 1899; Paul Douglas's study of real wages in the United States since (Douglas 1930), which gave data for 1899 or 1900; and the 1901 cost-of-living survey conducted by Carroll Wright, U.S. Commissioner of Labor (U.S. Commissioner of Labor 1903: Table II-B, pp. 264–82). In the cost-of-living survey, only frequencies for grouped intervals of income were given, and so means for intervals were assumed. (For example, the mean for the interval $400–499 was assumed to be $450.) A list of the occupations and imputed incomes is given in Table A.1. Occupations that were not available from the various sources are assigned an income, either the average for the occupational category as a whole or the average for a similar occupation for which an average income was known. The most important exception was farmers, for whom income depended on type and size of farm, crop prices, harvest size, etc. It was felt that too much uncertainty was associated with this occupation to make an imputation.

No adjustment was made to the incomes directly for obvious variations by age and sex. Adjustments for this were made separately during the analysis. An estimate of age/earnings profile was made from the 1889–90 U.S. Commissioner of Labor Survey on income and expenditures, from which an index was made (U.S. Commissioner of Labor 1890, 1891; Haines 1979c). The index values were: age 10–19: .700; 20–29: .955; 30–39: 1.086; 40–49: 1.099; 50–59: .910; 60 and over: .726, with the base being the overall mean. On the basis of this observed pattern, it was decided to include a parabolic function of husband's age in the regression analysis (i.e., husband's age and husband's age squared). The lower level of female incomes was generally taken into account in the low incomes of predominantly female occupations, such as milliners, seamstresses, and domestic servants. A correction factor of .705 for lower female incomes in mixed occupations was imputed from Lebergott (1964:488).

In addition to average incomes, occupational averages with respect to months unemployed were also assigned to each individual on the basis of the individual's occupation. The unemployment variables were the average months unemployed for that occupation and the proportion of the occupation reporting some unemployment in the twelve months prior to the census. These results were tabulated from the census sample only for males aged 10 and over. The occupation-specific values for average months unemployed and proportion reporting some months unemployed are also given in Table A.1, along with the frequencies for each occupation.

TABLE A.1
Imputed Income and Estimated Number of Months Unemployed for Men in Various Occupations: U.S., 1900

Code	Occupation	Frequency	Imputed annual income ($)	Source	Avg. months unemployed	Proportion reporting at least one month unemployed
	Agricultural pursuits	13,691	334	CW	0.78	0.20
6	Farm & Plantation Laborers	2,836	255	PD	1.50	0.38
7	Farm Labor (family)	2,976	255	PD	1.39	0.37
8	Garden & Nursery Labor	43	255	PD	1.06	0.21
11	Dairy Workers	35	255	PD	0.21	0.03
16	Farmers & Planters	7,101	NI	—	0.29	0.07
17	Farmers (family)	318	NI	—	0.35	0.11

Code	Occupation	Frequency	Imputed annual income ($)	Source	Avg. months unemployed	Proportion reporting at least one month unemployed
18	Farm, Plantation Overseers	21	750	CW	0.21	0.05
21	Gardeners	59	413	CW	1.29	0.27
22	Florists, Nurserymen, Vinegrowers	20	593	CW	0.28	0.06
23	Fruit Growers	17	334	CW	0.00	0.00
26	Lumbermen & Raftsmen	87	356	CW	1.13	0.39
31	Stock Raisers	50	334	CW	0.00	0.00
32	Stock Herders & Drovers	59	334	CW	1.65	0.43
36	Turpentine Farmers & Labor	40	334	CW	1.15	0.33
41	Wood Choppers	23	400	CW	0.80	0.25
47	Agricultural—not specified	6	334	CW	2.00	0.50
	Professional service	1,530	865	CW	0.78	0.17
56	Actors	18	865	CW	1.18	0.36
57	Professional Showmen	16	865	CW	1.87	0.33
58	Theatrical Managers	2	865	CW	0.00	0.00
61	Architects	8	1,000	S	0.00	0.00
62	Designers, Draftsmen, Inventors	23	1,000	S	0.48	0.14
66	Engineers (civil)	14	1,033	CW	1.85	0.31
67	Engineers (mechanical, electrical)	22	979	CW	1.21	0.26
68	Engineers (mining)	5	979	CW	0.00	0.00
69	Surveyors	7	1,200	S	1.43	0.29
71	Authors & Scientists	8	1,000	S	0.75	0.25
72	Librarians & Assistants	8	1,100	CW		
73	Chemists, Assayers, Metallurgy	11	974	SL	0.00	0.00
76	Officials (national)	52	605	SL	0.00	0.00
77	Officials (state)	3	605	SL	0.00	0.00
78	Officials (county)	17	605	SL	0.00	0.00
79	Officials (city)	12	605	SL	0.45	0.09
81	Physicians, Surgeons	175	1,000	S	0.11	0.02
82	Teachers	537	590	CW	2.87	0.64
83	Professors (college, univ.)	12	1,200	S	4.29	0.71
86	Veterinary Surgeons	14	1,200	S	0.64	0.18
87	Professional (not specified)	9	865	CW	3.50	0.50
91	Artists, Teachers of Art	31	1,050	CW	0.12	0.06
92	Clergymen	128	730	PD	0.34	0.07
93	Dentists	32	900	CW	0.22	0.04
94	Electricians	63	837	CW	0.30	0.09
96	Journalists	38	928	CW	0.52	0.06
97	Lawyers	149	1,200	S	0.24	0.04
98	Musicians, Teachers of Music	116	670	CW	0.82	0.20
	Domestic & personal service	7,539	243/332	SL	1.64	0.40
106	Janitors	76	552	CW	0.33	0.10
107	Sextons	4	488	CW	0.00	0.00

Code	Occupation	Frequency	Imputed annual income ($)	Source	Avg. months unemployed	Proportion reporting at least one month unemployed
111	Elevator Tenders	15	469	CW	0.00	0.00
112	Laborers (coal yard)	2	373	CW	2.00	0.50
113	Laborers (general)	3,464	373	CW	2.04	0.50
114	Longshoremen	33	540	CW	2.41	0.48
116	Stevedores	11	540	CW	2.10	0.60
121	Laundry Work (hand)	500	209	SL	0.39	0.08
122	Laundry Work (steam)	20	551	CW	0.20	0.10
126	Nurses (trained)	14	450	CW	0.00	0.00
127	Nurses (not specified)	211	209	SL	0.67	0.11
128	Midwives	6	243	SL		
131	Servants	2,022	243	SL	0.69	0.19
132	Waiters	113	509	CW	1.31	0.31
136	Soldiers	143	450	S	0.23	0.15
137	Sailors	9	467	CW	1.67	0.67
138	Marines	1	450	S	0.00	0.00
141	Watchmen, Policemen	137	592/887	CW	0.32	0.08
142	Firemen	21	874	CW	0.00	0.00
146	Bootblacks	9	430	CW	0.33	0.11
147	Hunters, Trappers, Guides	12	334	S	0.00	0.00
148	Domestic Service (not specified)	17	243	SL	0.60	0.10
151	Barbers & Hairdressers	160	605	CW	0.41	0.09
152	Bartenders	130	647	CW	0.70	0.12
153	Boarding- & Lodging-House Keepers	82	500	S	1.29	0.14
154	Hotel Keepers	72	750	S	0.35	0.06
156	Housekeepers & Stewards	132	350/725	CW	0.33	0.11
157	Restaurant Keepers	23	750	CW	0.00	0.00
158	Saloon Keepers	100	750	S	0.01	0.01
	Trade & transportation	5,939	620/639 510/505	CW SL	0.48	0.11
206	Agents (insurance & real estate)	157	743	CW	0.23	0.04
207	Agents (not specified)	130	758	CW	0.60	0.11
211	Bankers & Brokers (stock)	107	1,500	S	1.78	0.16
212	Brokers (commercial)	16	1,200	S	0.00	0.00
216	Boatmen & Canalmen	12	500	CW	2.00	0.42
217	Pilots	3	942	CW	0.00	0.00
218	Sailors	78	467	CW	0.94	0.27
221	Clerks & Copyists	844	714	CW	0.44	0.10
222	Clerks (shipping)	36	600	S	0.16	0.03
223	Letter & Mail Carriers	30	919	CW	0.43	0.04
226	Draymen, Teamsters, Expressmen	625	546	CW	0.74	0.19
227	Carriage & Hack Drivers	66	555	CW	0.15	0.05
231	Foremen (livery stable)	2	669	CW	0.00	0.00
232	Foremen (steam railroad)	54	646	CW	0.08	0.04
233	Foremen (street railway)	2	690	CW	0.00	0.00

Code	Occupation	Frequency	Imputed annual income ($)	Source	Avg. months unemployed	Proportion reporting at least one month unemployed
234	Foremen (not specified)	15	823	CW	0.00	0.00
241	Merchants (boots, shoes)	20	1,100	SL	0.77	0.15
242	Merchants (cigars, tobacco)	15	1,100	SL	0.00	0.00
243	Merchants (clothing)	21	1,100	SL	0.12	0.06
244	Merchants (coal & wood)	18	1,100	SL	0.00	0.00
246	Merchants (drugs, medicines)	66	1,100	SL	0.44	0.07
247	Merchants (dry goods, notions)	52	1,100	SL	0.00	0.00
248	Merchants (general store)	30	1,100	SL	0.00	0.00
249	Merchants (groceries)	176	1,100	SL	0.02	0.01
251	Merchants (liquors, wines)	13	1,100	SL	0.00	0.00
252	Merchants (lumber)	26	1,100	SL	0.00	0.00
253	Merchants (produce, provisions)	88	1,100	SL	0.23	0.08
254	Merchants (not specified)	351	1,100	SL	0.28	0.06
256	Bundle & Cash Boys	17	400	S	0.50	0.13
257	Messengers	46	500	CW	0.79	0.12
258	Office Boys	21	400	S	0.95	0.10
261	Bank Officials, Cashiers	26	1,500	CW	0.63	0.05
262	Officials (insurance & trust cos.)	6	1,500	CW	0.00	0.00
263	Officials (trade cos.)	12	1,500	CW	0.00	0.00
264	Officials (transportation cos.)	41	1,500	CW	0.00	0.00
266	Steam RR Baggagemen	13	708	CW	0.82	0.18
267	Steam RR Brakemen	99	638	CW	0.31	0.14
268	Steam RR Conductors	52	944	CW	0.21	0.09
269	Steam RR Engineers, Firemen	126	992/711	CW	0.45	0.10
271	Steam RR Laborers	351	462	CW	1.04	0.30
272	Steam RR Station Agents, Employees	58	843	CW	0.12	0.06
273	Steam RR Switchmen, Yardmen	49	682/533	CW	0.02	0.02
276	Stenographers	123	780	CW	0.08	0.03
277	Typewriters	11	780	CW	0.00	0.00
281	Street Railway Conductors	20	654	CW	0.75	0.10
282	Street Railway Drivers	1	650	CW	0.00	0.00
283	Street Railway Laborers	7	462	CW	1.00	0.40
284	Street Railway Motormen	43	634	CW	0.32	0.11
291	Telegraph Operators	76	742	CW	0.40	0.10
292	Telephone Operators	29	500	CW	0.00	0.00
301	Bookkeepers & Accountants	344	819	CW	0.45	0.09
302	Commercial Travelers	123	1,010	CW	0.31	0.09
303	Hostlers	78	581	CW	0.83	0.22
304	Hucksters & Peddlers	103	400	CW	0.73	0.18
306	Livery-Stable Keepers	28	502	CW	0.00	0.00
307	Wholesale Merchants, Dealers	94	1,100	SL	0.23	0.04
308	Packers & Shippers	56	534	CW	1.19	0.34
309	Porters & Helpers (stores)	79	521	CW	0.88	0.18
311	Salesmen & Saleswomen	635	680	CW	0.38	0.07

Code	Occupation	Frequency	Imputed annual income ($)	Source	Avg. months unemployed	Proportion reporting at least one month unemployed
312	Telegraph & Telephone Linemen	16	681	CW	0.46	0.08
313	Undertakers	19	689	CW	0.18	0.06
321	Auctioneers	2	620	S	0.00	0.00
323	Newspaper Carriers	9	483	CW	0.63	0.13
324	Weighers, Gaugers, Measurers	1	600	CW	0.00	0.00
326	Trade & Transport (not specified)	8	631	CW	1.83	0.50
331	Conductors (not specified)	31	799	CW	0.39	0.11
332	Railroad Employees (not specified)	33	639	CW	0.50	0.19
	Building trades	1,586	661	CW	2.07	0.47
416	Carpenters & Joiners	782	630	CW	2.00	0.47
417	Ship Carpenters	24	638	CW	1.30	0.25
418	Apprentices (carpentry)	2	425	CW	4.00	0.50
421	Masons	197	775	CW	3.12	0.65
422	Masons' Laborers	12	356	CW	1.82	0.55
423	Apprentices (mason)	2	519	CW	0.00	0.00
426	Painters, Glaziers, Varnishers	300	624	CW	2.14	0.49
427	Painters (carriages)	26	627	CW	0.77	0.27
431	Paper Hangers	26	651	CW	2.36	0.44
436	Plasterers	49	712	CW	3.50	0.70
441	Plumbers, Steam Fitters	130	850	CW	0.85	0.21
442	Apprentice Plumbers	11	489	CW	2.50	0.50
446	Roofers & Slaters	13	615	CW	1.23	0.31
447	Apprentice Roofers	1	412	CW	—	—
450	Mechanics (not specified)	11	661	CW	1.67	0.22
	Chemicals	42	560	CW	0.49	0.14
466	Oil-Well Employees	23	560	CW	0.63	0.21
467	Oil-Works Employees	7	560	CW	0.71	0.14
471	Chemical-Works Employees	3	560	CW	0.00	0.00
472	Fertilizer Makers	1	560	CW	0.00	0.00
473	Powder & Cartridge Makers	6	560	CW	0.00	0.00
474	Salt-Works Employees	2	560	CW	—	—
486	Brick Makers	44	500	CW	2.48	0.60
487	Tile Makers	6	483	CW	1.33	0.33
491	Glass Workers	57	740	CW	2.18	0.67
492	Marble & Stone Cutters	83	781	CW	1.54	0.36
493	Potters	14	747	CW	0.67	0.25
	Fishing & mining	857	—	—	1.99	0.50
506	Miners (coal)	367	482	CW	2.24	0.60
507	Miners (gold & silver)	44	841	CW	1.10	0.35
508	Miners (not specified)	283	482	CW	1.67	0.41
509	Quarrymen	68	532	CW	1.98	0.45
510	Fishermen & Oystermen	95	550	CW	2.44	0.49

Code	Occupation	Frequency	Imputed annual income ($)	Source	Avg. months unemployed	Proportion reporting at least one month unemployed
	Food products	375	607	CW	0.67	0.14
526	Fish Curers & Packers	1	570	CW	3.00	1.00
527	Meat, Fruit Canners, Preservers	10	570	S	1.00	0.17
528	Meat Packers, Curers, Picklers	19	570	CW	0.61	0.17
529	Sugar Makers, Refiners	4	586	S	0.25	0.25
531	Food Preparers (not specified)	9	607	CW	0.00	0.00
536	Bakers	93	629	CW	0.68	0.15
537	Butchers	119	607	CW	0.75	0.13
538	Butter & Cheese Makers	31	650	CW	0.56	0.15
539	Confectioners	42	586	CW	0.52	0.08
541	Millers	47	796	CW	0.74	0.18
	Iron & steel industry	1,138	685	CW	0.89	0.21
556	Blacksmiths	281	689	CW	0.87	0.17
557	Blacksmiths' Apprentices	12	507	CW	0.36	0.09
561	Iron & Steel Workers	240	665	CW	1.24	0.30
562	Molders	97	735	CW	1.13	0.28
566	Machinists	326	736	CW	0.64	0.15
567	Machinists' Apprentices	22	485	CW	0.63	0.21
571	Steam-Boiler Makers	40	754	CW	1.29	0.18
572	Steam-Boiler Helpers	9	511	CW	1.14	0.14
576	Stove, Furnace, Grate Makers	20	665	S	0.88	0.31
577	Tool & Cutlery Workers	42	881	CW	0.56	0.15
578	Wheelwrights	29	700	CW	0.85	0.19
579	Wire Workers	20	674	CW	0.35	0.18
	Leather products	364	600	CW	1.33	0.29
606	Boot & Shoe Factory Operatives	112	649	CW	2.05	0.57
607	Shoemakers	130	452	CW	1.15	0.22
610	Harness & Saddle Makers	54	594	CW	0.37	0.07
616	Leather Curriers	22	537	CW	3.14	0.50
617	Leather Tanners	35	555	CW	0.79	0.17
621	Trunk Makers	6	503	CW	0.00	0.00
622	Leather Case, Pocketbook Makers	5	617	CW	0.00	0.00
	Liquors & beverages	48	676	CW	1.05	0.20
636	Bottlers	21	558	CW	0.83	0.22
641	Brewers & Maltsters	22	764	CW	1.00	0.16
642	Distillers & Rectifiers	5	800	CW	2.25	0.25
	Lumber products	411	572	CW	1.19	0.31
656	Saw & Planing Mill Workers	156	572	CW	1.50	0.36
657	Lumber-Yard Employees	20	572	CW	1.81	0.50
661	Basket Makers	8	470	CW	1.86	0.43

Code	Occupation	Frequency	Imputed annual income ($)	Source	Avg. months unemployed	Proportion reporting at least one month unemployed
662	Box Makers (wood)	8	462	CW	1.75	0.25
663	Furniture Manufactory Employees	37	582	CW	1.15	0.24
664	Piano & Organ Makers	16	662	CW	0.67	0.33
666	Woodworkers (not specified)	74	550	CW	0.60	0.23
671	Cabinet Makers	50	662	CW	0.78	0.22
672	Coopers	42	541	CW	1.32	0.34
	Other metal products	351	665	CW	0.82	0.24
706	Brass Workers	33	644	CW	0.92	0.16
707	Brass Molders	11	756	CW	0.64	0.18
711	Clock-Factory Operatives	4	450	CW	0.00	0.00
712	Watch-Factory Operatives	23	883	CW	0.67	0.06
713	Clock & Watch Repairers	6	900	S	1.50	0.33
716	Gold & Silver Workers	12	607	CW	1.89	0.56
717	Jewelry Manufactory Employees	19	660	CW	0.25	0.17
722	Tinners & Tinware Makers	94	656	CW	0.60	0.23
723	Apprentice Tinsmiths	1	439	CW	0.00	0.00
726	Copper Workers	7	775	CW	1.00	0.29
727	Electroplaters	10	800	CW	0.38	0.13
728	Gunsmiths, Locksmiths	17	610	CW	0.80	0.27
729	Lead & Zinc Workers	2	665	CW	0.00	0.00
732	Metalworkers (not specified)	112	665	CW	1.07	0.30
	Paper & printing	368	743	CW	0.71	0.14
756	Printers & Pressmen	154	720	CW	0.69	0.13
757	Lithographers	10	877	CW	0.00	0.00
758	Compositors	57	784	CW	0.73	0.16
759	Electrotypers, Stereotypers	6	950	CW	0.00	0.00
761	Apprentice Printers	3	482	CW	3.67	0.33
766	Bookbinders	51	713	CW	0.68	0.11
767	Box Makers (paper)	18	530	CW	0.00	0.00
768	Engravers	7	960	CW	1.17	0.33
769	Paper & Pulp Mill Operatives	62	579	CW	0.82	0.16
	Textiles	1,790	530	CW	1.14	0.29
806	Bleachery Operatives	6	417	CW	1.00	0.40
807	Dye-Works Operatives	24	460	CW	0.87	0.17
811	Carpet-Factory Operatives	30	565	CW	1.21	0.36
812	Cotton-Mill Operatives	260	523	CW	1.17	0.27
813	Hosiery, Knitting-Mill Operatives	49	530	CW	0.44	0.11
814	Silk-Mill Operatives	72	577	CW	0.57	0.20
816	Woolen-Mill Operatives	72	502	CW	0.90	0.26
821	Hemp- & Jute-Mill Operatives	1	502	S	—	—
822	Linen-Mill Operatives	2	502	S	0.00	0.00
823	Print-Works Operatives	6	502	S	0.20	0.20

Code	Occupation	Frequency	Imputed annual income ($)	Source	Avg. months unemployed	Proportion reporting at least one month unemployed
824	Rope & Cordage Factory Operatives	5	502	S	0.00	0.00
826	Worsted-Mill Operatives	7	502	CW	2.25	0.25
827	Textile (not specified)	122	530	CW	1.21	0.25
831	Dressmakers	411	280	SL	2.25	0.50
832	Apprentice Dressmakers	2	188	SL	—	—
836	Milliners	117	389	SL	0.00	0.00
837	Apprentice Milliners	1	245	SL	—	—
841	Tailors & Tailoresses	265	599	CW	1.21	0.35
842	Apprentice Tailors	2	405	CW	4.00	0.50
846	Hat & Cap Makers	31	640	CW	1.61	0.35
847	Seamstresses	165	288	CW	1.00	0.20
848	Shirt, Collar, Cuff Makers	51	388	PD	1.06	0.35
851	Carpet (rag) Makers	1	400	CW	—	—
852	Lace & Embroidery Makers	14	388	PD	1.00	0.25
853	Sail, Awning & Tent Makers	6	681	CW	1.40	0.40
854	Sewing Machine Operators	5	550	CW	—	—
856	Textile Workers (not specified)	63	530	CW	1.44	0.36
	Miscellaneous industries	2,457	—	—	0.75	0.19
906	Manufacturers & Officials	221	1,250	S	0.20	0.04
907	Builders & Contractors	67	1,200	S	0.49	0.12
908	Publishers of Books/Maps/Papers	9	1,100	S	0.00	0.00
909	Officials of Mining Cos.	15	1,500	S	0.00	0.00
911	Broom & Brush Makers	22	503	CW	1.82	0.35
912	Charcoal, Coke, & Lime Burners	13	520	CW	0.91	0.18
913	Engineers & Firemen (not locomotive)	253	749/595	CW	0.80	0.19
914	Glove Makers	10	641	CW	0.50	0.25
916	Model & Pattern Makers	20	794	CW	0.35	0.12
917	Photographers	34	823	CW	0.69	0.14
918	Rubber-Factory Operatives	36	488	CW	1.05	0.40
919	Tobacco- & Cigar-Factory Operatives	190	603	CW	1.05	0.28
921	Upholsterers	37	606	CW	1.61	0.39
926	Apprentices (not specified)	44	373	S	0.74	0.13
927	Artificial-Flower Makers	3	373	S	—	—
928	Button Makers	15	557	CW	0.57	0.29
929	Candle, Soap, Tallow Makers	5	450	S	0.50	0.25
931	Corset Makers	14	450	S	0.00	0.00
932	Cotton Ginners	1	450	S	2.00	1.00
933	Electric Light & Power Employees	19	676	CW	0.00	0.00
934	Gas-Works Employees	9	676	CW	1.44	0.33
936	Piano & Organ Tuners	2	867	CW	0.00	0.00
937	Straw Workers	1	450	S	—	—
939	Umbrella & Parasol Makers	7	450	S	0.00	0.00

Code	Occupation	Frequency	Imputed annual income ($)	Source	Avg. months unemployed	Proportion reporting at least one month unemployed
941	Well Borers	8	650	CW	2.57	0.71
942	Whitewashers	10	312	CW	4.50	0.90
943	Unspecified	253	450	S	0.82	0.28
946	Uncodable employment	532	450	S	0.74	0.17
947	Housekeeper, Steward, Domestic Resident	389	243	S	0.00	0.00
951	Officials, Societies & Institutions	10	1,200	S	1.11	0.11
952	Managers, Officials, Proprietors	53	1,200	S	0.17	0.05
953	Government Officials (level unknown)	7	790	SL	0.86	0.14
954	Inspectors	6	775	CW	0.50	0.25
955	Foremen	28	823	CW	1.11	0.21
956	Box Makers (type unknown)	37	496	CW	0.79	0.26
957	Vehicle Makers, Repairers (type unknown)	77	657	CW	0.71	0.18
	Nonoccupational codes	61,748	—	—	2.82	0.36
961	At school	13,724	NI	—	2.22	0.41
962	Housewife	307	NI	—		
963	Retired	132	NI	—	6.69	0.60
964	Landlord	167	1,100	S	1.97	0.19
966	Invalid (physical or mental)	49	NI	—	7.20	0.60
967	Inmate	528	NI	—	2.35	0.41
969	Nun	15	NI	—		
969	Other nonoccupation	379	NI	—	6.14	0.64
976	Child Labor (farm)	42	NI	—	0.29	0.14
977	Child Labor (domestic)	6	NI	—		
978	Child Labor (other)	26	NI	—	0.00	0.00
998	Illegible	215	NI	—	0.72	0.16
999	No occupation reported	46,158	NI	—	3.09	0.36
	Total	100,438	—	—	1.02	0.24

Note: Incomes were imputed from the 1901 cost-of-living survey (U.S. Commissioner of Labor 1903), given as CW; Lebergott 1964, given as SL; and Douglas 1930, given as PD. The code S means taken from a similar occupation or group average. NI means not included. The results for average months unemployed and proportion with some unemployment are for males aged 10 and over, who had a nonblank report for months unemployed.

APPENDIX B

THE STATE EARNINGS INDEX

TO ACCOUNT for spatial income variation, an index of state earnings was constructed. One obvious choice would be the 1900 state personal income estimates of Easterlin (1957). These estimates, however, are heavily influenced by the occupational structure of a state. Since we have information on an individual's occupation, we seek a measure of occupation-specific wage levels, aggregated across occupations using a set of weights that is identical for all states. For this purpose, we utilize the earnings data presented by Lebergott (1964: Tables A-23 to A-29) by state for 1899–1900 for six selected occupations or industries (farm laborers, common laborers, domestic service, cotton manufacture, woolen manufacture, and iron and steel manufacture). To obtain comparable estimates from that source, monthly wages of farm laborers were multiplied by 12; the weekly wages of domestic workers were multiplied by 52; and the daily wages of common laborers were multiplied by 5.6 days per week and 44 weeks per year. The earnings of the textile and metal workers were already on an annual basis. Thus, farm laborers and domestic service workers were assumed to have had a full year's employment, while common laborers were not. Not all occupations or industries were represented for all states. There were 48 states (data for Alaska and Hawaii were not available) and the District of Columbia. A total of 186 cells resulted. The following dummy variable regression equation was estimated:

$$Ln(Y_{ij}) = B_0 + \Sigma_{i=1}^{6} B_i I_i + \Sigma_{j=1}^{49} B_j S_j ,$$

where $Ln(Y_{ij})$ = natural log of earnings for occupation/industry i and state j;

B = coefficient;

I_i = dummy variable for occupation or industry i ($i = 1 \ldots 6$);

S_j = dummy variable for state j ($j = 1 \ldots 49$).

The regression results are presented in Table B.1. Three models are given. Model I includes only the occupational dummy variables. The omitted category is iron and steel manufacture. It had the highest average earnings, so that all the coefficients are negative deviations from iron and steel manufacturing incomes. The constant term is thus, in this case, the natural logarithm of the state average of iron and steel earnings per worker. Model II includes only dummy variables for states. The reference category is California, which had the highest average income in this sample. The constant term is therefore the logarithm of the average earnings in California, and the dummy variables measure deviations from it. Finally, Model III includes both occupational and state dummy variables.

A perusal of Table B.1 reveals that occupation is much more successful in explaining variation than is location (i.e., state of residence). The R^2 for Model I is .594 and R^2 adjusted for degrees of freedom is .583, whereas the R^2 for Model II, with only the state dummy variables, is only .292 and the adjusted R^2 only .045. The Model II equation is not even jointly significant at a 5 percent level, as measured by the F-ratio (which is only 1.180). Nonetheless, Model III, which has both occupational and state dummy variables, is *much* more successful than either of the other two in explaining variation in earnings per worker. It has an R^2 of .916 and an adjusted R^2 of .882, and it is jointly significant at a 1 percent level (as measured by the F-ratio). The conclusion that can be drawn is that, although occupation is a better predictor of earnings per worker than state of residence, both sets of variables belong in the model.

The estimated coefficients in Model III permit the estimation of predicted average state workers' annual earnings, holding constant occupational and industry composition at their averages over all states. The estimates are given in Table B.2. In that table the values of $Ln(Y)$ and Y are given and are converted to an index, dividing each value by the $Y(= 244)$ for the whole sample. This is the index used in the regressions in Chapter 4. One advantage of using the Lebergott (1964) data is that the types of earnings estimates produced are rather close in nature to those derived from the 1901 cost-of-living survey (U.S. Commissioner of Labor 1903), Douglas's study of wages (1930), and other estimates from Lebergott that were used to impute income for individual occupations. The estimated values of the state earnings index were assigned to each worker on the basis of state of residence for the regression analysis.

For purposes of comparison, Table B.2 also includes the Easterlin estimates of state-level income per capita for 1899–1900. The correlation between them is quite reasonable, with a zero-order correlation of .810 and a Spearman rank order correlation of .819.

TABLE B.1

Equations Predicting Earnings in Various Occupations and States of Residence: U.S., 1899–1900

	(1)		(2)		(3)	
	Coefficient	Significance	Coefficient	Significance	Coefficient	Significance
Independent variables:						
Constant	6.1121	NC	5.9545	NC	6.5496	NC
Occupation						
Farm laborer	− 0.8376	***			− 0.9532	***
Common laborer	− 0.3117	***			− 0.2759	***
Domestic servant	− 1.1511	***			− 1.1516	***
Cotton manufacture	− 0.5626	***			− 0.4932	***
Woolen manufacture	− 0.4630	***			− 0.4468	***
Iron & steel mfg.	NI	NI			NI	NI
State						
Maine			− 0.3562	—	− 0.2872	***
New Hampshire			− 0.3035	—	− 0.2346	**
Vermont			− 0.4135	*	− 0.3445	***
Massachusetts			− 0.1713	—	− 0.2130	**
Rhode Island			− 0.2799	—	− 0.2110	*
Connecticut			− 0.2226	—	− 0.2644	**
New York			− 0.2539	—	− 0.2956	***
New Jersey			− 0.2661	—	− 0.3078	***
Pennsylvania			− 0.2475	—	− 0.2892	***
Ohio			− 0.3140	—	− 0.3557	***
Indiana			− 0.3672	—	− 0.4090	***
Illinois			− 0.2238	—	− 0.2535	**
Michigan			− 0.3361	—	− 0.3658	***
Wisconsin			− 0.2960	—	− 0.3257	***
Minnesota			− 0.4082	—	− 0.2965	***
Iowa			− 0.5130	*	− 0.4013	***
Missouri			− 0.3376	—	− 0.3672	***
North Dakota			− 0.3861	—	− 0.0281	—
South Dakota			− 0.4532	—	− 0.0952	—
Nebraska			− 0.4448	*	− 0.2464	**
Kansas			− 0.5679	*	− 0.3695	***
Delaware			− 0.4351	**	− 0.4556	***
Maryland			− 0.5169	*	− 0.5586	***
Dist. Columbia			− 0.2846	—	− 0.6038	***
Virginia			− 0.6286	**	− 0.6703	***
West Virginia			− 0.3871	—	− 0.4168	***
North Carolina			− 0.9608	***	− 0.8918	***
South Carolina			− 1.0373	***	− 0.9140	***
Georgia			− 0.9341	***	− 0.9758	***
Florida			− 0.9309	***	− 0.7326	***
Kentucky			− 0.4875	**	− 0.5292	***
Tennessee			− 0.7152	***	− 0.7569	***
Alabama			− 0.6714	***	− 0.8327	***
Mississippi			− 0.7969	***	− 0.8498	***
Arkansas			− 0.9369	***	− 0.7385	***
Louisiana			− 0.9261	***	− 0.7277	***
Oklahoma			− 0.7954	**	− 0.4374	**

TABLE B.1 *(cont.)*

	(1)		(2)		(3)	
	Coefficient	Significance	Coefficient	Significance	Coefficient	Significance
Texas			−0.5158	**	−0.5455	***
Montana			−0.0012	—	0.3568	**
Idaho			−0.1314	—	0.2266	—
Wyoming			−0.0795	—	0.2785	—
Colorado			−0.3233	—	0.0347	—
New Mexico			−0.5563	—	−0.1983	—
Arizona			−0.1285	—	0.2295	—
Utah			−0.2211	—	0.1369	—
Nevada			−0.0117	—	0.3463	*
Washington			−0.2474	—	0.1106	—
Oregon			−0.3377	—	−0.0203	—
California			NI	NI	NI	NI
N	186		186		186	
R-square	0.594		0.292		0.916	
Adjusted R-square	0.583		0.045		0.882	
F-ratio	52.690	***	1.180	—	27.233	***

Source: Data from Lebergott 1964.

Note: The dependent variable is the log of annual earnings in a particular occupation/state-of-residence category. A one-tailed significance test was used in models 1 and 2. A two-tailed significance test was used in model 3. NC = not calculated; NI = not included; *** = significant at least at a 1 percent level; ** = significant at least at a 5 percent level; * = significant at least at a 10 percent level; — = not significant at least at a 10 percent level.

TABLE B.2
Estimates of Annual Earnings Levels by State: U.S., 1899–1900

	Estimates derived from Table B.1		Easterlin's estimates	
State	Annual earnings ($)	Ratio to national average	Annual income ($)	Ratio to national average
Alabama	163	0.6680	88	0.4356
Arizona	471	1.9303	321	1.5891
Arkansas	179	0.7336	89	0.4406
California	374	1.5328	365	1.8069
Colorado	388	1.5902	318	1.5743
Connecticut	287	1.1762	278	1.3762
Delaware	237	0.9713	220	1.0891
Dist. Columbia	205	0.8402	—	—
Florida	180	0.7377	112	0.5545
Georgia	141	0.5779	86	0.4257
Idaho	470	1.9262	221	1.0941
Illinois	291	1.1926	260	1.2871
Indiana	249	1.0205	182	0.9010

TABLE B.2 (cont.)

State	Estimates derived from Table B.1		Easterlin's estimates	
	Annual earnings ($)	Ratio to national average	Annual income ($)	Ratio to national average
Iowa	251	1.0287	202	1.0000
Kansas	259	1.0615	187	0.9257
Kentucky	221	0.9057	120	0.5941
Louisiana	181	0.7418	128	0.6337
Maine	281	1.1516	187	0.9257
Maryland	214	0.8770	204	1.0099
Massachusetts	303	1.2418	304	1.5050
Michigan	260	1.0656	185	0.9158
Minnesota	278	1.1393	207	1.0248
Mississippi	160	0.6557	84	0.4158
Missouri	259	1.0615	188	0.9307
Montana	535	2.1926	415	2.0545
Nebraska	293	1.2008	212	1.0495
Nevada	529	2.1680	395	1.9554
New Hampshire	296	1.2131	214	1.0594
New Jersey	275	1.1270	277	1.3713
New Mexico	307	1.2582	148	0.7327
New York	279	1.1434	323	1.5990
North Carolina	153	0.6270	72	0.3564
North Dakota	364	1.4918	209	1.0347
Ohio	262	1.0738	222	1.0990
Oklahoma	242	0.9918	114	0.5644
Oregon	382	1.5656	248	1.2277
Pennsylvania	280	1.1475	250	1.2376
Rhode Island	303	1.2418	293	1.4505
South Carolina	150	0.6148	74	0.3663
South Dakota	340	1.3934	183	0.9059
Tennessee	176	0.7213	101	0.5000
Texas	217	0.8893	138	0.6832
Utah	429	1.7582	183	0.9059
Vermont	265	1.0861	190	0.9406
Virginia	192	0.7869	110	0.5446
Washington	418	1.7131	296	1.4653
West Virginia	247	1.0123	117	0.5792
Wisconsin	270	1.1066	179	0.8861
Wyoming	495	2.0287	311	1.5396
Total	244	—	202	—

Source: Table B.1 and Easterlin 1957.

APPENDIX C

THE MORTALITY INDEX

THE MORTALITY INDEX used to analyze the American data in Chapters 3–5 takes the form of the ratio of child deaths to expected child deaths. It is computed for each currently married woman who reported that she had borne at least one child and whose reported duration of current marriage was less than 25 years. When women are combined into a group, the ratio consists of the sum of child deaths to women in that group divided by the sum of expected child deaths among those women.

The number of child deaths (D) that have occurred to woman i is found simply by subtracting her reported number of surviving children, S_i, from her reported number of children ever born, P_i:

$$D_i = P_i - S_i.$$

The expected number of child deaths for woman i is based upon her reported number of children ever born, P_i, and the expected proportion dead among children ever born to women in her duration of marriage category. The categories used are 0–4, 5–9, 10–14, 15–19, and 20–24 years. For woman i in marital-duration category j, the expected number of child deaths, ED_{ij}, is found by

$$ED_{ij} = P_i \times EPD_j.$$

Finally, the expected proportion of children who have died among women in marital-duration category j is based upon equations of the type first developed by William Brass and Jeremiah Sullivan to translate proportions dead into life table measures of survivorship. These equations are of the form:

$$q(2) = PD(0–4) \times K(0–4),$$
$$q(3) = PD(5–9) \times K(5–9),$$
$$q(5) = PD(10–14) \times K(10–14),$$
$$q(10) = PD(15–19) \times K(15–19), \text{ and}$$
$$q(15) = PD(20–24) \times K(20–24),$$

where $q(x)$ is the cumulative probability of dying before age x in the underlying life table, $PD(j)$ is the proportion dead among children ever born in marital duration category j (0–4, 5–9, . . . 20–24), and $K(j)$ is a multiplier (close to unity) that is appropriate for women in marital duration category j.

The multiplier is a function of $\bar{P}(0–4)$, $\bar{P}(5–9)$, and $\bar{P}(10–14)$, the mean parities of all women in marital durations 0–4, 5–9, and 10–14 years. The multipliers are designed to take account of the marital-duration profile of childbearing. For example, in a population in which childbearing is unusually "late" within marriage (i.e., where $\bar{P}(5–9)/\bar{P}(0–4)$ is unusually high), children born to women of a particular marital duration will have been exposed to morality for an unusually short period of time. Hence, a particular value of $PD(j)$ will translate into an unusually high value of $q(x)$: the same proportion dead will translate into higher mortality and poorer survivorship than is typically the case, and $K(j)$ will be unusually high.

For present purposes, we invert the normal procedure. Rather than translate observed proportions dead into estimated life table measures, we translate a given life table into expected proportions dead. In other words, we rewrite the estimating equations as

$$EPD(0–4) = q(2)/K(0–4),$$
$$EPD(5–9) = q(3)/K(5–9),$$
$$EPD(10–14) = q(5)/K(10–14),$$
$$EPD(15–19) = q(10)/K(15–19), \text{ and}$$
$$EPD(20–24) = q(15)/K(20–24).$$

Formulas for estimating $K(j)$ are drawn from United Nations 1983a: Table 56. In applying these equations, we use values of $\bar{P}(0–4)$, $\bar{P}(5–9)$, and $\bar{P}(10–14)$ for all women of those marital durations in the census sample. Finally, the life table values of $q(2)$, $q(3)$ . . . $q(15)$ are taken from Coale and Demeny's (1966) Model West life table, level 13.0 (with males and females combined in the ratio of 1.05 to 1.00). This level provides a good fit to the data for women in marital durations 0–24, with a ratio of the number of dead children to the expected number of dead children of 1.0088 for this group as a whole in the sample.

Implicit in this procedure is the assumption that social and environmental conditions will act multiplicatively on the $q(x)$ function through age 15. Trussell and Preston (1982) show that this multiplicative assumption is highly accurate within same model life table systems: populations with higher mortality have, to a close approximation, $q(x)$ functions that are constant multiples of those in lower mortality populations within the same model life table system. We have demonstrated in Chapter 2 that the Model West system is very appropriate to American mortality conditions at the turn of the century, as it has proven to be subsequently.

At West level 13.0, $q(5)$ is .191, the infant mortality rate is .129, and life expectancy at birth is 48.5 years. Other values of the mortality

TABLE C.1

Values of Certain Mortality Functions in Model West Life Tables
Corresponding to Particular Values of the Child Mortality Index

Child mortality index	$q(5)$	Infant mortality rate	Life expectancy at birth (years)	"West" level
.6000	.113	.081	57.7	16.8
.8000	.152	.105	52.9	14.8
1.0088	.191	.129	48.5	13.0
1.2000	.227	.152	44.7	11.5
1.4000	.265	.177	40.8	9.9
1.6000	.303	.203	37.2	8.4

index can also be mapped into these functions by reference to the West model life table system (see Table C.1).

For example, if a group has a mortality index of .80, the implied $q(5)$ is approximately .152. As we argue in Chapter 2, and as is implied by the position of $q(5)$ in the middle of our estimation equations, $q(5)$ is the most robustly estimated life table function onto which the mortality index can be mapped. Values of $q(5)$ are not very sensitive to the choice of standard life table (West level 13.0). If the West model life table system is appropriate for a group, then the mortality index can also be translated into the group's levels of the infant mortality rate and life expectancy at birth, functions whose identification is more dependent upon assumptions about the nature of relationships among age-specific death rates within the group.

NOTES

CHAPTER ONE

1. This result refers to the surviving-children method using the West life table. (See Chapter 2.)

2. The states were Connecticut, Massachusetts, New Hampshire, New Jersey, New York, Rhode Island, and Vermont.

3. Industrial structure was defined as the proportion of males aged 10 and over employed in mines and quarries; in metals, etc.; in woodworking, etc.; in brickmaking, etc.; in skins and hides, etc.; in textiles; and as mechanics and laborers.

4. Evidence from England and Wales in 1911 also reveals a monotonic inverse relationship between child mortality and number of rooms per family (see Table 5.1).

CHAPTER TWO

1. The Death Registration Area was formed in 1900 from states and cities where tests revealed that death registration was at least 90 percent complete and where a uniform death certificate had been adopted (Cassedy 1965). It consisted originally of Maine, Vermont, New Hampshire, Massachusetts, Rhode Island, Connecticut, New York, New Jersey, Michigan, Indiana, the District of Columbia, and selected cities not in these jurisdictions. In this chapter, numerical results for the Death Registration Area refer to the 10 states just enumerated and the District of Columbia, collectively referred to by Glover (1921) as the "Original Registration States."

2. The mortality statistics for the Death Registration Area itself reveal considerably higher mortality in urban areas and among blacks (Glover 1921).

3. Comparable questions on children ever born and children surviving were asked in the 1890 census, but unfortunately most of those original schedules were lost in a fire in 1921. The questions were asked again in the 1910 census, but the results were not then tabulated or used. A project was finally undertaken in conjunction with the 1940 census that retabulated and analyzed the 1910 data for children ever born (U.S. Bureau of the Census 1943, 1944, 1945). But the information on children surviving was never tabulated or used.

4. Comparisons of various age, sex, race, and nativity distributions with published data using a series of chi-square tests revealed generally statistically insignificant differences.

5. This "woman" file contained the census information on the woman herself, that of her husband and matched own-children when present, and selected characteristics of the area of residence. The actual matching procedure was carried out at the University of Washington, under the supervision

of Avery Guest and Stephen Graham. We are grateful to them for making this file available.

6. For additional details on these procedures and on this methodology, see Preston and Palloni 1978. An application to 1900 census data for the anthracite mining region of Pennsylvania is made in Haines 1977.

7. This is based on the formula that the variance of a binomial distribution is $p \times q \times n$, where p = the probability of the outcome occurring (i.e., in this case, a child death); $q = (1 - p)$; and n = the number of cases (or trials). The standard deviation is the square root of the variance.

8. Because of the small number of children ever born in the census sample for several states and territories, some had to be combined. Thus Arizona, Nevada, and New Mexico were combined into one unit, as were Idaho, Montana, and Wyoming. Oklahoma and Indian Territory were taken as one unit. The District of Columbia was used as a unit of observation. Alaska and Hawaii were excluded. There are thus 45 observations in total.

9. Among the states with positive residuals:

State	Residual	Registration coverage in the 1900 census (percent)
Pennsylvania	4.43	41.1
Ohio	2.48	31.9
Maryland	3.85	44.3
Delaware	11.99	41.4
California	0.16	41.1
Wisconsin	0.70	20.9

Registration coverage is from Condran and Crimmins 1979: Table 2.

CHAPTER THREE

1. The male and female life tables for this level of mortality were combined by weighting the $1(x)$ column of the life tables by 0.5122 for males and 0.4878 for females on the assumption of a sex ratio at birth of 105 males per 100 females.

2. An example would be a case in which mortality has been declining in the past and in which the intention is to compare the wives of farmers to those of farm laborers. If farmers and their wives were, on average, older and of higher marital duration than farm laborers and their wives, then the index of child mortalty for farmers will tend to be somewhat overstated relative to that for farm laborers. Since farmers tended to have lower child mortality, the effect in this instance would be to decrease the differential.

3. Note that, to estimate the significance of a difference in child mortality between two groups, the t-test is

$$t = \frac{q_A(5) - q_B(5)}{\sqrt{\dfrac{S_A{}^2}{n_A} + \dfrac{S_B{}^2}{n_B}}}$$

where s_i^2 is the sample variance of $q(5)$ in group i and n_i is the number of births in group i.

4. Note that in this chapter we use the 1900 census definition of an urban place, which has a minimum size of 1,000 inhabitants. Several tabulations in earlier chapters used a size criterion of 2,500 for the purpose of establishing comparability over time.

5. The enumerators' instructions were to answer "Yes" in the "Can Read" column for any person aged 10 and over who could read in any language. A "No" was entered otherwise. All children below age 10 were to be given a blank. A similar instruction was made for the column "Can Write." "The inquiries . . . are intended to show the literacy of all persons 10 years of age and over, and should be answered according as they are able to read or write the language ordinarily spoken by them" (U.S. Bureau of the Census 1979:37). We adopt a definition of literacy requiring the ability to both read and write.

6. The proportions of illiterate women by race and ethnicity in the total sample population were: total, 11.9 percent; white, 7.1 percent; native white, 5.0 percent; native white with native mother, 5.7 percent; native white with foreign-born mother, 2.3 percent; foreign-born white, 14.8 percent; black, 51.4 percent.

7. Of the total households in the 1900 census sample (27,069 in number), 84.4 percent contained no extended family and 62.2 percent were husband/wife units (with or without children).

CHAPTER FOUR

1. Race is not included for the husband since, in the sample, there were almost no cases of racial intermarriage and hence race of husband and wife are nearly perfectly collinear.

2. Although state real income may be conceptually superior to state nominal income, the adjustment for price levels introduces additional error into the variables. Perhaps for this reason, the F-ratio for the equation using nominal income (8.875) exceeds that for the equation using real income (8.813). Consequently, we use nominal income for the basic presentations in this chapter. Some of the regional mortality differences that remain when nominal income is controlled will, therefore, reflect differences in price levels among the regions.

3. George Alter raised with us the possibility that results we presented regarding region (especially the low mortality levels in the South Atlantic) and working wives may be confined to the black population. To test this possibility, we reran equation (4) of Table 4.1 for whites alone. Results are not appreciably altered on these or other variables, although the mortality

advantage of the *rural* South is smaller when results are confined to the white population.

4. We wish to thank Timothy Guinnane for this suggestion.

5. Actually, a very small fraction of the population was Asian or had an unknown race, so three categories of this variable are recognized in the statistical analysis.

6. The F-ratio in this case is a measure of the statistical significance of the change in R^2 caused by removing a variable from the full model.

CHAPTER FIVE

1. The singulate mean age at first marriage was calculated from data on age, sex, and marital status from the 1911 Census of England and Wales, according to Hajnal's method (Hajnal 1953).

2. These categories are based on relatively "rough and ready" occupational groupings of the Registrar General, T.H.C. Stevenson. For a critique, see Armstrong 1972:203–6 and Szreter 1984. An extended treatment of childhood mortality by occupation of parents is given in Haines 1985.

3. The six county boroughs for Ireland were Dublin, Belfast, Cork, Londonderry, Limerick, and Waterford.

4. This result uses the mortality of the six county boroughs as the urban child mortality level and of the rest of Ireland as the rural figure. The standardization to England's urban percentage is thus .78 (.2058) + .22 (.1226) = .187.

5. As a check on the data for England and Wales, the differentials from the census estimates were compared to those from the first vital statistics tabulation (1911) of the infant mortality rate by the eight social-class categories used by the Registrar General at that time (Great Britain 1913b:73, 88). The results are as follows (indexed to a total of 100):

Social class	Census	Vital statistics
Professional, Higher White-Collar	65	61
Farmers & Lower White-Collar	83	85
Skilled Manual Workers	95	90
Semi-skilled Manual Workers	100	97
Unskilled Manual Workers	122	122
Textile Workers	120	119
Miners	128	128
Agricultural Workers & Related	79	78
Total	100	100

The two sets of results are highly correlated, despite the fact that the census results apply to children as well as infants, while the vital statistics apply only to infants. Further, the vital statistics data come from only one year of experience (1911) and are thus subject to more variability. The results apply to slightly different periods as well: the vital statistics to 1911 and the census index to about 1907–8. In addition, the 1911 census results apply to current occupation, which may have differed from occupation in the past. The zero-order correlation between the mortality index for 116 detailed occupational categories in the census and the infant mortality rate for the same categories from the 1911 vital statistics indicates a quite close relationship ($r = 0.939$). Overall, the census mortality index seems to give an excellent picture of relative mortality by occupation of father for England and Wales just after the turn of the century.

6. Income measures are not strictly comparable between the United States and England. American incomes were largely yearly incomes from the 1901 Commissioner of Labor Survey, while English incomes were full-time equivalent annual earnings. Nonetheless, the relative incomes, as given by the index, should be independent of level. The index reflects higher relative incomes among most English professionals. A conversion rate of $4.85 per pound sterling was used, the prevailing rate under the gold standard. The difference in child mortality levels between England and the United States for specific occupational groups was tested for statistical significance. To do this, several steps were necessary. First, the index values were normalized so that the national average values were 1.0000. Second, these normalized values were converted to $q(5)$ values by multiplying them by the $q(5)$ value in the standard American model life table (West model, level 13, both sexes combined assuming a sex ratio at birth of 1.05; $q(5) = .19119$). This basically reduced both sets of differentials to a common mortality *level*. Third, it was assumed that these $q(5)$ values approximately followed a binomial process where $q(5) = p$ and $\delta = [p(1 - p)/n]^{1/2}$, where n was the number of children ever born to that occupational group. Finally, the statistical difference of these values was tested using the formula

$$t = (p_{us} - p_{ew})/(\delta^2_{us} + \delta^2_{ew})^{1/2}.$$

This yielded the following t-statistics:

Textile workers	.177
Miners	4.559
Agricultural laborers	
(a) Total	6.629
(b) U.S. native white	1.569
Teachers	2.582
Clergy	2.236
Clerks (commercial and business)	2.702
Physicians and surgeons	3.468

All but textile workers and native white agricultural laborers showed differences that were significant at least at a five percent level (two-tailed test).

7. For the United States, each of the occupational codes, based on the 1900 census coding system, was assigned an average annual income. Again, farmers are excluded because it was felt that the earnings of agricultural laborers (for whom an estimate was made) were not representative of farmers, and no good way could be found to capture the effect of differences in returns

from capital and land, a major component of farm incomes. The dates covered were in the range 1899–1901. (See Appendix A.) All estimates for grouped data were aggregated up from the sample.

For England and Wales, the period covered was 1901–14, but most of the estimates applied to 1906. The British earnings data come mostly as weekly, not average annual, earnings. In view of the difficulty of determining differences in weeks worked, it was decided to calculate full-time equivalent earnings by multiplying the average weekly earnings by 52, the practice of two of the sources (Williamson 1982b:36–37; Routh 1965:60–61). Consequently, the results for Britain are not comparable in level to those for the United States, although the years 1899–1901 were years of fairly low unemployment in the United States (U.S. Bureau of the Census 1975: Series D 85–86). Data were taken for England, or England and Wales, rather than for Great Britain whenever possible. (A number of the estimates included data for Scotland, but the results are dominated by the English data.) The estimates were made for 116 occupations or occupational groups. Any reaggregations—of social classes, for instance—were from these 116 groups. Groups for whom estimates were not available were farmers and a number of proprietors, such as retail merchants. Most professional and manual workers were covered, constituting about 75 percent of the male labor force in England and Wales.

8. There are small discrepancies in the occupations that could be used to estimate earnings inequalities, so that the result is not definitive. In particular, the absence of data for "proprietors" in England and Wales might have biased downwards the income level of the lower white-collar group, although the effect on measures of overall inequality is unclear. The groups actually included in the category for England and Wales are: Farmer's Sons; Officers of Local Authorities; Goldsmiths and Silversmiths; Watchmakers and Clockmakers; Bakers and Confectioners. Missing were such groups as: Coffee and Eating House Keepers; Inn and Hotel Keepers; Publicans; Boarding and Lodging House Keepers; Dealers and Merchants in various products (for example, coal, timber, wood, cork, bark, boots and shoes, corn, flour, seed); Drapers; General Shopkeepers; Grocers; Greengrocers; Tobacconists; Milksellers and Dairymen; Cheesemongers and Buttermen; Fishmongers, Poulterers and Game Dealers; Clothiers and Outfitters.

9. Using a 5000-inhabitant cut-off to define an urban place in the U.S. makes the U.S. definition as close as possible to that in England. The urban proportion in our sample for the U.S. is .37, and in England it was .73. The variance in proportion urban is $U(1 - U)$, where U is the percentage living in urban places. The variance is thus .172 in England and Wales and .233 in the U.S. The differences are not large, and the fact that the variance is greater in the U.S. offsets the fact that the sensitivity to urban residence was greater in England.

10. To clarify a bit more formally, suppose that mortality is a simple linear function of two variables:

$$M_i = a + bY_i + cU_i.$$

Then it can be shown that the variance in mortality is equal to

$$\sigma_M^2 = b^2\sigma_Y^2 + c^2\sigma_U^2 + 2bc\,\text{COV}_{Y,U}.$$

The difference between values of σ_M^2 for two countries can be decomposed into a series of terms involving coefficients and variances of independent variables. The basic terms involving the variance in urban proportions (U) will disappear if δ_U^2 is the same in both countries. Also, since b is nearly the same in the two countries, the contribution of differences in δ_Y^2 will simply be weighted by b^2. We don't implement this scheme formally because of non-linearities and differences in measurement in the two countries, but the logic underlies our analysis.

11. For an additional example, when variables representing the percentages of various occupations that are black, have literate wives, and have foreign-born wives are added to Model 2 for the United States, only the percentage of blacks is significant, with a coefficient of 10.1.

12. The total number of "expected deaths" among offspring of the intelligentsia is 130.2, apportioned in the following way: physicians, surgeons, and dentists, 35.6; clergymen, 32.3; teachers, 26.0; lawyers, 22.4; and pharmacists, 13.9.

REFERENCES

Abbott, S. W. 1899. "A Massachusetts Life Table for the Five Years 1893–97." In Massachusetts State Board of Health, *Thirtieth Annual Report: 1895*, pp. 810–27. Boston.

———. 1900. *The Past and Present Condition of Public Hygiene and State Medicine in the United States*. Boston: Wright & Potter Printing Company.

Ackerknecht, E. H. 1973. *Therapeutics from the Primitives to the 20th Century with an Appendix: History of Dietetics*. New York: The Hafner Press.

Adams, S. H. 1906. *The Great American Fraud*. New York. Partially reprinted in Bremner 1971, pp. 882–83.

Addams, J. 1910. *Twenty Years at Hull-House*. Macmillan: New York.

Altendorfer, M. E. 1947. "Relationship between Per Capita Income and Mortality in the Cities of 100,000 or More Population." *Public Health Reports* 62(48):1681–91.

American Public Works Association. 1976. *History of Public Works in the United States, 1776–1976*. Chicago: American Public Works Association.

Anderson, L. 1984. "Hard Choices: Supplying Water to New England Towns." *The Journal of Interdisciplinary History* 15(2) (Autumn):211–34.

Andrews, F. M., J. N. Morgan, J. A. Sonquist, and L. Klem. 1973. *Multiple Classification Analysis*. 2nd ed. Ann Arbor: Institute for Social Research, University of Michigan.

Antonovsky, A. 1967. "Social Class, Life Expectancy and Overall Mortality." *Milbank Memorial Fund Quarterly* 45(2), pt. 1:31–73.

Antonovsky, A., and J. Bernstein. 1977. "Social Class and Infant Mortality." *Social Science and Medicine* 11(8/9) (May):453–77.

Apple, R. 1980. "To Be Used Only under the Direction of a Physician: Commercial Feeding and Medical Practice, 1870–1940." *Bulletin of the History of Medicine* 54(2):402–17.

———. 1981. *How Shall I Feed My Baby? Infant Feeding in the United States, 1870–1940*. Ann Arbor: University Microfilms.

Armstrong, W. A. 1972. "The Use of Information about Occupation." In E. A. Wrigley, ed., *Nineteenth Century Society: Essays in the Use of Quantitative Methods for the Study of Social Data*, pp. 191–310. Cambridge: Cambridge University Press.

Ashby, H. 1922. *Infant Mortality*. 2nd ed. Cambridge: Cambridge University Press.

Atkinson, A. B. 1970. "On the Measurement of Inequality." *Journal of Economic Theory* 2(3) (September):244–63.

Atwater, W. O., and C. D. Woods. 1897. *Dietary Studies with Reference to the Food of the Negro in Alabama in 1895 and 1896*. U.S. Department of Agriculture, Office of Experiment Stations Bulletin 38. Washington, D.C.: G.P.O.

Avery, R. C. 1981. *Model Life Table and Stable Population Generation Program*. Ithaca, N.Y.: Cornell University, International Population Program.

Aykroyd, W. R. 1971. "Nutrition and Mortality in Infancy and Early Childhood: Past and Present Relationships." *American Journal of Clinical Nutrition* 24:480–87.

Baker, S. J. 1939. *Fighting for Life*. New York: Macmillan. Reprinted in part in Bremner 1971, pp. 16–18.

Barr, M. W. 1905. "Results of Asexualization." *Journal of Psycho-Asthenics* 9:129. Reprinted in Bremner 1971, pp. 856–57.

Becker, G. S. 1975. *Human Capital*. 2nd ed. New York: Columbia University Press.

Behm, H. 1979. "Socioeconomic Determinants of Mortality in Latin America." In United National/World Health Organization, *Proceedings of the Meeting on Socioeconomic Determinants and Consequences of Mortality*, pp. 139–65. El Colegio de Mexico, Mexico City, 19–25 June 1979.

Benjamin, B. 1964. "The Urban Background to Public Health Changes in England and Wales, 1900–1950." *Population Studies* 17(3):225–48.

Bennett, M. K., and R. H. Pierce. 1961. "Change in the American National Diet, 1879–1959." *Food Research Institute Studies* 2(2):97–118.

Blake, N. M. 1956. *Water for the Cities: A History of the Urban Water Supply Problem in the United States*. Syracuse, N.Y.: Syracuse University Press.

Blau, Francine D. 1980. "Immigration and Labor Earnings in Early Twentieth Century America." *Research in Population Economics* 2:21–41.

Blumberg, R. L. 1988. "Income under Female Versus Male Control." *Journal of Family Issues* 9(1):51–84.

Bogue, D. J. 1959. *The Population of the United States*. Glencoe, Ill.: The Free Press.

Bowditch. H. I. 1877. *Public Hygiene in America*. Boston: Little, Brown, and Company.

Bradley, F. S., and M. A. Williamson. 1918. *Rural Children in Selected Counties of North Carolina*. U.S. Department of Labor Children's Bureau Rural Child Welfare Series, 2. Washington, D.C.: G.P.O.

Brass, W. 1975. *Methods for Estimating Fertility and Mortality from Limited and Defective Data*. Chapel Hill, N.C.: Carolina Population Center.

Bremner, R. H., ed. 1971. *Children and Youth in America: A Documentary History*. Vol. 2: 1866–1932. Cambridge, Mass.: Harvard University Press.

———, ed. 1974. *Care of Dependent Children in the Late Nineteenth and Early Twentieth Centuries*. New York: Arno Press.

Brend, W. A. 1917. "Infant Mortality." *Medical Research Council Special Report Series No. 10*. London: H. M. Stationery Office.

Brieger, G. H. 1966. "American Surgery and the Germ Theory of Disease." *Bulletin of the History of Medicine* 40:135–45.

Briggs, A. 1956–57. "Middle Class Consciousness in English Politics, 1780–1846." *Past and Present* 9:65–74.

Bryant, A. P. 1898. "Some Results of Dietary Studies in the United States." In *United States Department of Agriculture Yearbook*, pp. 439–52. Washington, D.C.: G.P.O.

Cain, L. P. 1972. "Raising and Watering a City: Ellis Sylvester Chesbrough and Chicago's First Sanitation System." *Technology and Culture* 13:353–72.
———. 1974. "Unfouling the Public's Nest: Chicago's Sanitary Diversion of Lake Michigan Water." *Technology and Culture* 15:594–613.
———. 1977. "An Economic History of Urban Location and Sanitation." *Research in Economic History* 2:337–89.
Caldwell, J. C. 1979. "Education as a Factor in Mortality Decline: An Examination of Nigerian Data." *Population Studies* 33(3) (November):395–414.
———. 1981. "Influence of Maternal Education on Infant and Child Mortality: Levels and Causes." Paper presented at the Symposium on Literacy, Education, and Health Development, University of Michigan, Ann Arbor, 17–19 March.
Caldwell, M. 1988. *The Last Crusade: The War on Consumption, 1862–1954*. New York: Atheneum.
Cassedy, J. H. 1962a. *Charles V. Chapin and the Public Health Movement*. Cambridge, Mass.: Harvard University Press.
———. 1962b. "The Flamboyant Colonel Waring: An Anticontagionist Holds the American Stage in the Age of Pasteur and Koch." *Bulletin of the History of Medicine* 36:163–76. Reprinted in Leavitt and Numbers 1978, pp. 305–12.
———. 1965. "The Registration Area and American Vital Statistics: Development of a Health Research Resource, 1885–1915." *Bulletin of the History of Medicine* 39(3):221–31.
Chapin, C. V. 1901. *Municipal Sanitation in the United States*. Providence, R.I.: Snow and Furnhum.
———. 1910. *The Sources and Modes of Infection*. New York: J. Wiley and Sons.
———. 1919. "The Control of Midwifery." In Chenery and Merritt 1984, pp. 157–63. Reprint of U.S. Department of Labor, Children's Bureau, *Standards of Child Welfare*, Report of the Children's Bureau Conferences, May and June 1919. Bureau Publication no. 60. Washington, D.C.: Department of Labor.
Chenery, H., and M. Syrquin. 1975. *Patterns of Development, 1950–1970*. London: Oxford University Press.
Chenery, W. L., and E. A. Merritt, eds. 1974. *Standards of Child Welfare*. New York: Arno Press.
Cheney, R. A. 1984. "Seasonal Aspects of Infant and Childhood Mortality: Philadelphia, 1865–1920." *Journal of Interdisciplinary History* 14(3) (Winter):561–85.
Clelland, J. G., and J. K. van Ginneken. 1988. "Maternal Education and Child Survival in Developing Countries: The Search for Pathways of Influence." *Social Science and Medicine* 27(12):1357–68.
Coale, A. J., and P. Demeny. 1966. *Regional Model Life Tables and Stable Populations*. Princeton, N.J.: Princeton University Press.
Coale, A. J., and N. W. Rives, Jr. 1973. "A Statistical Reconstruction of the Black Population of the United States 1880–1970: Estimates of True Numbers by Age and Sex, Birth Rates, and Total Fertility." *Population Index* 39(1) (January):3–36.

Coale, A. J., and M. Zelnik. 1963. *New Estimates of Fertility and Population in the United States: A Study of Annual White Births from 1855 to 1960 and of Completeness of Enumeration in the Censuses from 1880 to 1960*. Princeton, N.J.: Princeton University Press.

Cochrane, S. H. 1980. "Educational Differentials in Mortality of Children." Paper presented at the annual meetings of the Population Association of America, 10–12 April 1980, Denver, Colo.

Coit, H. L. 1893. *A Plan to Procure Cow's Milk Designed for Clinical Purposes*. Newark, N.J. Reprinted in part in Bremner 1971, pp. 867–69.

Cole, W. A. and P. Deane. 1965. "The Growth of National Incomes." In H. J. Habakkuk and M. Postan, eds. *The Cambridge Economic History of Europe*, vol. 6, pt. 1, pp. 1–55. Cambridge: Cambridge University Press.

Coleman, W. 1987. *Yellow Fever in the North: The Methods of Early Epidemiology*. Madison: University of Wisconsin.

Comstock, A. 1883. *Traps for the Young*. Reissued by Belknap Press of Harvard University Press, 1967. Reprinted in part in Bremner 1971, pp. 226–28.

Condran, G. A. 1980. "Ethnic Differences in Mortality in the Nineteenth Century: A Case Study of Philadelphia, 1880–81." Unpublished paper.

———. 1984. "An Evaluation of Estimates of Undernumeraation in the Census and the Age Pattern of Mortality, Philadelphia, 1880." *Demography* 21(1) (February):53–69.

Condran, G. A., and R. A. Cheney. 1982. "Mortality Trends in Philadelphia: Age- and Cause-Specific Death Rates, 1870–1930." *Demography* 19(1) (February):97–123.

Condran, G. A., and E. Crimmins-Gardner. 1976. "The United States Population in the Nineteenth Century: Mortality." Paper presented at the annual meetings of the Population Association of America, Montreal, Canada.

———. 1978. "Public Health Measures and Mortality in U.S. Cities in the Late Nineteenth Century." *Human Ecology* 6(1) (March):27–54.

Condran, G. A., and E. Crimmins. 1979. "A Description and Evaluation of Mortality Data in the Federal Census: 1850–1900." *Historical Methods* 12(1) (Winter):1–23.

———. 1980. "Mortality Differentials between Rural and Urban Areas of States in the Northeastern United States, 1890–1900." *Journal of Historical Geography* 6(2):179–202.

Condran, G. A., and Ellen A. Kramarow. 1990. "Low Child Mortality in the United States in the Early Twentieth Century: An Examination of a Jewish Immigrant Population." Unpublished paper, Population Studies Center, University of Pennsylvania.

Condran, G. A., H. Williams, and R. A. Cheney. 1984. "A Decline in Mortality in Philadelphia from 1870 to 1930: The Role of Municipal Services." *The Pennsylvania Magazine of History and Biography* 108 (April):153–77.

Conference on the Prevention of Infant Mortality. 1909. *Prevention of Infant Mortality*. Being the papers and discussions of a conference held at New

Haven, Conn., November 11, 12, 1909, under the auspices of the American Academy of Medicine. American Academy of Medicine.

Crandall, F. M., M.D. 1896. "Editor's Introduction." *Archives of Pediatrics* 13 (July).

Crimmins, E., and G. A. Condran. 1983. "Mortality Variation in U.S. Cities in 1900: A Two-Level Explanation by Cause of Death and Underlying Factors." *Social Science History* 7(1) (Winter):31–59.

Daley, A., and B. Benjamin. 1964. "London as a Case Study." *Population Studies* 17:249–62.

Dart, H. M. 1921. *Maternity and Child Care in Selected Rural Areas of Mississippi.* U.S. Department of Labor Children's Bureau Rural Child Welfare Series, 5. Washington, D.C.: G.P.O.

Davenport, C. B., and A. G. Love. 1921. *Statistics: Army Anthropology,* vol. 15, part 1, *The Medical Department of the United States Army in the World War.* Medical Department. U.S. Army. Washington, D.C.: G.P.O.

Davis, K. 1973. "Cities and Mortality." International Union for the Scientific Study of Population. *International Population Conference: Liege, 1973* 3:259–82. Liege: IUSSP.

Deane, P. 1979. *The First Industrial Revolution.* 2nd ed. Cambridge: Cambridge University Press.

Demeny, P., and P. Gingrich. 1967. "A Reconsideration of Negro-White Mortality Differentials in the United States." *Demography* 4(2):820–37.

Demos, J. 1986. *Past, Present and Personal: The Family and the Life Course in American History.* Oxford: Oxford University Press.

Devine, E. T. 1909. "The Waste of Infant Life." In Conference on the Prevention of Infant Mortality, *Prevention of Infant Mortality,* pp. 95–112. Conference held in New Haven, Conn., under the auspices of the American Academy of Medicine.

De Vries, J. 1984. *European Urbanization, 1500–1800.* Cambridge, Mass.: Harvard University Press.

Dorn, H. F. 1959. "Mortality." In P. M. Hauser and O. D. Duncan, eds., *The Study of Population: An Inventory and Appraisal,* pp. 437–71. Chicago: University of Chicago Press.

Douglas, P. H. 1930. *Real Wages in the United States, 1890–1926.* New York: Houghton Mifflin Company.

Dublin, L. I., and G. W. Baker. 1920. "The Mortality of Race Stocks in Pennsylvania and New York." *Quarterly Publication of the American Statistical Association* 17(129):13–44.

DuBois, W.E.B. 1899. *The Philadelphia Negro.* Reissued 1967. New York: Schocken Books.

Duffy, J. 1967. "The Changing Image of the American Physician." *Journal of the American Medical Association* 200:136–40. Reprinted in Leavitt and Numbers 1978, pp. 131–37.

———. 1971. "Social Impact of Disease in the Late 19th Century." *Bulletin of the New York Academy of Medicine* 47:797–811. Reprinted in Leavitt and Numbers 1978, pp. 395–402.

Duffy, J. 1974. *A History of Public Health in New York City, 1866–1966.* New York: Russell Sage Foundation.

Durand, J. D. 1980. "Comment." In R. A. Easterlin, ed., *Population and Economic Change in Developing Countries,* Conference Report no. 30, Universities-National Bureau Committee for Economic Research, pp. 341–47. Chicago: University of Chicago Press.

Dye, N. S. 1987. "Modern Obstetrics and Working-Class Women: The New York Midwifery Dispensary, 1890–1920." *Journal of Social History* 20:49–64.

Dye, N. S., and D. B. Smith. 1986. "Mother Love and Infant Death, 1750–1920." *Journal of American History* 73:329–53.

Dyehouse, C. 1979. "Working Class Mothers and Infant Mortality in England, 1895–1914." *The Journal of Social History* 12(2) (Winter):248–67.

Easterlin, R. A. 1957. "State Income Estimates." In E. S. Lee, A. R. Miller, C. P. Brained, and R. A. Easterlin, *Population Redistribution and Economic Growth in the United States, 1870–1950,* vol 1, *Methodological Considerations and Reference Tables,* pp. 703–59. Philadelphia: American Philosophical Society.

————. 1960. "Interregional Difference in Per Capita Income, Population, and Total Income, 1840–1950." In *Trends in the American Economy in the Nineteenth Century,* pp. 73–140. National Bureau of Economic Research, Studies in Income and Wealth, vol. 24. Princeton, N.J.: Princeton University Press.

————. 1961. "Influences on European Overseas Emigration before World War I." *Economic Development and Cultural Change* 9(3) (April):331–49.

————. 1968. "Economic Growth: An Overview." *International Encyclopedia of the Social Sciences,* vol. 4: 395–408. New York: Macmillan.

————. 1977. "Population Issues in American Economic History: A Survey and Critique." In R. Gallman, ed., *Recent Developments in the Study of Business and Economic History: Essays in Honor of Herman E. Krooss,* pp. 131–58. Greenwich, Conn.: JAI Press.

Eblen, J. E. 1974. "New Estimates of the Vital Rates of the United States Black Population during the Nineteenth Century." *Demography* 11(2) (May):301–19.

Eldridge, H. T., and D. S. Thomas. 1964. *Population Redistribution and Economic Growth: United States, 1870–1950.* Vol. 3, *Demographic Analyses and Interrelations.* Philadelphia: American Philosophical Society.

Elliot, E. B. 1857. "On the Law of Human Mortality That Appears to Obtain in Massachusetts with Tables of Practical Value Deduced Therefrom." *Proceedings of the American Association for the Advancement of Science.* Eleventh Meeting. Part A: 51–81.

England and Wales. 1914. Registrar General. *Census of England and Wales. 1911.* Vol. 10, *Occupations and Industries,* part 2. London: H.M.S.O.

————. 1923. Registrar General. *Census of England and Wales, 1911.* Vol. 13, *Fertility of Marriage,* part 2. London: H.M.S.O.

Ewbank, D. 1987. "History of Black Mortality and Health before 1940." *The Milbank Quarterly* 65, suppl. 1:100–128.

Ewbank, D., and S. H. Preston. 1989. "Personal Health Behavior and the Decline in Infant and Child Mortality: The United States, 1900–30." Forthcoming in Proceedings of the Health Transition Workshop, Canberra, Australia, 15–19 May.

Farley, R. 1970. *Growth of the Black Population: A Study of Demographic Trends.* Chicago: Markham.

Ferguson, T. 1964. "Public Health in Britain in the Climate of the Nineteenth Century." *Population Studies* 17(3):213–24.

Fisher, I. 1899. "Mortality Statistics of the United States Census." In American Economic Association, *The Federal Census: Critical Essays*, Publications of the American Economic Association, new series, no. 2, pp. 121–69. New York: Macmillan.

———. 1909. *Report on National Vitality, Its Wastes and Conservation.* Bulletin of the Committee of One Hundred on National Health. Prepared for the National Conservation Commission. Washington, D.C.: G.P.O.

Fogel, R. W. 1986. "Nutrition and the Decline in Mortality since 1700: Some Additional Preliminary Findings." National Bureau of Economic Research, Working Paper no. 1802 (January).

———. 1988. "The Escape from Hunger and Early Death: Europe and America, 1750–2050." Unpublished manuscript.

Fogel, R. W., S. L. Engerman, and J. Trussell. 1982. "Exploring the Use of Data on Height: The Analysis of Long-Term Trends in Nutrition, Labor Welfare and Labor Productivity." *Social Science History* 6(4) (Fall):401–21.

Fogel, R. W., S. L. Engerman, R. Floud, R. A. Margo, K. Sokoloff, R. H. Steckel, J. Trussell, G. C. Villaflor, and K. W. Wachter. 1983. "Secular Changes in American and British Stature and Nutrition." *The Journal of Interdisciplinary History* 14(2) (Autumn):445–81.

Fogel, R. W., S. L. Engerman, J. Trussell, R. Floud, C. L. Pope, and L. T. Wimmer. 1978. "The Economics of Mortality in North America, 1650–1910: A Description of a Research Project." *Historical Methods* 11(2):75–108.

Forman, S. E. 1906. "Conditions of Living among the Poor." *Bulletin of the Bureau of Labor*, no. 64, pp. 593–698. Washington, D.C.: G.P.O.

Forster, C., and G.S.L. Tucker. 1972. *Economic Opportunity and White American Fertility Ratios, 1800–1860.* New Haven: Yale University Press.

Fox, E. G. 1919. "Rural Problems." In Chenery and Merritt 1974, pp. 186–94. Reprint of U.S. Department of Labor, Children's Bureau, *Standards of Child Welfare*, Report of the Children's Bureau of Conferences, May and June 1919. Bureau Publication no. 60. Washington, D.C.: Department of Labor.

Frissell, H. B., and I. Bevier. 1899. *Dietary Studies of Negroes in Eastern Virginia in 1897 and 1898.* U.S. Department of Agriculture, Office of Experiment Stations Bulletin, 71. Washington, D.C.: G.P.O

Furstenberg, F. F., Jr., T. Hershberg, and J. Modell. 1975. "The Origins of the Female-Headed Black Family: The Impact of the Urban Experience." *Journal of Interdisciplinary History* 6(2):211–33.

Galishoff, S. 1980. "Triumph and Failure: The American Response to the Urban Water Supply Problem, 1860–1923." In Melosi 1980, pp. 35–57.

Ginsberg, C. 1983. "Sex-Specific Child Mortality and the Economic Value of Children in Nineteenth Century Massachusetts." Dissertation, University of California, Berkeley.

Glass, D. V. 1964. "Some Indicators of Differences between Urban and Rural Mortality in England and Wales and Scotland." *Population Studies* 17(3):263–67.

Glover, J. W. 1921. *United States Life Tables, 1890, 1901, 1910, and 1901–1910.* Washington, D.C.: G.P.O.

Goldin, C. 1981. "Family Strategies and the Family Economy in Late Nineteenth Century: The Role of Secondary Workers." In Hershberg 1981, pp. 277–310.

Goldin, C., and D. O. Parsons. 1987. "Industrialization, Child Labor, and Family Economic Well-Being." Unpublished manuscript.

Goldsmith, J. R. 1980. "Mortality and Working Conditions in Industry." In Samuel H. Preston, ed., *Biological and Social Aspects of Mortality and the Length of Life*, pp. 173–98. Liege, Belgium: Ordina.

Graff, H. J. 1979a. *The Literacy Myth: Literacy and Social Structure in the Nineteenth Century City.* New York: Academic Press.

———. 1979b. "Literacy, Education, and Fertility, Past and Present: A Critical Review." *Population and Development Review* 5(1) (March):105–35.

Graham, S. 1980. *1900 Public Use Sample: User's Handbook.* Center for Studies in Demography and Ecology, University of Washington, Seattle, Wash. (July).

Great Britain. 1909–1913. Board of Trade. "Report of an Enquiry by the Board of Trade into Earnings and Hours of Labour of Workpeople in the United Kingdom in 1906." House of Commons, Sessional Papers, cols. 4545, 4844, 5986, 5196, 5460, 5814, 6953, 6556. London: H.M.S.O.

———. 1913a. *Census of Ireland, 1911.* General Report, with Tables and Appendix. London: H.M.S.O.

———. 1913b. *Seventy-Fourth Annual Report of the Registrar General of Births, Deaths, and Marriages in England and Wales, 1911.* London: H.M.S.O. [Command Papers 6578.]

Grossman, M. 1972. *The Demand for Health: A Theoretical and Empirical Investigation.* National Bureau of Economic Research, Occasional Paper no. 119. New York: Columbia University Press.

Gutman, R. 1956. "The Accuracy of Vital Statistics in Massachusetts, 1842–1901." Ph.D. dissertation, Columbia University.

Hadley, J. 1982. *More Medical Care, Better Health?* Washington, D.C.: The Urban Institute Press.

Haines, M. R. 1977. "Mortality in Nineteenth Century America: Estimates from New York and Pennsylvania Census Data, 1865 and 1900." *Demography* 14(3) (August):311–31.

———. 1979a. "The Use of Model Life Tables to Estimate Mortality for the United States in the Late Nineteenth Century." *Demography* 16(2) (May):289–312.

————. 1979b. *Fertility and Occupation: Population Patterns in Industrialization*. New York: Academic Press.

————. 1979c. "Industrial Work and the Family Life Cycle, 1889–1890." *Research in Economic History* 4:289–356.

————. 1980. "Fertility and Marriage in a Nineteenth Century Industrial City: Philadelphia, 1850–1880." *The Journal of Economic History* 40(1) (March):151–58.

————. 1985. "Inequality and Childhood Mortality: A Comparison of England and Wales, 1911, and the United States, 1900." *The Journal of Economic History* 45(4) (December):885–912.

————. 1989a. "A State and Local Consumer Price Index for the United States in 1890." *Historical Methods* 22:97–105.

————. 1989b. "Consumer Behavior and Immigrant Assimilation: A Comparison of the United States, Britain, and Germany, 1889/90." National Bureau of Economic Research Working Paper Series on Historical Factors in Long Run Growth, Working Paper no. 6. Cambridge, Mass.: NBER.

Haines, M. R., and B. A. Anderson. 1986. "Late Nineteenth Century Demography in the United States." Paper presented at the 1986 Conference of the Soviet-American Bilateral Committee on Quantitative History. New Orleans, La., 17–19 December.

————. 1988. "New Demographic History of the Late Nineteenth-Century United States." *Explorations in Economic History* 25(4):341–65.

Hajnal, J. 1953. "Age at Marriage and Proportions Marrying." *Population Studies* 7(3) (November):111–36.

Hamilton, A. 1909. "Excessive Child-bearing as a Factor in Infant Mortality." In Conference on the Prevention of Infant Mortality 1909, pp. 74–80.

Handlin, O. 1973. *The Uprooted*. 2nd ed., enlarged. Boston: Little, Brown and Company.

Hedger, C. 1909. "The Relation of Infant Mortality to the Occupation and Long Hours of Work for Women." In Conference on the Prevention of Infant Mortality 1909, pp. 32–41.

Hempel, C. G. 1966. *Philosophy of Natural Science*. Englewood Cliffs, N.J.: Prentice-Hall.

Henderson, C. R. 1901. *The Relief and Care of Dependent Children*. Boston. Reprinted in part in Bremner 1974, pp. 98–120.

Hershberg, T., ed. 1981. *Philadelphia: Work, Space, Family, and Group Experience in the Nineteenth Century*. New York: Oxford University Press.

Hershberg, T., A. Burstein, E. P. Ericksen, S. W. Greenberg, and W. L. Yancey. 1981. "A Tale of Three Cities: Blacks, Immigrants, and Opportunity in Philadelphia, 1850–1880, 1930, 1970." In Hershberg 1981, pp. 461–91.

Hewitt, M. 1958. *Wives and Mothers in Victorian Industry*. London: Rockliff.

Higgs, R. 1971. "Race, Skills and Earnings: American Immigrants in 1909." *The Journal of Economic History* 31(2) (June):420–28.

————. 1973. "Mortality in Rural America, 1870–1920: Estimates and Conjectures." *Explorations in Economics History* 10(2) (Winter):177–95.

Higgs, R. 1977. *Competition and Coercion: Blacks in the American Economy, 1865–1914*. Cambridge: Cambridge University Press.

———. 1979. "Cycles and Trends of Mortality in Eighteen Large American Cities, 1871–1900." *Explorations in Economic History* 16(4) (October):381–408.

Higgs, R., and D. Booth. 1979. "Mortality Differentials within Large American Cities in 1890." *Human Ecology* 7(4) (December):353–70.

Hill, K., H. Zlotnik, and J. Durch. 1981. "Simple Procedures for Reducing the Effects of Age Errors on Indirect Demographic Estimation Techniques." Paper presented at the annual meetings of the Population Association, Washington, D.C.

Hill, P. J. 1975. "Relative Skill and Income Levels of Native and Foreign Born Workers in the United States." *Explorations in Economic History* 12(1) (January):47–60.

Hills, J. L. 1909. "Dietary Studies in Vermont Farmers' Families." In *Dietary Studies in Rural Regions*. U.S. Department of Agriculture Office of Experiment Stations Bulletin, no. 221, pp. 7–19. Washington, D.C.: G.P.O.

Hobcraft, J. N., J. W. McDonald, and S. O. Rutstein. 1985. "Demographic Determinants of Infant and Early Child Mortality: A Comparative Analysis." *Population Studies* 39(3):363–85.

Hoffman, F. L. 1896. *Race Traits and Tendencies of the American Negro*. Publications of the American Economic Association, vol. 11(1, 2, and 3):1–329. Published for the American Economic Association by the Macmillan Company, New York.

Hollingsworth, T. H. 1964. "The Demography of the British Peerage." *Supplement to Population Studies*, vol. 18, part 2, pp. iv–108.

Hollingsworth, J. R. 1981. "Inequality in Levels of Health in England and Wales, 1891–1971." *Journal of Health and Social Behavior* 22(3) (September):268–83.

Hollopeter, W. C. 1906. "The Pediatric Outlook." *Transactions of the Section of Diseases of Children, American Medical Association*: 15–18. Reprinted in Bremner 1971, pp. 820–21.

Holmes, G. K. 1907. *Meat Supply and Surplus, with Consideration of Consumption and Exports*. Department of Agriculture Bulletin, no. 55. Washington, D.C.: G.P.O.

Holt, L. Emmett. 1896. *The Diseases of Infancy and Childhood for the Use of Students and Practitioners of Medicine*. New York: D. Appleton and Company.

———. 1897. "The Medical Report: A Survey of Ten Years' Work." Babies Hospital of New York, *Tenth Annual Report*: 34–40. Reprinted in Bremner 1971, pp. 832–36.

Howard, W. T. 1924. *Public Health Administration and the Natural History of Disease in Baltimore, Maryland, 1797–1920*. Washington, D.C.: Carnegie Institution.

Humphreys, N. A. 1887. "Class Mortality Statistics." *Journal of the Royal Statistical Society* 50, pt. 2 (June):255–92.

Jacobi, A. 1889. *The Relations of Pediatrics to General Medicine. Transactions of* the *American Pediatric Society*. Vol. 1, pp. 15–17. Reprinted in part in Bremner 1971, pp. 898–901.

———. 1890. "Introductory." In J. M. Keating, *Cyclopedia*, vol. 1, pp. 7–10. Philadelphia. Reprinted in Bremner 1971, pp. 817–19.

———. 1909. "The Improvement of the Poor Sick Children: General Principles." In W. J. Robinson, ed., *Collectanea Jacobi*, vol. 6, pp. 349–53. New York. Reprinted in Bremner 1971, pp. 831–32.

Jacobson, P. H. 1957. "An Estimate of the Expectation of Life in the United States in 1850." *Milbank Memorial Fund Quarterly* 35(2) (April):197–201.

Johansson, S. R. 1987. "Neglect, Abuse, and Avoidable Death: Parental Investment and the Mortality of Infants and Children in the European Tradition." In R. J. Gelles and J. B. Lancaster, eds., *Child Abuse and Neglect: Biosocial Dimensions*, pp. 57–93. New York: Aldine De Gruyter.

Johansson, S. R., and S. H. Preston. 1979. "Tribal Demography: The Hopi and Navaho Populations as Seen through Manuscripts of the U.S. Census of 1900." *Social Science History* 3(1):1–33.

Johnson, R. C. 1978. "The 1900 Census Sampling Project: Methods and Procedures for Sampling and Data Entry." *Historical Methods* 11(4) (Fall):147–51.

Kadin, M. L. 1982. "Modernization and the Social Inequality of Death in the United States, 1910–1970." Ph.D. dissertation, Department of Sociology, Brown University.

Katz, M. B. 1986. *In the Shadow of the Poorhouse*. New York: Basic Books.

Keyfitz, N., and W. Flieger. 1968. *World Population: An Analysis of Vital Data*. Chicago: University of Chicago Press.

Kintner, H. J. 1982. "The Determinants of Infant Mortality in Germany from 1871 to 1933." Ph.D. dissertation, University of Michigan.

———. 1985. "Trends and Regional Differences in Breastfeeding in Germany from 1871 to 1937." *Journal of Family History* 20 (Summer):163–82.

———. 1987. "The Impact of Breastfeeding Patterns on Regional Differences in Infant Mortality in Germany, 1910." *The European Journal of Population* 3(2):1–29.

Kiple, K. F., and V. H. King. 1981. *Another Dimension to the Black Diaspora: Diet, Disease, and Racism*. Cambridge: Cambridge University Press.

Kitagawa, E. M., and P. M. Hauser. 1973. *Differential Mortality in the United States*. Cambridge, Mass.: Harvard University Press.

Knodel, J., and E. van de Walle. 1967. "Breast Feeding, Fertility, and Infant Mortality: An Analysis of Some Early German Data." *Population Studies* 21(2) (September):109–31.

———. 1979. "Lessons from the Past: Policy Implications of Historical Fertility Studies." *Population and Development Review* 5 (June):217–45.

Kobrin, F. E. 1966. "The American Midwife Controversy: A Crisis of Professionalization." *Bulletin of the History of Medicine* 40:350–63. Reprinted in Leavitt and Numbers 1978, pp. 217–25.

Koplik, H. 1902. *The Diseases of Infancy and Early Childhood. Designed for the Use of Students and Practitioners of Medicine*. New York: Lea Brothers and Company.

Kunitz, S. J. 1974. "Professionalism and Social Control in the Progressive Era: The Case of the Flexner Report." *Social Problems* 22(1):15–27.

————. 1983. "Speculations on the European Mortality Decline." *Economic History Review*, n.s. 36:349–64.

————. 1984. "Mortality Change in America, 1620–1920." *Human Biology* 56(3):559–82.

————. 1986. "Mortality since Malthus." In D. Coleman and R. Schofield, eds., *The State of Population Theory*, pp. 279–302. Oxford: Basil Blackwell.

Kuznets, S. 1966. *Modern Economic Growth: Rate, Structure, and Spread*. New Haven: Yale University Press.

Laurie, B., T. Hershberg and G. Alter. 1981. "Immigrants and Industry: The Philadelphia Experience, 1850–1880." In Hershberg 1981, pp. 93–119.

Leavitt, J. W. 1979. "Politics and Public Health: Smallpox in Milwaukee, 1894–95." In S. Reverby and D. Rosner, eds., *Health Care in America: Essays in Social History*, pp. 84–101. Philadelphia: Temple University Press.

————. 1986. *Brought to Bed: Childbearing in America, 1750–1950*. New York. Oxford University Press.

Leavitt, J. W., and R. L. Numbers, eds. 1978. *Sickness and Health in America: Readings in the History of Medicine and Public Health*. Madison: University of Wisconsin Press.

Lebergott, S. 1964. *Manpower in Economic Growth: The American Record since 1800*. New York: McGraw-Hill.

————. 1976. "Are the Rich Getting Richer? Trends in U.S. Wealth Concentration." *The Journal of Economic History* 36(1) (March):147–62.

Lentzner, H. R. 1987. "Seasonal Patterns of Infant and Child Mortality in New York, Chicago and New Orleans: 1870–1919." Dissertation, University of Pennsylvania.

Letchworth, W. P. 1897. "Dependent Children and Family Homes." In *Proceedings of the National Conference of Charities and Corrections*, pp. 94–105. Reprinted in Bremner 1974.

Lewi, M. J. 1902. "What Shall Be Done with the Professional Midwife?" *Transactions of the Medical Society of the State of New York*: 282–84. Reprinted in Bremner 1971, pp. 983–85.

Lindenbaum, S. 1983. "The Influence of Maternal Education on Infant and Child Mortality in Bangladesh." Unpublished paper. International Centre for Diarrheal Disease Research, Bangladesh.

Lindert, P. H. 1983. "Who Owned Victorian England?" Agricultural History Center, Working Paper Series, no. 12 (February). University of California, Davis.

Logan, W.P.D. 1954. "Social Class Variations in Mortality." In United Nations, *Proceeding of the World Population Conference, Rome, 1954* 1:185–213.

McCusker, J. J., and R. R. Menard. 1985. *The Economy of British America, 1607–1789*. Chapel Hill: University of North Carolina Press.

McGouldrick, Paul F., and M. B. Tannen. 1977. "Did American Manufacturers Discriminate against Immigrants before 1914?" *The Journal of Economic History* 37(3) (September):723–46.

McKeown, T. 1976. *The Modern Rise of Population*. New York: Academic Press.

McKeown, T., and R. G. Brown. 1955. "Medical Evidence Related to English Population Changes in the Eighteenth Century." *Population Studies* 9(2) (November):119–41.

McKeown, T., R. G. Brown, and R. G. Record. 1972. "An Interpretation of the Modern Rise of Population in Europe." *Population Studies* 26(3) (November):345–82.

McKeown, T., and R. G. Record. 1962. "Reasons for the Decline of Mortality in England and Wales during the Nineteenth Century." *Population Studies* 16, pt. 2:94–122.

McKinlay, J. B., and S. M. McKinlay. 1977. "The Questionable Contribution of Medical Measures to the Decline of Mortality in the United States." *Health and Society* 55 (Summer):405–28.

Margo, R., and G. C. Villafor. 1987. "The Growth of Wages in Antebellum America: New Evidence." *Journal of Economic History* 47(4):873–95.

Matthiesen, P. 1972. "Application of the Brass-Sullivan Method to Historical Data." *Population Index* 38(4):403–9.

Maulitz, R. C. 1979. "Physician Versus Bacteriologist: The Ideology of Science in Clinical Medicine." In Vogel and Rosenberg 1979, pp. 91–107.

Mayer, A. J., and R. V. Marks. 1954. "Differentials in Infant Mortality, by Race, Economic Level and Cause of Death, for Detroit: 1940 and 1950." *Human Biology* 26 (May):143–55.

Meckel, R. A. 1985. "Immigration, Mortality, and Population Growth in Boston, 1840–1880." *The Journal of Interdisciplinary History* 15(3) (Winter):393–417.

————. 1990. *Save the Babies: American Public Health Reform and the Prevention of Infant Mortality, 1850–1929*. Baltimore: The Johns Hopkins University Press.

Meech, L. S. 1898. *System and Tables of Life Insurance*. Rev. ed. New York: The Spectator Company.

Meeker, E. 1972. "The Improving Health of the United States, 1850–1915." *Explorations in Economic History* 9(4) (Summer):353–73.

————. 1974. "The Social Rate of Return on Investment in Public Health, 1880–1910." *The Journal of Economic History* 34(2) (June):392–421.

————. 1976. "Mortality Trends of Southern Blacks, 1850–1910: Some Preliminary Findings." *Explorations in Economic History* 13(1) (January):13–42.

————. 1980. "Medicine and Public Health." In G. Porter, ed., *Encyclopedia of American Economic History*, vol. 3, pp. 1058–67. New York: Charles Scribner's Sons.

Meeker, E., and R. Higgs. 1976. "Economic-Demographic Interactions and Trends in Black America, 1850–1910." Discussion Paper no. 76–3. Seattle, Wash.: Institute for Economic Research.

Melosi, M. V., ed. 1980. *Pollution and Reform in American Cities, 1870–1930*. Austin: University of Texas Press.

Mitchell, B. R., and P. Deane. 1971. *Abstract of British Historical Statistics*. Cambridge: Cambridge University Press.

Modell, J., and T. K. Hareven. 1973. "Urbanization and the Malleable Household: An Examination of Boarding and Lodging in American Families." *Journal of Marriage and the Family* no. 35 (August):467–79.

Moore, E. 1917. *Maternity and Infant Care in a Rural County of Kansas*. U.S. Department of Labor, Chldren's Bureau, Rural Child Welfare Series no. 1. Washington, D.C.: G.P.O.

Morawetz, D. 1977. *Twenty-Five Years of Economic Development*. Baltimore: The Johns Hopkins University Press.

Moriyama, I. M., and L. Guralnick. 1956. "Occupational and Social Class Differences in Mortality." *Trends and Differentials in Mortality*. New York: Milbank Memorial Fund.

Morris, J. N., and J. A. Heady. 1955. "Social and Biological Factors in Infant Mortality—5. Mortality in Relation to Father's Occupation, 1911–1950." *The Lancet* (March 12):554–60.

Morse, J. L. 1906. "The Protection of Infants and Young Children from Tuberculosis Infection." *Transactions of the National Association for the Study and Prevention of Tuberculosis*, pp. 624–26. Reprinted in Bremner 1971, pp. 890–92.

Mosley, H. W. 1985. "Will Primary Health Care Reduce Infant and Child Mortality? A Critique of Some Current Strategies, with Special Reference to Africa and Asia." In J. Vallin and A. Lopez, eds., *Health Policy, Social Policy and Mortality Prospects*, pp. 103–38. Liege, Belgium: Ordina.

Mosley, H. W., and L. Chen. 1984. "An Analytical Framework for the Study of Child Survival in Developing Countries." In W. H. Mosley and L. Chen, eds., *Child Survival: Strategies for Research*, pp. 25–48. New York: Cambridge University Press.

Newsholme, A. 1913. *Second Report on Infant and Child Mortality*. 42nd Annual Report of Local Government Board, 1912–13. Supplement in Continuation of Report of the Medical Officer of the Board.

North, C. E. 1921. "Milk and Its Relation to Public Health." In M. P. Ravenel, ed., *A Half Century of Public Health*, pp. 236–89. New York: Public Health Association American.

Okun, B. 1958. *Trends in Birth Rates in the United States since 1870*. Baltimore: The Johns Hopkins University Press.

Omran, A. R. 1971. "The Epidemiologic Transition: A Theory of the Epidemiology of Population Change." *Milbank Memorial Fund Quarterly* 49, pt. 1:509–38.

Ovington, M. W. 1905. "The Negro Home in New York." *Charities* 15:25–26. Reprinted in Bremner 1971, pp. 18–19.

Pagnini, D., and S. P. Morgan. 1988. "Intermarriage and Social Distance among U.S. Immigrants at the Turn of the Century." Unpublished manuscript, Population Studies Center, University of Pennylvania.

Pamuk, E. R. 1985. "Social Class Inequality in Mortality from 1921 to 1972 in England and Wales." *Population Studies* 39(1) (March):17–31.

Paradise, V. I. 1919. *Maternity Care and the Welfare of Young Children in a Home-steading County in Montana*. U.S. Department of Labor, Children's Bureau, Rural Child Welfare Series no. 3. Washington, D.C.: G.P.O.

Park, E. H., and E. Holt. 1903. "Report upon the Results with Different Kinds of Pure and Impure Milk in Infant Feeding in Tenement Houses and Institutions of New York City: A Cultural and Bacteriological Study." *Archives of Pediatrics* 20(12):881–909.

Patterson, J. T. 1986. *America's Struggle against Poverty, 1900–1985*. Cambridge, Mass.: Harvard University Press.

Pellegrino, E. D. 1979. "The Sociocultural Impact of Twentieth-Century Therapeutics." In Vogel and Rosenberg 1979, pp. 245–66.

Peller, S. 1965. "Births and Deaths among Europe's Ruling Families since 1500." In D.V. Glass and D.E.C. Eversley, eds., *Population in History: Essays in Historical Demography*, pp. 87–100. London: Edward Arnold, Ltd.

Pessen, E. 1973. *Riches, Class and Power before the Civil War*. Lexington, Mass.: D. C. Heath.

Phelps, E. B. 1909. "Discussion." In Conference on the Prevention of Infant Mortality 1909, pp. 41–43.

Phelps Brown, H. 1977. *The Inequality of Pay*. Berkeley: University of California Press.

Pleck, E. 1978. "A Mother's Wages: Income Earning among Married Italian and Black Women, 1897–1911." In M. Gordon, ed., *The American Family in Socio-Historical Perspective*, pp. 490–510. New York: St. Martin's Press.

Preston, S. H. 1975. "The Changing Relation between Mortality and Level of Economic Development." *Population Studies* 29(2) (July):231–48.

———. 1976. *Mortality Patterns in National Populations: With Special Reference to Recorded Causes of Death*. New York: Academic Press.

———. 1980. "Causes and Consequences of Mortality Declines in Less Developed Countries during the Twentieth Century." In R. A. Easterlin, ed., *Population and Economic Change in Developing Countries*, pp. 289–341. Conference Report no. 30. Universities-National Bureau Committee for Economic Research. Chicago: University of Chicago Press.

———. 1985. "Resources, Knowledge, and Child Mortality: A Comparison of the U.S. in the Late Nineteenth Century and Developing Countries Today." *Proceedings*, International Population Conference, International Union for the Scientific Study of Population, Florence, Italy, 5–12 June 1985. 4:373–88.

———. 1985. "Mortality and Development Revisited." *Population Bulletin of the United Nations* no. 18:34–40.

Preston, S. H., and A. A Farah. 1982. "Child Mortality Differentials in Sudan." *Population and Development Review* 8(2) (June):365–83.

Preston, S. H., and M. R. Haines. 1984. "New Estimates of Child Mortality in the United States in 1900." *Journal of the American Statistical Association* 79(386):272–81.

Preston, S. H., M. R. Haines and E. Pamuk. 1981. "Effects of Industrialization and Urbanization on Mortality in Developed Countries." In International Union for the Scientific Study of Population, *International Population Conference, Manila, 1981: Solicited Papers*, vol. 2, pp. 233–54. Liege: IUSSP.

Preston, S. H., N. Keyfitz, and R. Schoen. 1972. *Causes of Death: Life Tables for National Populations*. New York: Seminar Press.

Preston, S. H., and A. Palloni. 1978. "Fine-Tuning Brass-type Mortality Estimates with Data on Ages of Surviving Children." In United Nations, *Population Bulletin of the United Nations*, no. 10–1977, pp. 72–91. New York: United Nations.

Preston, S. H., and E. van de Walle. 1978. "Urban French Mortality in the Nineteenth Century." *Population Studies* 32(2):275–97.

Ransom, R. L., and R. Sutch. 1977. *One Kind of Freedom: The Economic Consequences of Emancipation*. Cambridge: Cambridge University Press.

Ravenel, Mazyck P. 1921. *A Half-Century of Public Health*. New York: American Public Health Association.

Richmond, P. A. 1954. "American Attitudes towards the Germ Theory of Disease (1860–1880)." *Journal of the History of Medicine*: 428–54.

Riis, J. 1890. *How the Other Half Lives*. New York: Charles Scribner's Sons.

———. 1892. *The Children of the Poor*. New York: Charles Scribner's Sons.

Rochester, A. 1923. *Infant Mortality: Results of a Field Study in Baltimore, Maryland. Based on Births in One Year*. U.S. Children's Bureau Publication no. 119. Washington, D.C.: G.P.O.

Rose, J. C. 1989. "Biological Consequences of Segregation." *Journal of Economic History* 49(2):351–60.

Rosen, G. 1958. *A History of Public Health*. New York: MD Publications, Inc.

Rosenberg, C. E. 1979. "The Therapeutic Revolution: Medicine, Meaning, and Social Change in Nineteenth-Century America." In Vogel and Rosenberg 1979, pp. 3–25.

———. 1987. *The Care of Strangers*. New York: Basic Books.

Rosenkrantz, Barbara. 1972. *Public Health and the State: Changing Views in Massachusetts, 1842–1936*. Cambridge, Mass.: Harvard University Press.

Rotch, T. M. 1891. "Iconoclasm and Original Thought in the Study of Pediatrics." *Transactions of the American Pediatric Society* 3:6–9. Reprinted in Bremner 1971, pp. 819–20.

Rothstein, W. G. 1972. *American Physicians in the Nineteenth Century: From Sects to Science*. Baltimore: The Johns Hopkins University Press.

Routh, G. 1965. *Occupation and Pay in Great Britain, 1906–60*. London: Cambridge University Press.

Royster, Dr. 1924. "Discussion." *Transactions of the American Pediatric Society* 36:52. Reprinted in Bremner 1971, p. 976.

Rubinstein, W. D. 1977. "Wealth, Elites, and the Class Structure of Modern Britain." *Past and Present* 76:99–126.

Rutstein, S. O., A. E. Sommerfelt, and J. Schoemaker. 1988. "Who Uses Maternal and Child Health Services? Evidence from the Demographic and Health Surveys." Paper presented to the Expert Group Meeting on Child Survival Programs, Johns Hopkins University, Baltimore. 21–22 November 1988.

Sanderson, W. 1978. "New Estimates of the Decline in the Fertility of White

Women in the United States, 1800–1920." Formal memorandum, Center for Research in Economic Growth Memorandum no. 225. Department of Economics, Stanford University.

Schmeltz, U. O. 1971. *Infant and Early Childhood Mortality among Jews of the Diaspora*. Jerusalem. Institute of Contemporary Jewry, The Hebrew University.

Schultz, T. W. 1981. *Investing in People: The Economics of Population Quality*. Berkeley, Calif.: University of California Press.

Schwartz, H. 1909. "Discussion." In Conference on the Prevention of Infant Child Mortality 1909, pp. 165–69.

Sedgwick, W. T., and J. S. MacNutt. 1910. "On the Mills-Reincke Phenomenon and Hazen's Theorem Concerning the Decrease in Mortality from Diseases Other than Typhoid Following the Purification of Public Water-Supplies." *Journal of Infectious Diseases* 7(4):489–564.

Seutemann, K. 1894. "Kindersterblichkeit sozialer Bevolkerungsgruppen, insbesonders Provinzen." In F. J. Neumann, ed., *Beitrage zur Geschichte der Bevolkerung in Deutschland seit dem Anfange dieses Jahrhunderts*, Band 5, pp. 1–167. Berlin.

Shaftel, N. 1978. "A History of the Purification of Milk in New York, or, 'How, Now, Brown Cow?' " In Leavitt and Numbers 1978, pp. 275–91. Originally published in *New York State Journal of Medicine* 58 (1958):911–28.

Shapiro, S., E. R. Schlesinger, and R.E.L. Nesbitt, Jr. 1968. *Infant, Perinatal, Maternal, and Childhood Mortality in the United States*. Cambridge, Mass.: Harvard University Press.

Sherbon, F. B., and E. Moore. 1919. *Maternity and Infant Care in Two Rural Counties in Wisconsin*. U.S. Department of Labor, Children's Bureau, Rural Child Welfare Series no. 4. Washington, D.C.: G.P.O.

Shryock, R. H. 1947. *The Development of Modern Medicine: An Interpretation of the Social and Scientific Factors Involved*. New York: Knopf.

————. 1957. *National Tuberculosis Association, 1904–54: A Study of the Voluntary Health Movement in the United States*. New York: National Tuberculosis Association.

Smith, D. S. 1978. "A Community-Based Sample of the Older Population from the 1880 and 1900 United States Manuscript Censuses." *Historical Methods* 11(2) (Spring):67–74.

————. 1983. "Differential Mortality in the United States before 1900." *Journal of Interdisciplinary History* 13(4) (Spring):735–59.

Smuts, R. W. 1959. *Women and Work in America*. New York: Columbia University Press.

Starr, P. 1982. *The Social Transformation of American Medicine*. New York: Basic Books.

Steckel, R. H. 1988. "The Health and Mortality of Women and Children, 1850–1860." *The Journal of Economic History* 47(2):333–45.

Stocks, P. 1938. "The Effect of Occupation and its Accompanying Environment on Mortality." *Journal of the Royal Statistical Society* (London) 101, pt. 4:669–708.

Stockwell, E. 1963. "A Critical Examination of the Relationship between Socioeconomic Status and Mortality." *American Journal of Public Health* 53(6):956–64.

Stolnitz, G. 1955. "A Century of International Mortality Trends: I." *Population Studies* 9:24–55.

Stone, E. A. 1912. "The Midwives of Rhode Island." *The Providence Medical Journal* 13:58–59. Reprinted in Bremner 1971, pp. 988–89.

Suliman, S. 1983. "Estimation of Levels and Trends of U.S. Adult Black Mortality during the Period 1870–1900." Dissertation, University of Pennsylvania.

Sullivan, J. M. 1972. "Models for the Estimation of the Probability of Dying between Birth and Exact Ages in Early Childhood." *Population Studies* 26(1) (March):79–97.

Swedlund, A. C. 1985. "Infant and Childhood Mortality in the Nineteenth Century United States: A View from Franklin County, Massachusetts." Paper prepared for Conference on the Health and Disease of Populations in Transition, Werner-Gren Foundation for Anthropological Research, 19–27 October, Santa Fe, New Mexico.

Szreter, S. 1984. "The Genesis of the Registrar-General's Social Classification of Occupations." *The British Journal of Sociology* 35(4):522–46.

———. 1988. "The Importance of Social Intervention in Britain's Mortality Decline c.1850–1914: A Reinterpretation of the Role of Public Health." *Social History of Medicine* 1:1–37.

Taeuber, C., and I. B. Taeuber. 1958. *The Changing Population of the United States*. New York: Wiley.

Tanner, J. M. 1981. *A History of the Study of Human Growth*. Cambridge: Cambridge University Press.

———. 1982. "The Potential of Auxological Data for Monitoring Economic and Social Well-Being." *Social Science History* 6(4) (Fall):571–81.

Tarr, J. A., J. McCurley, and T. F. Yosie. 1980. "The Development and Impact of Urban Wastewater Technology: Changing Concepts of Water Quality Control, 1850–1930." In Melosi 1980, pp. 59–82.

Taylor, A. J., ed. 1975. *The Standard of Living in Britain in the Industrial Revolution*. London: Methuen.

Tentler, L. W. 1979. *Wage-Earning Women: Industrial Work and Family Life in the United States, 1900–1930*. New York: Oxford University Press.

Thompson, W. S., and P. K. Whelpton. 1933. *Population Trends in the United States*. New York: McGraw-Hill.

Titmuss, R. M. 1943. *Birth, Poverty, and Wealth*. London: Hamish Hamilton Medical Books.

Trussell, T. J. 1975. "A Re-estimation of the Multiplying Factors for the Brass Technique for Determining Childhood Survivorship Rates." *Population Studies* 29(1) (March):97–107.

Trussell, J., and S. Preston. 1982. "Estimating the Covariates of Childhood Mortality from Retrospective Reports of Mothers." *Health Policy and Education* 3:1–43.

United Nations. 1973. *The Determinants and Consequences of Population Trends:*

New Summary of Findings on Interaction of Demographic, Economic, and Social Factors. New York: United Nations.

——. 1982. *Levels and Trends of Mortality since 1950.* New York: United Nations.

——. 1983a. *Indirect Techniques for Demographic Estimation.* Manual X. New York: United Nations.

——. 1983b. *World Population Prospects as Assessed in 1982.* Population Division, unpublished printout (November). New York: United Nations.

——. 1985. *Socioeconomic Differentials in Child Mortality in Developing Countries.* Population Study no. 97. New York: United Nations.

U.S. Bureau of the Census. 1886. *U.S. Census of Population: 1880.* Vol. 10, part 2, "Vital Statistics: Mortality." Washington, D.C.: G.P.O.

——. 1902a. *U.S. Census of Population: 1900.* Vol. 1, part 2, "Population." Washington, D.C.: G.P.O.

——. 1902b. *U.S. Census of Population: 1900,* Vol. 4, "Vital Statistics." part 2, "Statistics of Deaths." Washington, D.C.: G.P.O.

——. 1904. *United States Census, 1900.* Special Reports. "Occupations of the Twelfth Census." Washington, D.C.: G.P.O.

——. 1918. *Negro Population, 1790–1915.* Washington, D.C.: G.P.O.

——. 1943. *U.S. Census of Population: 1940.* "Differential Fertility, 1940 and 1910: Fertility for States and Large Cities." Washington, D.C.: G.P.O.

——. 1944. *Sixteenth Census of the United States: 1940 Population.* "Differential Fertility, 1940 and 1910: Standardized Fertility Rates and Reproduction Rates." Washington, D.C.: G.P.O.

——. 1945. *United States Census of Population: 1940.* "Population: Differential Fertility 1940 and 1910: Women by Number of Children Ever Born." Washington, D.C.: G.P.O.

——. 1966. *Long Term Economic Growth, 1869–1965: A Statistical Compendium.* Washington, D.C.: G.P.O.

——. 1971. *The Methods and Materials of Demography,* vols. 1 and 2. By H. S. Shryock, J. S. Siegel, and Associates. Washington, D.C.: G.P.O.

——. 1972. *U.S. Census of Population: 1970.* Vol. 1, part 1, section 1, " Number of Inhabitants: United States Summary." Washington, D.C.: G.P.O.

——. 1975. *Historical Statistics of the United States: Colonial Times to 1970.* Washington, D.C.: G.P.O.

——. 1979. *Twenty Censuses: Population and Housing Questions, 1790–1980.* Washington, D.C.: G.P.O.

——. 1980. *Social Indicators III: Selected Data on Social Conditions and Trends in the United States* (December). Washington, D.C.: G.P.O.

U.S. Bureau of Labor, Department of Commerce and Labor. 1906. *Bulletin of the Bureau of Labor,* no. 65:1–368. Washington, D.C.: G.P.O.

U.S. Commissioner of Labor. 1890. *Sixth Annual Report of the Commissioner of Labor, 1890.* Part 3, "Cost of Living." U.S. Congress, House of Representatives, House Executive Document 265, 51st Congress, 2nd session. Washington, D.C.: G.P.O.

——. 1891. *Seventh Annual Report of the Commissioner of Labor, 1891.* Part 3,

"Cost of Living." U.S. Congress, House of Representatives, House Executive Document 232, 52nd Congress, 1st session. Washington, D.C.: G.P.O.

————. 1903. *18th Annual Report of the Commissioner of Labor.* "Cost of Living and Retail Prices of Food." Washington, D.C.: G.P.O.

Uselding, P. 1976. "In Dispraise of Muckrakers: United States Occupational Mortality, 1890–1910." *Research in Economic History* 1:334–71.

Usher, D. 1973. "An Imputation to the Measure of Economic Growth for Changes in Life Expectancy." In M. Moss, ed., *The Measurement of Economic and Social Performance*, pp. 193–232. New York: Columbia University Press.

Vallin, J. 1979. "Socioeconomic Determinants of Mortality in Industrialized Countries." In United Nations/World Health Organization, *Proceedings of the Meeting on Socioeconomic Determinants and Consequences of Mortality*, pp. 19–25. El Colegio de Mexico, Mexico City, June 1979. New York: United Nations.

Vinovskis, M. 1972. "Mortality Rates and Trends in Massachusetts before 1860." *The Journal of Economic History* 32(1) (March):184–213.

————. 1978. "The Jacobson Life Table of 1850: A Critical Re-examination from a Massachusetts Perspective." *Journal of Interdisciplinary History* 8(4) (Spring):703–24.

————, ed. 1979. *Studies in American Historical Demography.* New York: Academic Press.

————. 1981. *Fertility in Massachusetts from the Revolution to the Civil War.* New York: Academic Press.

Vogel, M. J. 1979. "The Transformation of the American Hospital, 1850–1920." In S. Reverby and D. Rosner, eds., *Health Care in America: Essays in Social History*, pp. 105–16. Philadelphia: Temple University Press.

————. 1980. *The Invention of the Modern Hospital: Boston, 1870–1980.* Chicago: University of Chicago Press.

Vogel, M. J., and C. E. Rosenberg, eds. 1979. *The Therapeutic Revolution: Essays in the Social History of American Medicine.* Philadelphia: University of Pennsylvania Press.

Von Pirquet, C. 1909. "The Relation of Tuberculosis to Infant Mortality." In Conference on the Prevention of Infant Mortality 1909, pp. 25–29.

Wait, C. E. 1909a. "Dietary Studies of Families Living in the Mountain Region of Eastern Tennessee." In *Dietary Studies in Rural Regions*, pp. 21–116. U.S. Department of Agriculture Office of Experiment Stations Bulletin no. 221. Washington, D.C.: G.P.O.

————. 1909b. "Discussion of American Rural Dietaries." In *Dietary Studies in Rural Regions*, pp. 137–42. U.S. Department of Agriculture Office of Experiment Stations Bulletin no. 221. Washington, D.C.: G.P.O.

Ward, D. 1971. *Cities and Immigrants: A Geography of Change in Nineteenth Century America.* New York: Oxford University Press.

Watterson, P. 1986. "The Role of the Environment in the Decline of Infant Mortality: An Analysis of the 1911 Census of England and Wales." *Journal of Biosocial Science* 18:457–70.

————. 1988. "Infant Mortality by Father's Occupation from the 1911 Census of England and Wales." *Demography* 25(2):289–306.

Weber, A. F. 1899. *The Growth of Cities in the Nineteenth Century: A Study in Statistics*. New York: Macmillan Company.

Wende, E. 1900. "Report on the Cause and Prevention of Infant Mortality." *Pediatrics* 9:101–9, 144–53, 177–85.

Whipple, G. E. 1921. "Fifty Years of Water Purification." In M. P. Ravenel, ed., *A Half Century of Public Health*, pp. 161–80. New York: American Public Health Association.

White, H. C. 1909. "Dietary Studies in Georgia." In *Dietary Studies in Rural Regions*, pp. 117–36. U.S. Department of Agriculture Office of Experiment Stations Bulletin no. 221. Washington, D.C.: G.P.O.

White House Conference on Child Health and Protection. 1931. *Health Protection for the Preschool Child*. New York: The Century Company. Reprinted in part in Bremner 1971, pp. 1080–83.

Wiebe, R. H. 1967. *The Search for Order: 1877–1920*. New York: Hill and Wang.

Wile, I. S. 1909. "Educational Responsibilities of a Milk Depot." In Conference on the Prevention of Infant Mortality 1909, pp. 139–53.

Williamson, J. G. 1982a. "Was the Industrial Revolution Worth It? Disamenities and Death in Nineteenth Century British Towns." *Explorations in Economic History* 19:221–45.

————. 1982b. "The Structure of Pay in Britain, 1710–1911." *Research in Economic History* 7:1–54.

————. 1984. "British Mortality and the Value of Life, 1781–1931." *Population Studies* 38(1) (March):157–72.

————. 1985. *Did British Capitalism Breed Inequality?* Boston: Allen and Unwin.

Williamson, J. G., and P. Lindert. 1980. *American Inequality: A Macroeconomic History*. New York: Academic Press.

Wilson, W. A. 1966. "On Mortality Trends by Occupation and Social Class." In *Official Documents . . . European Population Conference*. Strasbourg, 30 August–6 September 1966, vol. 1, p. 14. (CDE(66)C18).

Winslow, C.E.A. 1909. "The Educational Session, Introductory Remarks by the Chairman." In Conference on the Prevention of Infant Mortality 1909, pp. 223–25.

Wohl, A. S. 1983. *Endangered Lives: Public Health in Victorian Britain*. Cambridge, Mass.: Harvard University Press.

Woodbury, R. M. 1925. *Causal Factors in Infant Mortality: A Statistical Study Based on Investigations in Eight Cities*. Washington, D.C.: G.P.O.

————. 1926. *Infant Mortality and Its Causes*. Baltimore: The Williams and Williams Company.

Woods, R. 1985. "The Effects of Population Redistribution on the Level of Mortality in Nineteenth Century England and Wales." *Journal of Economic History* 45(3) (September):645–51.

Woods, R., and J. Woodward, eds. 1984. *Urban Disease and Mortality in Nineteenth Century England*. New York: St. Martin's Press.

Woods, R. I., and P.R.A. Hinde. 1987. "Mortality in Victorian England: Models and Patterns." *Journal of Interdisciplinary History* 17:62–85.

Woods, R. I., P. A. Watterson, and J. H. Woodward. 1988. "The Causes of Rapid Infant Mortality Decline in England and Wales, 1861–1921, Part I." *Population Studies* 42(3):343–66.

World Bank. 1980. *Poverty and Human Development*. New York: Oxford University Press.

World Bank. 1984. *World Development Report 1984*. New York: Oxford University Press.

World Health Organization. 1978. *Social and Biological Effects on Perinatal Mortality*. Vol. 1. Budapest: Statistical Publishing House.

Wright, Gavin. 1986. *Old South, New South: Revolutions in the Southern Economy since the Civil War*. New York: Basic Books.

Wrigley, E. A. 1961. *Industrial Growth and Population Change: A Regional Study of the Coalfield Areas of Northwest Europe in the Later Nineteenth Century*. Cambridge: Cambridge University Press.

———. 1969. *Population and History*. New York: McGraw-Hill.

Yasuba, Y. 1962. *Birth Rates of the White Population of the United States, 1800–1860: An Economic Analysis*. Baltimore: The Johns Hopkins University Press.

Zelnik, M. 1969. "Age Patterns of Mortality of American Negroes: 1900–02 to 1959–61." *Journal of the American Statistical Association* 64 (June):433–51.

Zunz, O. 1982. *The Changing Face of Inequality: Urbanization, Industrial Development, and Immigrants in Detroit, 1880–1920*. Chicago: University of Chicago Press.

INDEX BY AUTHOR

INDEX BY SUBJECT